Child Survivors of the Holocaust

Paul Valent was born in Bratislava (now Slovakia) in 1938. His parents came from well-to-do Jewish families. During World War II, in the wake of increasing persecution, the family escaped to Budapest, Hungary, where they spent the war as Aryans. The parents were caught at one time and escaped from a cattle wagon bound for Auschwitz. During this time the child Paul was hidden on the family farm.

The family migrated to Melbourne, Australia, in 1949. Dr Valent studied medicine at Melbourne University and psychiatry in London. He practiced as a psychiatrist for three years in Israel.

On his return to Australia, in his work as a psychotherapist Dr Valent worked at amalgamating psychoanalytic and trauma therapies. His work for over two decades as director of psychological services to emergency departments in teaching hospitals made him aware of the relevance of a biopsychosocial outlook to trauma. He has also been at the forefront in disaster work in Australia, and he founded and is current past president of the Australasian Society for Traumatic Stress Studies. Dr Valent has treated survivors — adults, children, and second generation survivors, as well as survivors from many other traumas. In 1990 he founded the Child Survivors of the Holocaust group in Melbourne, with which he is still closely associated.

In the latter years Dr Valent has worked to integrate traumatology, but the Holocaust and his child survivor experiences have remained the guiding benchmarks to other traumas. He has written widely on child survivors and other topics in professional journals and texts. His other books are *From Survival to Fulfillment; A Framework for the Life-Trauma Dialectic* and *Trauma and Fulfillment Therapy; A Wholist Framework.*

Child Survivors
of the Holocaust

PAUL VALENT

BRUNNER-ROUTLEDGE
NEW YORK & LONDON

Published in 2002 by
Brunner-Routledge
29 West 35th Street
New York, NY 10001

Published in Great Britain by
Brunner-Routledge
11 New Fetter Lane
London EC4P 4EE

Brunner-Routledge is an imprint of the Taylor & Francis Group.

First published in 1993 by William Heinemann Australia, a part of Reed
Books, Australia
22 Salmon Street, Port Melbourne, Victoria 3207
A division of Reed International Books Australia Pty Limited

10 9 8 7 6 5 4 3 2 1

Cataloging–in–Publication Data is available from the Library of Congress.

ISBN 0–415–93335–8

This book is dedicated to child survivors everywhere. It is also dedicated to the memory of those who did not survive.

Contents

—•—

Acknowledgements

— • —

This book could not have been written without the support of many different people. First I thank those who helped me discover myself as a child survivor: Sarah Moskovitz, Judith Kestenberg and Tom Paterson. I thank Judith for encouraging me to write, and Sarah for her generosity in supporting me to write this book following her own book on child survivors, *Love Despite Hate*.

I especially thank each and every child survivor in this book who gave of themselves so unstintingly in their interviews and thereafter.

I thank Stan Marks for his encouragement and guidance in the conception of this book. I thank Louise Adler for her sensitive editing and support, and Adrienne Ralph and Belinda Byrne who contributed greatly toward the quality of this book. I would also like to thank the La Trobe Library for kind permission to reproduce Elizabeth Gilliam's photograph of Eva Marks.

Then there are those silent people whose support was so necessary. Firstly I thank my parents for ensuring my survival.

I thank my friends for their encouragement and for tolerating my withdrawal into my task. I give heartfelt thanks to my children, Dani, Ariel and Amy, for their unerring support, tolerance and good humour.

I would especially like to thank my wife Julie for providing the light and normal side of life while I was immersed in its dark side. Without her love, support and encouragement this book would not have been written.

Foreword

— • —

During the research for my book *Schindler's Ark* (now known in the United States as *Schindler's List*), I met and interviewed a number of survivors of the Holocaust who had been children at the time of their ordeal. It took only a short time to see that they were the most damaged of any group of survivors, the group to whom the very term *survivors* applied most questionably.

As one of them described it: he had been a normal child in an average middle-class Polish family, and took that as the known world, when overnight he was brutally driven out and went with his parents into the ghetto. He would no sooner begin to invest himself in the ghetto and its people, than it would be disbanded with the greatest ferocity, and with loss of life amongst his peers. Then he would repeat the process of identification with the forced labour camp and its inhabitants, and again find that the people around him, in whom he invested his very identity, disappeared or else were killed before his eyes. And finally he went to the *Vernichtungslager*, the death camp, where once again he hopelessly tried to find a solidity where all was in brutal flux.

He was aware that as a survivor, he was a mere remnant, and the huge conundrum faced by his child mind was whether to trust the world ever again.

Paul Valent has marshalled the voices of ten such child survivors. Their accounts are full of heartbreaking salient detail. Can we sustain for example the memory of Eva G, small child, fourteen days in a cattle truck to reach Teresienstadt? Of Richard chased by guard dogs in the Lublin ghetto? And all the separations, deaths and beatings they beheld? And in their suffering the continual suffering of all the uncomprehending children who are the butt of any government's cruel policy.

Valent's commentary on these memories of now-middle-aged survivors is admirably balanced. For there is a great ambiguity in the Holocaust. It is singular among slaughters since it is a case of a government using all its instrumentalities to achieve genocide through an industrial process. And yet many liberals shy away from this perception, believing that by acknowledging the moral uniqueness of the Holocaust, the policies of the Israeli government are validated. These child survivors' stories do not directly confront this issue, but they do add authority to those, like me, who believe that the impulse for the creation of a Jewish State was an utterly valid one given the horrors remembered and recorded here. The Holocaust must be remembered by all of us, even by those who do not always agree with Israeli policy. The relationship between Israel and the rest of the world would be more balanced as a result of all of us acknowledging the unique nature of the Holocaust than it will be by us denying, for political reasons, that it happened or that it has provided the Israeli state with too much leverage.

Child Survivors makes fascinating reading and will be seen as possessing universal import.

Tom Keneally

Preface

—•—

Since publication of the Australian edition many of the aims of the book have been fulfilled. First, as the books sold out rapidly many thousands of people became informed about how major traumas can affect children. Second, hopefully the book contributed to some prevention of consequent child traumas, such as in priority treatment given to children in a number of recently war torn countries. However, we are also unfortunately becoming ever more aware that children are still very widely traumatized.

The book may have contributed to enhanced recognition of child survivors of the Holocaust in the last seven years. One hears less frequently, "But you were too young to be affected." They are less frequently confused with second generation children of survivors. With difficulty they have had claims recognized along with adults for compensation as Holocaust survivors, orphans and slave laborers. They have recognized themselves more and formed child survivor groups around the world with international conferences in many countries.

On a more personal level many individuals whether Holocaust or other childhood trauma survivors, expressed gratitude for this book. It gave them insights and words for the first time for their own traumas. It helped them to see how early traumas pervaded their later life, and it helped them to move on. Adults who survived childhood sexual and other severe traumas particularly identified with child survivors of the Holocaust.

In the larger context, the social climate has become more open to recognition of childhood abuse, and trauma generally. Surprisingly, too, interest in the Holocaust has increased. This may be because the important issues arising from it are more discernible and digestible from a distance of time. Steven Spielberg's film *Schindler's List* (based on Thomas Keneally's *Schindler's Ark*) and later the Shoah Foundation with its tens of thousands of testimonies also gave impetus to Holocaust awareness. Yet counterforces have been active too — revisionists who deny the Holocaust, and those who claim that children's memories of sexual abuse have been falsely implanted by therapists.

In the academic field trauma has become a more accepted field of study, including childhood trauma, and transgenerational transmission of trauma. Arguably child survivors of the Holocaust are the most fertile group for such studies as the sources of their traumas are well documented and they have been followed up now for almost sixty years. They serve as a benchmark for childhood traumas. For instance, the way child survivors of the Holocaust remembered and did not remember can be compared to the way survivors of childhood sexual abuse recall their traumas. It is gratifying that *Child Survivors* has been used for a number of academic theses around the world. In my own work, my knowledge of child survivors of the Holocaust contributed seminally to my subsequent books, *From Survival to Fulfillment; A Framework for the Life-Trauma Dialectic* and *Trauma and Fulfillment Therapy; A Wholist Framework.* These books cover theoretical and practical concepts of trauma.

So what is the need for this second edition? If no other reason, over the latter years a constant demand for the out-of-print book has persisted, and many booksellers and individuals have asked for another edition. More importantly, the stories in the book have not lost their value, and with the extra distance of time they may have become even more valuable. For instance, they can contribute to questions of the roots of morality, memory, resilience, and more specific scientific questions of roots of psychosomatic symptoms, psychiatric illnesses and transgene rational transmission of trauma.

Just like in *Schindler's List* the little girl epitomized the Holocaust, the children in this book epitomize vividly the different facets of Holocaust horror. They do so from different ages, ranging from baby to adult ways of viewing and remembering.

The stories have not lost relevance, freshness, vibrancy or poignancy. Though the subjects in the book have progressed in their lives in the last seven years (in the main they have painfully clawed out more life for themselves), their original stories stand just as true today as seven years ago. To preserve their organic wholeness and power, I decided not to alter the stories in this edition, except for typographical errors. However, I have made some alterations in the commentaries, which bring them up to date with current knowledge.

As they read the book, I suggest that readers pace themselves according to what is comfortable for them. From experience some read the stories voraciously as they help them to understand themselves. Others have found a slower pace more comfortable, as each story requires extensive assimilation.

Lastly, I would again like to thank the child survivors in this book. They were anxious about laying themselves bare in this book, but they have been gratified with the responses to their stories both from family and friends, and more distant readers. They continue to wish that their stories may help others.

Introduction

— • —

The death of one child is difficult to comprehend. The murder of one child is even harder. The murder of one and a half million children is impossible to understand. And yet Nazi leaders decreed that, along with all Jewish adults, all Jewish children were to be exterminated.

The annihilation was near complete. Less than ten per cent of Jewish children survived in Nazi-occupied Europe. This may be the most massive extermination of a group of people in history, as well as the most unequal contest ever. The nature of the annihilation was also unprecedented. Children were not spared any of the suffering and torture meted out to adults. On the contrary, because they could not obey orders and work, they were dealt with more harshly. For instance, in round-ups they were thrown out of windows and hauled by their hair into trucks. Children were not spared segregation, stigmatisation, having to wear a star, overcrowding, hiding, round-ups, mass shootings, deportations, slave labour, concentration camps, torture, medical experimentation, humiliation and murder. Many died through deliberately induced starvation, cold and disease.

I did not know that a million and a half children died in the Holocaust until quite recently. I had vague memories of two boy twins with whom I had played who just disappeared. There was a general but unformed sense which I had at the time of people disappearing. I have photographs of three cousins with whom I had stayed on the farm when my parents were deported by the Nazis who disappeared. But even while I was with my parents the dread of disappearances remained unformed. Why dread? Because as a four year old, I had already experienced the disappearance of our live-in housemaid. And other frightening things had already happened. I remember clearly even now the fear when we crossed the border at night and how the next day I was given a new identity, a new history of my short life. My body became a source of fear. I was told that under no circumstances must I expose my penis. I did not understand about circumcision or why I had to pretend a new story of myself. But I absorbed my parents' admonitions that if I made a mistake something dreadful would happen.

Something dreadful did happen. Two men in trenchcoats approached my parents in the street. After some talking my parents told me that they were going to buy some ice cream with these gentlemen and would be back in ten minutes. Somehow I knew I should not protest. My parents picked me up from my uncle's farm two and a half months later and we spent the rest of the three years hiding in Budapest as Aryans. I was seven at the end of the war. It has taken much inner searching and two trips to reconstruct and flesh out this time, especially the two and a half months of separation. It was necessary for me to revisit and understand my past as it was the source of much later anguish.

Children want to express their inner turmoil to the outside world. I started to write a book at the age of nine. I wanted to convey something of my hidden fears and to convince the world to cease persecuting me and my parents and other good innocent people. I had to stop writing after a page and a half because I knew too little about the war and about myself. But a part of me has always been writing this book.

Not that I knew it. I became convinced that I was lucky. After all, I had lived through the war, my parents were intact and I had always been loved and cared for. If anyone had cause for complaint it was my parents. It was they who had escaped a cattle car bound for Auschwitz after their arrest, they who lost so many family members. My job was to strive to be an Australian. I followed football and drank beer.

I studied medicine and later psychiatry. I became involved in other people's traumas. I married and had children. I was successful. But still something deep down inside kept bothering me. It always had.

At a conference in 1989 I met Sarah Moskovitz. I did not know at the time that she had written about child survivors and that she together with Dr Judith Kestenberg were the discoverers of child survivors. On the way to a panel of child survivors she asked me, 'Are you a child survivor?'

'No,' I replied. 'My parents were survivors.'

'Where were you during the war?'

'Budapest.'

'How old were you at the end of the war?'

'Seven.'

'So you are a child survivor.'

'But I have not been in concentration camps.'

'It does not matter. You are a child survivor.'

I met at the panel another child survivor who had been in Budapest during the war. We talked and talked. We must have been like two Martians meeting our own kind for the first time. We found that we had felt similarly and we had extracted similar meanings from our situations. Through each other we both felt suddenly more human.

I wanted to continue this experience and for others to benefit similarly, so I founded a child survivor group in Melbourne. We tell and record our stories and discuss issues arising out of our stories. We ran an international conference recently. There is a sense of family at child survivor meetings. Everyone can be genuine.

It is a difficult task to integrate traumas and to use them as a source of wisdom and means to help others. For me, perhaps it is not an exaggeration to say that from the little boy's marginalisation and need to understand, there developed an adult with some capacity to question, learn and teach in the fields of stress and trauma, and to integrate answers into medicine and psychiatry. For instance, in liaison psychiatry I found that people's medical illnesses were intricately connected with their psychological and social upheavals. During my stay in Israel I found that, contrary to general opinion, the Six Day War had marked and varied effects on both soldiers and civilians. In a bushfire population I saw the evolution of survivor guilt and depression, and of physical illnesses. And in my psychotherapy work I found more and more how forgotten childhood traumas pervaded my patients' lives. Of course none of these discoveries were extraordinarily original, but they gave me a perspective from which to view both non-Holocaust and Holocaust patients. The latter included adult, second-generation and child survivors.

I found that though the meanings people made of the traumas

varied, *all* people shared similar types of distress following their traumas. However, where child survivors of the Holocaust varied from their counterparts was that their traumas, and those of their parents, were relatively stark and well-documented compared to other groups such as incest victims. Thus the distress of Holocaust survivors was like a clear standard against which the distress of others could be compared.

Child survivors of the Holocaust do not like to establish a hierarchy of suffering among themselves. Nor do I wish to say that their trauma and distress is greater than that of other groups. But, generally speaking, child survivors of the Holocaust did suffer multiple and severe traumas in most horrible circumstances and their distress has been widespread, even if unacknowledged till recently. But rather than concentrate on the enormity of these traumas, I suggest we use them to shed light on the widespread abuse and subsequent distress of children everywhere. I found that wherever I looked in my medical or psychiatric practice, children bore silent and unacknowledged witness to their sufferings in many ways throughout their lives.

So this book is the culmination of a mutual desire, shared by myself and the interviewees, for child survivors to have their traumas documented, recognised, understood and prevented in the future. We hoped to help all children with similar traumas, and to provide a framework for understanding trauma more generally.

The interviewees and I were very aware that our individual needs were less important than the complete veracity and authenticity of the individual stories. The interviewees were therefore very open and honest. My own survivor experience facilitated empathy and trust. Yet I was careful to not mix my story in with those of the others.

Nevertheless, my past experience had made me aware of certain issues which were followed up with each interviewee. These issues included the following questions: do children remember what happened? How important are memories, and is it better to have them or to forget? What makes one remember or forget? What difference does the age of the child make to the outcome in survivors? What is the influence of parents in traumatic situations? What do children do to survive, how do they cope? What do they suffer, and how do their traumas influence their lives? Do these experiences lead to physical and mental illnesses, and which ones? How are survivors' identities, values, and moral and religious outlooks affected? What is the effect of their traumas on the next generation?

In order to answer some of the above questions I needed to have a range of stories. So I chose to include in this book people from a variety of backgrounds, with differences in age, gender, country of survival, type of persecution and survival of parents. I included those from within and without our child survivor group, though the majority belong to it. I included two siblings to indicate the differences which can occur even within the same family. I also included two non-related children of different ages who were in the same camp. Some skews in representativeness had to occur in such a small sample. For instance three children survived in France.

No one whom I asked to be interviewed refused. All the subjects agreed readily to be interviewed. The interviews took place on a single day, with only interviewer and subject present and took between two and a half and seven hours. There was usually only one interruption, for refreshments. The interviews were both audiotaped and videotaped.

Each interviewee was told that the audiotape would be used in Judith Kestenberg's child survivor research project and the videotape would be a record whose use would be determined in the future. Each person was told that they could refuse either recording method. None did. Each interviewee was told that they could delete sensitive information after the recordings if they wished, as long as the deletion and its reasons were recorded. Otherwise they could use pseudonyms, but the records had to be true. No deletions were requested. One interviewee requested to be anonymous.

My impression was that the interviewees soon disregarded both recording devices and immersed themselves in a personal communication with me. For instance, they often continued speaking without interruption while I changed tapes or when we had refreshments.

After obtaining their consents, my only instruction to the interviewees was to tell their stories. I interrupted as little as possible, only to clarify details, and occasionally to ask, 'How did you feel about this?' In the second part we reviewed the story and saw what influence wartime experiences had in later life. Here I asked more direct questions and referred to feelings and meanings, but still allowed the flow of the story as much as possible. This part often took as long as the first part.

After the interview we wound down, often over a cup of tea. Within a week I communicated with the interviewees to see how they felt. They usually said that they had been stirred up for a few days but were settling. They were pleased to have given the interview. Most had not delved as deeply or comprehensively into their stories previously and had found it worthwhile to have done so.

Throughout the book I used child survivors' own recorded words as much as possible. However, for readability I have omitted redundant words and repetitions and as the subjects struggled to find words for their experiences I wrote down the most cogent solutions to those struggles rather than the whole process. Nevertheless, when it seemed important to demonstrate that process, I included it.

I gave the edited transcripts of the interviews to the interviewees. They only corrected technical points such as dates and places. I was most impressed that no one wanted changes to any matters of substance however painful they might have been. There were only three exceptions to this. One was a homosexual experience by one of the subjects, an illness of one of the children, and a traumatic experience of one of the survivors' children. In each case the deletions were made for the sakes of other people's confidentiality and they did not affect the substance of the survivors' stories. Some were initially doubtful about publishing feelings about their parents who were still alive. However, as they saw that this was an important part of their stories they wished these feelings to be included and to work out their feelings with their parents directly. No one suggested any alterations to my comments at the end of their stories.

I showed each person the copy of the final story after making their own corrections and including the editor's suggestions which were only technical. They agreed to the final copy without exception. On the whole, most found reading their stories as coherent wholes both involving and sometimes shocking. They often looked at themselves with more respect than previously for what they had survived and how they had achieved it.

Finally, for whom is this book written? As I was writing the book, I was aware of my various roles. I was acting as an historian of a significant aspect of the Second World War which had been omitted from other historical writings; I was a child survivor myself; but I was also a conceptualiser, a doctor, psychologist and scientific philosopher. I realised that the people in this book threw up questions for us all in our own struggles to find meaning from extraordinary events.

This book may be of interest to historians and especially those interested in the Holocaust. It should be of interest to professionals interested in the effects of trauma, and especially of the effects of trauma on children. However, sometimes it is worth observing in depth a period of history or a group of people because they reflect more starkly than usual *general* human tendencies. Not only do our child survivors alert us to similar groups of children who suffer major turmoils, but they alert us to our own broader humanity as well. For who has not suffered trauma in childhood, even if on a smaller scale? Child survivors may contribute to our own self-knowledge, by helping us to acknowledge the roots of our patterns of thinking, behaviour, moral outlooks and values.

Readers may be deeply stirred by the child survivors' stories. If distressed I suggest readers take time out and read the book in digestible fractions. On the other hand, others may skim through the book or put it down and distract themselves. Thus readers may reflect the child survivors' own responses. My hope, and the hope of those in this book, is that to some extent each reader will derive some extra knowledge and compassion for him or herself, and for other children.

Eva S.

—•—

'UNLESS I TURN UP

IN ONE OF YOUR

TINS OF MEAT'

$\mathcal{E}$VA SLONIM HAD told her story briefly two and a half years earlier to the child survivor group, and then stayed away. It was a striking story of humiliation and pain told with dignity, but with only a thin protective skin. I suggested this interview with trepidation. However, Eva readily accepted, saying she had been preparing herself for years to tell her story. She said that she had not read anything about the Holocaust because she wanted her testimony to be 'pure'. She warned that for that reason her dates would be subjective and possibly inaccurate.

I arrived at a modern wealthy house in the centre of Caulfield. Eva herself was elegant, and looked younger than her age.

I WAS BORN IN Bratislava, Czecho-
slovakia, on 29th of August 1931. For me life before the war was very
much like life is now in Australia. We were very well off. We lived
opposite the President's palace. My father had a large textile business.
We had a maid and a German nurse in our household caring for us.
I was molly-coddled, I suppose. For example, my nurse always
accompanied me to school which was only ten minutes away. Though
I attended the orthodox day school, I had many non-Jewish friends,
with whom I felt totally equal. Our life was very nice until 1938 or
1939, when we started to receive word from my mother's parents in
Austria that things were very difficult for them there.

'But even in Slovakia there started some anti-Semitic outbursts.
I was seven or eight when my brother kept saying that he was assaulted
on his way to school. My parents did not believe him. They blamed
him for picking fights, and admonished him to be a good boy.

'I could not stand this any more, so one day I stole out of the
house, and I saw to my horror that as soon as Kurtie turned the
corner, four to six youths took his cap off, punched him, threw him
to the ground, and left him. He was totally powerless. Then he just
picked up his things. I had this terrible feeling, so I ran home and
told my parents what I had seen. They said, "Ha, this could never
happen in Czechoslovakia." My father said, "We were born here! My
parents were born here!" "But I saw it!" I cried. "Oh, well, we'll
report it to the police." This is how unprepared and unbelieving we
were when this whole thing unfolded on us.

'And yet my mother's family escaped Austria to Israel. In 1939 my father paid for the departures to Israel of all his employees. My father stayed because my aunty, who was a partner in the business, refused to leave and "live as a pauper" elsewhere, and also my father did not want to leave his ill parents.

'One day I stood in our dining-room, and I saw Germans marching in the street. My parents were horrified, stunned, devastated. But our German nurse, with whom I had shared a bedroom, whom I trusted and cared for till that day, jumped with joy, and exclaimed, "I am glad that I have lived to see this day!" That was my first great disappointment and feeling of being betrayed.

'The Germans were singing, "Today Germany is ours, tomorrow the world." ' Eva said the words in perfect German, the language she had learnt from her nurse. 'Suddenly our whole life was transformed. Three days later the Germans and their Slovak collaborators barged into my grandparents' flat downstairs. They assaulted my seventy year old grandfather, knocked out his teeth, and twisted the chain of his pocket watch around his neck. They dragged him like this, bleeding profusely, into our part of the house, and warned, "This will happen to you if you don't toe the line". We were in total shock.

'Then they came to arrest my father. I was in the room in bed with diphtheria. I started to cry hysterically at them taking my father away. One of the soldiers started to dance to humour me. I think they had a plan, and they wanted it to go smoothly, with people cooperating with them. Later they shot hysterical people, but at this time they still wanted to quieten me down.

'They did take my father away. My mother, and others like her, received a ransom notice. My mother sold property and paid the money, and luckily my father was returned. Others only received the ashes of their relatives, with warning notes to toe the line.

'Next they confiscated money in the bank. Edicts ordered us to hand over all our gold, silver, and jewellery. They gave my father receipts which were to fob us into believing that after the war our goods would be returned. In fact they just facilitated a more orderly handover than would have occurred had they just grabbed our property.

'The next edict ordered all Jewish boys over the age of sixteen to go into a "voluntary" labour force. They even gave a list of what they should bring — rucksacks, boots, etc. Again, one could rationalise that going to work was not the end of the world, that labour was needed in war, but why only Jewish boys?

'The next edict was for young girls over the age of sixteen. That was already more frightening, but they had to comply, because everyone's age, sex and address had been registered right at the start. If anyone did not turn up, they took hostages. The next edict took married couples without children. So people were left with no money, no youths. We were powerless. We did not realise at the time, no human mind could conceive, that all this was part of a most sinister plan.

'Then they confiscated businesses. Any gentile, any peasant could say, "I want Mr Weiss's [Eva's family name] business". So a Mr Josef Krampl said that. But because he was illiterate, he needed the Jew to run his shop. There was a scheme where such so-called "*arizators*" could have their Jews, and they were exempt from deportation.

'Krampl also took over our house. We moved into a semi-ghetto. The President, Tiso, and the Prime Minister, Tuka, were Catholic priests. Tiso pronounced on the radio that Jews were inferior creatures. As such, it was permissible to do away with them, according to the Bible. He exhorted the population to collaborate in this, not that they needed much encouragement.

'At school we were not allowed to use maps, so we used parts of the body instead. We had no idea what we were taught. One day all our teachers were taken away and the school was closed down. My old friends did not want to see me. Bank managers, solicitors, taxi drivers, suddenly refused to have dealings with us and despised us. Everyone dobbed us in, hated us. Nobody loved us. I felt greatly deceived by those I thought were my friends.

'One day when I was twelve, and by then not in good physical condition, I was walking in the street, trying to hide that humiliating star we had to wear by tilting my head. I recognised Tuka, having seen him walk in the park opposite our home in the past. He grabbed my arm, and kicked me in the stomach with his boot, saying, "There, little Jewish girl, now go on". The physical and emotional hurt! There was a priest who hurt a little Jewish girl! I took a tram home. Jews were only allowed in the standing area of trams. Unwittingly, feeling sick from the kick I sat down. A woman screamed, "Look, a Jewish girl sitting, get out!" So I stood up, but they punished me for sitting down by ordering me off the tram. They were all in it together in their hatred of us.'

Eva's impassive face belied her feelings.

'What did you feel during this time?'

'I felt intensely rejected, abandoned, inferior, humiliated. I felt hopeless and helpless.' These were the feelings which Eva had to suppress at the time.

'By now my father had lost his unrealistic optimism. He found hiding places for us all, for when the time came. No one volunteered to hide us out of kindness or charity, only for a lot of money. We lived in the ghetto now, always in fear of *razzias* [roundups].

'We had two rooms in the ghetto. My parents always helped others. At one stage we hid eighteen people in the two rooms, and we smuggled their excreta out in a bucket. On either side of all these people were my grandfather and grandmother dying on their beds. My grandfather was crying all the time, "My poor children are dead". My father forged letters in his brothers' names, but my grandfather saw through this ploy.

'My father also cared for the residents of an old age home in the ghetto. He even took away our milk to give it to them. I thought he was cruel to do that, I longed for that half a glass of milk a week. He gave away our clothes as well. I helped him to care for the old people.

'During this time I also became the clandestine messenger girl, working outside curfews, delivering money here and there. I was chosen because I had blonde hair, and did not look Jewish.

'This was in 1944, and I was twelve and a half. Things were very, very difficult. There were hardly any Jews left. My father had lost one hundred and eighty members of his family. My father's brother and family of four children, who had lived in the upper storey of our place, another brother with five children, all my father's cousins, they were all gone.

'I have never talked about how I felt at this stage. One day in the ghetto two men came dressed in SS uniforms. They told us they were Jews who had escaped from Auschwitz. They had worked in the *Sonderkommando* [body disposal unit], and they told us what was happening in Auschwitz. One of them lives in Melbourne now.

'So I knew things were very bad, and that the chances of us surviving were very, very small. Notwithstanding all that we were still religious, and I still had private lessons in German and in German literature. There was this strange dichotomy in my parents' minds. Crazy, from today's perspective.

'One night they came to get us. My father saw them coming and told my sister and me, in our nighties, to jump out the window into the garden, and to run wherever we could. But the house was surrounded and we were brought back into the house. My mother then faked a hysterical attack which convinced even us at the time. She was out of breath, apparently dying. They went to get a straitjacket for her. When the caretaker who guarded us went away for a minute, we all ran to our hiding place. My father had the foresight to get a flat, furnish it, and open a branch of his textile business in it for our German nurse. She was prepared to hide us temporarily now because my father threatened to tell the authorities if we were caught that her property was given to her as a favour by Jews.

'My father was issued another exemption paper because Mr Krampl still needed him, but he now called us all together. We were seven children. Kurti was the eldest and fifteen months older than I. Neomi was fifteen months younger than I, Marta three years younger than I. Then my mother lost two children, so Judith was six years younger than I, Renata and Ruth were ten and eleven years younger than I.

'My father said, "The chances of us all surviving are very, very minimal. I am sending the little children to Hungary with Mrs Tafon." We shaved their hair off, as they were officially boys, and drugged them with injections. I took off my star and accompanied them to the train. My six year old sister Judith was the next to go with Mrs Tafon. In those days people would report even a little child who displayed anxiety just in case he or she was Jewish. So we told Judith to look at Mrs Tafon when she waved to us. But she looked at us, and waved to Mrs Tafon.' This was one of the few times that Eva cried in the interview. 'That was the last time I ever saw her.

'By the time the Germans invaded Hungary, all the children were hidden there. Only I remained, to do my tasks. Father decided to gather the children back. He paid Mrs Tafon a lot of money, and she brought back Marta, Kurti and Neomi. We found out that the two little sisters were already interned. We told Mrs Tafon to look for Ruth, who had a birthmark on her leg, and bring her and the little girl with her back to us. She did manage to bribe her way into a camp in Budapest and got the two sisters out. However, Renata was dying of pneumonia. To show you the mercenary mind of the times, Mrs Tafon phoned my father and asked if she would still get her money for the child if she died. My father said, "Bring her back, dead or alive, and you'll get your money."

'I was put in a taxi to meet them at the border. I knew I was not allowed to display any emotions in front of the taxi driver. I arrived at the border and saw my very sick, emaciated, pock-marked sisters, and I must have displayed some emotion, because the taxi driver turned on me and said, "Oh, you're Jewish! I'll take you all to the Gestapo!" I protested, "I am not Jewish! They are my cousins, and they are not Jewish!" I managed to convince him. But there was this feeling, that he was after me. I was twelve, but they had to kill us all. He took us to near our place, and we walked home. After that we stopped lighting Sabbath candles, because we wanted to retrain the children to not know that they were Jewish. We nursed Renata back to health.

'But then I became very ill and the doctor said I had a touch of rheumatic fever. I had very inflamed tonsils and they needed to come out. Jews were not allowed to have hospital treatment, but there was an exempted Jewish doctor who was willing to treat me as an out-patient. I was put in this dentist's chair, and told to hold the tray for my blood. I could see in his glasses what he was doing. I was frightened of what was being done to me, and because I and my parents were there illegally.

'The nun passed him a needle for the local. The doctor said, "This needle is rusty." The nun . . . the *nun* said, "So what, she is only Jewish." He threw the needle away and asked for another one. This time he complained that it was blunt. "So what, I told you she is only Jewish." I wanted to get up, but he pushed me back into the chair. He took his own needle and injected me. And then I saw him peel my tonsils out, and then,' Eva became agitated, 'he attached a hook to my adenoids and pulled them out. The blood just dripped and I collected it. Then suddenly the doors of the theatre opened, and two

Germans came in. I did not know whether they came because of me, or for him, or because they were just sick themselves. But they dragged the doctor out. He was never seen again.

'The nuns just pushed me out of the chair, told me to wash myself at the basin, and get out. I felt very, very guilty because the doctor may have been taken away for trying to help me. I was in a bad state, and my parents begged the sisters to allow me to lie down for half an hour. "No Jews are allowed to lie down in this hospital. Get out!" We walked home for a good hour because we were not allowed on trams.

'My grandmother died and six months later my grandfather died. I helped to tie his jaw, dress him. Jewish burials were not allowed, so we buried him at night.' Eva breathed hard. 'There were few Jews left, and things became even worse. There were more surprise raids. My father gathered us again and said, "I don't think we have much time left. Kurt and Neomi you are going to hide in a place in the mountains, Eva and Marta, I found a place for you in Nitra [about one hundred kilometres away]." The two little ones were hidden in Ujlak, at the place of one of Count Esterhazy's servants.'

'How had you coped up to this time?'

'I coped day to day because there was so much to do, and it was urgent. I concentrated more on that than the fear I constantly felt. I was very scared that one day I would be taken away. Life was fear and something to do — look after grandmother, massage, feed, encourage grandfather to walk during his illness, help in the old age home, and work out how to share a chicken between eighteen people, giving my grandparents the best parts. I must have been traumatised when I buried my grandfather. But then I had to quickly help my mother with the children. And there was always something to cover up.

'When my father took us to the train to Nitra, he said, "You are on your own now. But we will keep in touch by you and me looking at the stars each night. And whatever hurts you or whatever you are afraid of, look at the stars, and I will listen to you, and answer you." And that was of very great help to me. Nevertheless, the separation felt final, terrible. And my father also said, "I have only one piece of advice, my child. If you are ever caught, don't admit that you are

Jewish, however much you are tortured. Because if you admit it, you will surely die. Otherwise you may have a chance to live." These words came to be embedded in my mind.

'I had papers, extracted from the German nurse, documenting that I was her sister. We lived in a flat all alone in great fear and anxiety. The nurse visited us sometimes, but she took away the meagre food and clothing which we had, and she never delivered the letters we wrote to our parents, so we lost contact with them.

'Marta could not speak Slovak or German, so we could not communicate. She scratched me out of frustration. I had to hold on to her at night, because she sleepwalked. Eventually she learned enough Slovak for us to understand each other, but not enough for her to converse with others.

'We went to church, prayed, went to confession, and visited the little sisters in Ujlak each Sunday, paying the man who looked after them. But we were running out of money, food and clothing. We were hungry. As well, everyone watched us. The neighbours reported us because they noticed that I did the housework on Fridays, never on Saturdays.

'The Germans came on many occasions to interrogate us, and I always managed to convince them that we were not Jewish. One day a high official with the death skull insignia interrogated me. After I convinced him, he offered me a job as a caretaker to his children. I asked him where he lived. "I live in Auschwitz," he said. I mastered my shock and horror, and passed the test. I said innocently, "Where is that?" "In Poland." I asked, "Why are you here now if you live in Poland?" "Because tomorrow we are mounting a surprise raid on all the Jews in Bratislava. There will not be a single Jew left when I finish tomorrow." My parents were in Bratislava.' Eva's voice shook. 'So I said that yes, I would like to work for him if my sister could come too. We agreed that he would return after he finished his job. He did not return.

'I had been too scared to attempt to make contact with my father previously, but as soon as the man left, I went to a public phone and rang 6236, my father's place of work. My father answered. I said, "There will be a raid tomorrow. Everybody will be liquidated." and I hung up. I know now that my father ran out of the shop and on his way home he told every Jewish person the news. All the Christians already knew. When my father arrived home, his house was already guarded by the caretaker, who was to make sure that no Jews left the house. But when his wife called him inside for a minute, my parents bolted, and went to their hiding place.

'A week or so later, the owners of our flat hid with us for a couple of days, in transit between hiding places. The day after they left we were buying our meagre rations at a stall when we saw a group of armed soldiers marching, led by the head of the *Hlinková Garda* [local Nazi party], and accompanied by an Alsatian dog. I still felt sufficient affinity for my country to think, "Oh, no, some more boys going to the front." But they turned into our block of flats. Marta and I wanted to run, but the stall holders said, "Don't you run! Go home, we are watching you." I told Marta to duck into the shop just before our house, but the whole street saw that these soldiers were coming for us, and the shopkeeper threw her out. We went home.

'The group of soldiers came in. Their leader pushed me against the wall, punched me in the temple with a knuckleduster, and said, "You are Jewish!" "I am not." My father's advice was at the forefront of my mind. He punched me again and said the same thing. I said I was not Jewish. He said to the Alsatian, "Get her!" I jumped on to a chair, and from there on to a cupboard. The man pulled me down and made me take off my skirt and pants, and put me across a chair, and hit me on my bottom with a rubber stick, the soldiers counting to twenty-five, and then another twenty-five behind my knees.' Eva was breathing heavily. 'I believe I screamed a lot. Then he pushed me against a wall and said, "Well, are you Jewish?" and I said, "No, I am not."

'Then in front of all the soldiers, I was so embarrassed, he opened my blouse, pinched my breasts, I was very sore, then he pinched my stomach, and screamed, "Well, are you Jewish?" "No, I am not! NOT!"' Eva looked frightened and cried. 'He said, "I have orders to kill all Christian girls, and keep Jews alive. What are you?" I said, "I am a Christian, and if all the Christians have to die, then kill me too." Then he said "Close those windows, I've had enough!" He put his revolver against my head and said this was my last chance. I said, "I am not Jewish." He put the gun away. He threw all our belongings down the stairs. They were then loaded on to the truck. Marta just cried and cried through all this, and luckily they left her alone.

'I had purposefully befriended a German girl who was the daughter of the *Obersturmtrupführer*. I thought that one day I could use her to testify that I was not Jewish. Lovely girl. As we were being pushed on to the truck, she came running, "Anča, Anča, what is the matter?" I said, "They think that I am Jewish." She said that her father was out of town. So I said, "Ring 4393, and tell my sister [the nurse] that everything has been taken away." You see, a non-Jew would not worry about being arrested for being Jewish, but would worry about property being taken away. That is how shrewd we had to be. We were not children. I don't know if we were grown-ups or animals.

'We were taken to a detention camp in Nitra. Only those who could work were given rations, so I had to share my rations with Marta. My work was sorting out confiscated Jewish property. We slept on wooden shelves with absolutely no bedclothes or covers. Every morning at four o'clock I was taken for interrogation to Mr Gombarik, the *Hlinková Garda* chief. To this day I keep waking each night at four o'clock, hearing the boots coming to get me. Each morning he systematically hit me with a knuckleduster, and pinched and kicked me. Then after all this torture he asked me if I would like to sleep with him. I was so naive, but I was suspicious of his request and said, "Sure, if you would like to sleep at my place, and if my sister can come along too." Thank God nothing came of it.

'He became more frustrated and angry with me, as I did not admit to being Jewish. He threatened that if I did not confess, he would send me to a camp where they would make tinned meat out of me, while if I confessed, he would be kind to me. I did not confess.

'He put a Jewish spy on me. As we were sorting, she picked up a *talith* [prayer shawl], and asked me what it was. I said "a blanket". A boy Simon, aged eighteen, who worked next to me whispered, "Don't tell, don't answer." She reported him, and the next day we all had to watch his public execution. And again I felt very, very guilty for being instrumental in his death because he tried to help me.

'Then they caught the nurse, my supposed sister. They roughed her up a bit, and she quickly denounced us. Marta and I were taken into a huge barrack flanked by soldiers. We had to walk the length of the barrack, at the end of which there was a quasi-tribunal. For two little children! There was Gombarik and his whole entourage. He said, "You are Jewish!" I said, "No, I told you I am not." He slapped me and I felt my face getting bigger and bigger. He said, "You are Eva Weiss from Bratislava," and he stated my address. I realised that he knew. There was no more point to deny, to fight. I said, "Yes."

'Just as I said it, in came the *Obersturmtrupführer.* "Hold it, hold it, I vouch for those girls. They are my girls, they are not Jewish." "Too late!" said Gombarik. "They have just admitted it." The next day Gombarik came to see us off at the train. He said, "Goodbye, Anča, my Christian friend, Eva my Jewish friend. We shall never see each other again." By then I was so angry, so hurt, so bruised, I really wanted to die. I said to him, "Unless I turn up in one of your tins of meat. Then think of me," and I got on the train.

'I still had a gold pen which I offered to a Slovak guard and asked him if he would let me jump the train. One so much wants to live that one tries anything. He agreed. "Would you shoot at me?" "Yes, but I would miss you." "But then others would shoot too," I suggested. He agreed, and said he could not influence them. I could not take the risk. We arrived in Sered.

'There they announced that they were looking for professional knitters. I said I was one, though I had never knitted a thing. I offered my services on condition that my sister stayed with me. They gave me this beautiful angora sweater to finish. I played with it till the train left. Then I tried to knit, and all the stitches unravelled. I got a very big hiding from the Jewish superintendent, and we were listed for the next day's transport. On the way to the holding room for the train, I saw an important looking SS man. I went to him saying I was falsely arrested for being Jewish, and I gave him a Christian name. He kicked me so hard that I fell to the ground. I learnt that his name was Bruner; he is currently in Syria. A hundred of us were forced to stand in the tiny holding room.

'On the train there was no room to move, and there was no food. There was a bucket in the middle for excreta. We all knew where we were going, and we were terrified. Marta and I felt extra vulnerable because we were the only children without parents, or a support group. We felt alone, orphaned. A man offered to throw me out of the train wrapped in blanket in return for a sexual favour which at the time I did not understand. It all seemed too impossible and risky, and I was too sore and frightened.

'The journey seemed to be very long. At stops we screamed, "Water! Water!" We were starved, thirsty, and run down. Some vomited, others soiled the floor. Some had heart attacks, and some were already dead. After seven days we arrived in Auschwitz.

'Someone picked up Marta who looked through the grille. She described chimneys and smoke. The smell was terrible. The train stopped and the doors were flung open. Soldiers came in and said, "All women, children and older people on the right, people over sixteen on the left. Some boys said to me, "Come with us. You could pass for sixteen." It is a horrible thing to be put to the test like that. But your will to live and the fear of death are so great, that you are even prepared to abandon your little sister. And she said to me, "Go, Eva. I can die by myself. Only one thing, remember the day of my death so you can say *kaddish* [memorial prayer] after me, and tell Mum and Dad which day I died." And I went . . . I went with the living.' Eva said this softly, puzzled, and sorrowful.

'As I went she tugged at my skirt, and said, "I am so frightened to die alone." I said, "All right, I'll stay with you, and from now on we'll never separate." And then they flung the doors open again, and shouted *"Raus! Raus!"* ["Out! Out!"], with dogs barking.

'The sight which greeted us was terrible. As we walked down the road we were flanked by prisoners behind barbed wires. They looked like insane animals, mad eyes looking out of shaven, emaciated bodies. I then made a vow — I was religious. I wanted to survive first, but I wanted God not to deny me my feelings, to make me inhuman like those bodies flanking me. I was as much afraid of losing my humanity as I was of death.

'Dr Mengele, though I did not know his name then, selected us to live. We were taken to a *Familienlager* [family camp]. From there I saw the old people I used to look after in the ghetto in a truck, obviously on their way to being exterminated. That first night we were very bewildered. There were rumours that they allowed us to live because the gas chambers were full, another because the war had ended. Marta stood on a bridge. Some Germans came and pushed her into the sewer. She was drowning there till some boys ran down and pulled her out, covered in excrement. There was no water to wash her with, so everyone donated their coffee instead.

'The *Blockelteste* [block leader], a Jewish man approached me to sleep with him. Again I did not know what he was talking about, but I told someone about it, at whose suggestion I hid among the ten people in my bunk, and covered myself with the dirty carpet we were given. After he could not find me, again, he took someone else.

'Our *kapo* [barrack leader] took a liking to me, and chose me to be his cook. He had a little room and it was warm there. I took off my shoes in order to save wear. My sister took them, and sold them for a piece of bread. But after she threw my shoes across the barbed wire, the woman said, "You're not going to live anyway, so I won't give you the bread." So I had to make myself shoes from cardboard.

'Three days later the *kapo* was in a very bad mood. He threw the things off the stove and burnt my arm, and screamed, "You know why I brought you here? Because you look like my daughter! And why are you alive, and not she?" And I pleaded, "But it's not my fault, I did not kill her." But he choked me and bashed me. And he took me to the latrines, I can still smell them, and he hit my head against the basin. He shrieked, "That's why I took you, not because I like you! You look like my daughter. Why are you alive?" ' Eva's voice faltered.

'Then my burnt arm was tattooed and we were taken by truck to what we were told were showers. We had to pass a huge concrete pit. Later I learnt that my sister Judith had been burnt in it. We had to undress in the chamber. I saw my teacher, whom I had revered so much, naked there. It was so humiliating to be naked. One Jewish inmate shaved our heads, another shaved the other parts. Then we were pushed out like animals. Some young women even paraded in desperation hoping to be noticed and to save their lives. Some people's will to live was so strong that they would stoop to anything. Others went to the gas chambers willingly because their children or parents were taken there. How one acted at the time depended on the fear and the will to live. That will to live was terrible,' said Eva with pained anguish, 'because it could make you choose yourself over others.

'We were hurled like animals into another chamber. Some screamed,

"This is the gas chamber!" We heard the door click shut and we were hermetically sealed off. We thought we were going to be gassed. But then water came, and we washed with the soap which we were told was made from humans. Another door opened. Petrol was poured on our heads. I was given a pair of soiled underpants, obviously having belonged to someone suffering their last agonies. The coat I was given missed a sleeve, and all the clothes were disgusting. But my little sister stole two of each garment.

'Then we were taken to the children's camp. The scene still haunts me. The mothers knocked on the door crying, "Can I see my baby?" and were torn away by the Germans, while the children cried all night. And this I'll take to my grave [Eva initially forbade this to be published], I am so ashamed of my own people. The *Blockelteste* (who now lives in Melbourne), took away the can of milk which was left for the children who were crying with hunger, fear and being alone. Another girl and I struggled with her, but she said "Look, you're not going to make it anyway, so give us a chance." And she took the milk away from us.

'We were separated into different groups. Marta and I were taken to the twins camp. Whether we were earmarked by Dr Mengele at the initial selection, or later, I do not know. There was a family of dwarves there on whom he experimented. There were different ways he chose children for experiments. One way was to order us to sit on beds and he chose us according to the way our legs hung. The most horrible way was to make us play "The farmer had a wife". Unbeknown to the child in the centre who chose another child, the chosen child was taken for experiments. Again you felt that you were instrumental in causing someone else's death. This dilemma was as difficult to live with as all the other traumas that were going on.

'Another time they called for volunteers to holiday in Switzerland. Some volunteered. You had to keep quiet about your suspicions about the ruse, because if others did not volunteer, they would take you. Another time an SS woman warned a boy she liked and we followed him to hide in the toilets while Dr Mengele came to choose.

'There was a five year old kid who rocked back and forth all day like a religious person. They came to get him. He turned around to me and said, "Please remember today, and say *kaddish* after me." I said, "But I don't know what date it is!" Then I said, "You know what, my number will be your *kaddish*." And he left quite happily.' Eva repeated with wonder and tears in her voice. 'And of course this [the tattooed number] is his *kaddish*. And when I die, I will have it taken out and embalmed, just as a testimony.

'There was a pregnant woman in the barrack. She gave Marta and me a teaspoon of her extra sugar rations. We calculated that we would live an extra month from this. We made similar calculations from a tablespoon of porridge. Another time someone threw a cigarette over from the men's camp. Martha took it and peddled it for bread. But having learnt the trick with my shoes, she ran away with the bread and peddled the cigarette again. That gave us some extra nutrition.

'One day Mengele took Marta, and I became hysterical. She was given injections, we do not know what. Then they took me to hospital for experiments. Each child shared a narrow bunk with another child, who spoke a different language. Nothing was given away, no detail was missed.

'I did not think that this was a research hospital. I thought we were there for extermination, because the children did not come back. And when I had been in the twins camp and had the job to carry the buckets from the toilets to the sewer, I went on the way into the chamber where they deposited the bodies after the experiments. I saw one of the boys who had been on my transport sitting naked with his cut off ear and arm placed next to him. You could see lungs and various organs. I realised they did horrific things. In the hospital I saw a boy across from my bunk who was in great pain, and his side literally burst open and his organs spilled out. I was very, very depressed. Many were bled to death. Mengele believed it was blood which caused twins. He knew nothing! All his experiments came to nothing! I am angry that he was given refuge on the basis that he might give useful medical information.

'Then there was a group of three year old children. I saw each being given a tablespoon of porridge, and then an injection. Each child just fell back dead. They must have finished the experiments on them.' Eva contained her emotions with effort. 'A woman gave birth to a child across from me. She delivered the baby herself. There was not a sound. She tied the umbilical cord and ran away. Dr Mengele came in and was hopping mad because the woman had gone. They sent a search party for her. He took the little baby, I can see it now. He injected the baby. It looked like a lame rabbit. He threw it across the barrack. My only relief was talking to the stars and my father.

'One day Dr Mengele came in and asked for my number. This Greek girl said '*Shalom*' as goodbye. I struggled because I knew this was my end. A number of people held me down. Dr Mengele came with a needle, and took my blood — one bottle, two bottles, another bottle. I thought, "I know what they will do with me." But after four bottles he stopped. He walked away and they left me alone.' Eva's voice sounded amazed. 'They told me my blood was going to be used for transfusing Germans.

'Both Marta and I were given injections regularly, I do not know what. But as adults both of us developed severe stomach cramp conditions of unknown cause, and we both had miscarriages. I had three. I can't prove that our conditions were related to those injections, but it seems more than a coincidence. I suffered serious vitamin deficiencies too, due to which I was never allowed to breastfeed.

'There was a mother and child in the hospital. They were not Jewish. They got Red Cross parcels with sardines. I have been mad on sardines ever since. They did not give us any, though I climbed up for the tails which they threw up. When the child died, it had a decent burial. We were jealous of being able to die with dignity instead of just in horror.

'One day suddenly we were given decent bedclothes, everything was cleaned up, our camp uniforms were replaced. A Red Cross delegation came and walked through like you do in a museum. One woman, also Eva, yelled, "Don't believe what you see, this is a showpiece! This is an extermination camp. This is an experimental section. Go and see the gas chambers, the other barracks." The Germans indicated that she was mad. The delegation did not talk to her, or any of us. Every day we hoped the world would come to know about us, that the Allies would bomb the camp. Nothing happened. The woman was publicly hung the next day. No one has ever heard of a Red Cross report.'

'How would you summarise your time with Dr Mengele?'

'My time with Dr Mengele was of terror, being petrified. I never dared to look in his eyes. I just thought I would not come out alive. I have no concept of how long we were there, but it could have been four to five weeks. We were in Auschwitz three months altogether.

'And yet while I was there, I made up my mind that if I survived I would have a large family and recreate what was constantly destroyed there.' Eva's posture indicated grief.

'One day Marta joyfully showed me a piece of shrapnel, indicating that the camp had been bombed. Our fear of bombs was nowhere near as great as our fear of Germans. Then one day we were lined up for Mengele to choose who could go on a long march and who could not. We understood that whoever remained in camp would be killed. By then I was very sick, through the blood letting, the injections, as well as typhoid and dysentery. Dr Mengele ruled me out and sent me to the barrack. But I went around the camp and the second time he selected me to march. But I had severe diarrhoea and no strength. I said to Marta, "You go on the march without me." She said, "Last time you came with me, this time I am coming with you." We went to the barrack followed by a number of children (I was a bit of a leader among the children). The Germans set the camp on fire and left.

'We were trapped between the furiously burning hospital and electrified fences. But suddenly there was a downpour of rain, and the fires went out. Then we realised that we were alone. Some people managed to raid the food stores. Thousands of people died from overeating, but I was too weak to go for the food. A few days later the Germans came back, and they took us on the march.

'Anyone who had stolen better clothes or blankets was soon shot. So was anyone who marched out of line, or helped anyone to walk. Even here there was this terrible problem of loyalty and responsibility. To what extent were you responsible for your friend or relative? Your instinct was to help, but you had to hold back, because that person was already dead, so . . . My sister and I tried to be inconspicuous in the middle of the marchers, and we pulled each other along. Thus we walked from Birkenau [the extermination section of Auschwitz] to Auschwitz.

'As we were taken to our barrack we saw hand-to-hand streetfights. Then we saw through the window that the Russians had won. They lined up the Germans, and told the inmates that they could do what they liked with them. They were not touched. Fifty years later I am still not sure whether this was because of fear, or weakness, or because we were not killers. I would like to think it was because we were not killers. I have no regrets about that, and I would still not kill them.' Eva let herself cry this time. 'No, I would not kill.

'A Russian soldier, who turned out to be Mr Stern from Bratislava, came upon us and told us to hide under a blanket to avoid being raped by the Russian soldiers. My face was wrinkled, my hand shrivelled. Mr Stern said, "When the Russians come, leave your finger outside the blanket to show them that you are an old woman." I did that and said in Polish-Russian that I was an old woman, and they left us alone.

'The Russians offered us all a bath. I was dirty from typhoid and lice, and I had a rash. I thought a bath would help. The Russians were our liberators, so I trusted them and I went. But they called me a Jewish parasite. They turned out to be basically anti-Semitic. I cannot tell you what that did to me. Again they shaved my hair, treated me with contempt. They did put me in hospital and gave me blood, but without any care and attention. I had a nightie which only reached my stomach and I could not get out of bed without embarrassment. My sister brought me *sholet* [a Jewish bean meal] and that was the first time that I ate non-kosher food voluntarily.

'I learnt Russian quickly. One day I overheard the Russians say that they would take all the children with them to Russia. That night Marta and I ran away. We travelled on open goods trains and trucks, wending our way toward Czechoslovakia. At nights we knocked on village doors, and we stayed overnight in stables. They usually gave us bread and milk to eat. Russian soldiers on the trains and in the streets were kind to children, so we had contradictory experiences of them. Someone gave us a little bottle of vodka, and told us that with it we could stop most trucks. We did, but again Marta had learnt not to give what she promised to give. So she withdrew the bottle, or cried, and they did not force her.' Eva laughed.

'One night I took off my shoes on a goods train. There was no toilet and this man emptied himself in my shoes. I slid into them. I wiped as best I could, but I stank. Thus we arrived at a refugee place on the Czechoslovak border. Food, bath were the priorities. Everyone had found someone to provide these for them except Marta and I. I asked a young Jewish man, "Can I have a shower at your place?" I am ashamed to report this, but this woman said to me, "You are a *chonte* [prostitute]." I asked "What is that?" "You can't have a bath at a man's place." "But I have nowhere else to have a bath." "I am going to tell your parents," she said. I did not even know whether I still had parents. What I missed, what hurt, what hurts,' Eva mixed her tenses 'is the lack of feeling toward two little children on their own. Why did the woman not explain kindly, just abused me?

'On my way to have this bath we heard that there was a pogrom, Poles killing Jews in the streets. So we ran back to the house.'

Eva's voice quivered. 'Then came the greatest moment after the war. An army truck came with members of the Jewish Brigade of the British army. They were Czechoslovaks who had emigrated to Israel and there they joined the British army. They said, "Come with us. You will never be alone again. We will take care of you. We will take you with us to Israel. This will never happen to our people again." They took us to Poprad [in Slovakia], to another refugee way station.

'Again we received no kindness from the people there, though we were given a weekly allowance of one hundred crowns. Marta and I had a craving for eggs, so we spent all our money on eggs, and were sick. We did not have the brains of adults. So we went back to begging in the villages again, still in camp uniforms. We got bread, milk and a stable.

'One day we knocked on a door, and this person whom my parents had hidden and helped a lot during the war, opened the door. I saw chocolate and food on the table. I exclaimed, "Chocolates! You know who we are." They were playing cards inside. "Could you . . . please . . . chocolates!" They said "No!" with indignation. "But you know my parents are wealthy, could you lend us some money, we'll pay you back." "No, get out!" Two of their relatives whom my parents had saved ran after us, and said, "We can take one of you, not both." Again a choice! Choose! I said, "Take my sister," and they took her, and found a place for me with a Jewish family. They looked after Marta well, but I still consider their behaviour in separating us as disgusting.

'I still wore camp clothes and clogs and I became a servant to the family where I stayed. The husband brought home material for a dress for me but the woman refused to make it. She was so unkind. Bratislava had not been liberated yet. She said, "I heard on the radio that your parents were shot in front of the State theatre. Now you have nobody. Nobody. I know you are very wealthy. Where is your money?" I said I did not know and she shook me in anger. Marta and I ran away that night. We continued hitchhiking on army trucks.

'In the next town a Dr Epstein recognised us, diagnosed us as having TB, and placed us in a hospital in the Tatra mountains. We were grateful not to have to beg, plead and ingratiate, and to be treated nicely. Our parents found us on a list of survivors, and they sent a Mr Korn to pick us up. But before he could haul us up to the back of the truck, it drove away and we had to hitchhike home.' The comic aspect of this was not lost on Eva.

'We arrived in Bratislava on a Sabbath morning, though we had no concept of time. Just as we arrived at our gate our father and brother were returning from synagogue. My father recognised us though my hair was only three centimetres long.' Eva's voice broke. 'It was a tremendous feeling. But it included being estranged. I could not kiss or cuddle, like an animal which had not been touched for a long time. I also resented the throng of refugees at our place, so that we hardly had anywhere to sleep. Though we did get some extra care, we were but a part of a large camp in our own home. And he kept bringing other sick children home. My father had vowed that if Marta and I survived, he would devote one year of his life to refugees. But I felt a bit resentful, unjustifiably so.

'Slowly we settled in. We all survived except Judith. My mother had Rosanna in the last days of the war.

'My parents arranged for us to see someone for our psychological welfare. I vaguely remember a clinic and talking about the war. We were sent to Switzerland to help our TB.

'Unfortunately, Kurti drowned while we were there. He was the leader of a *Bnei Akiva* [a religious Zionist youth organisation] group. His life's ambition was to live in Israel, and he spoke fluent Hebrew. He was my parents' pride and joy. The group was on an excursion beside the Danube. Because Kurti was very religious, he went to swim on his own, away from the girls. He got into difficulties and yelled for help. But at the same time the group was afraid that some nearby Russian soldiers would attack the girls. The boys in charge had to make a quick choice, and they chose to protect the girls. They did not know whether they could rescue my brother, but they were sure they could save the girls. They told me this only two years ago. It has haunted them all their lives. My parents had another child, Hannah, to replace him.'

'We came to Australia in 1948. It was sheer bewilderment. The food, facilities, having pets, were inconceivable novelties. One time Neomi and I spent all our money on lipstick and face make-up in Coles and had no money for our fares home. We created a stir in the community being seven girls. But my father allowed us out only with another sister present. And by ten he called the police if we were not home. There were funny moments like when a cat had kittens in my father's bed, and when my mother signed blindly permission for us to have our teeth out at school.

'My father brought some money with him, and he started a wafer factory. There was this man we knew who offered to manage it, promising that he would replace my father's lost son, but we lost a lot of money under his management. I worked extremely hard in my father's factory, carrying fifty kilogram sacks of flour (unbeknown to my father) so he would not have to do it. It was still the creed of old people first. In a rescue drill on the boat to Australia we pleaded for our parents to be taken first.

'I always had an ardent desire to study. I had a thirst for knowledge and I was intelligent, but, as I used to say, I was ignorant in seven languages. But being the oldest I was not given a chance, though I did study matriculation in night school after fourteen hours of work, and I passed.

'I overcame my resentment at being in Australia and not in Israel, and I was one of the founders of *Bnei Akiva* here. My group was my first crowd. Through it I met my husband, who was Australian-born. We married when I was twenty-one. I completed a secretarial/business course. In my first job my boss dictated a love letter which I wrote phonetically. I survived being sacked because my accounting was good.

'Later I worked in the physiology department at Melbourne University. I translated articles on kidney experiments on sheep from French and German, and typed our own experiments, which replicated them. I found it interesting that the doctors had psychological reasons to be involved in these experiments. One of the doctors had lost his wife through nephritis. He was so gentle that he always over-injected the animals and they died. It was a very nice, interesting environment for me.

'My sister Neomi developed nephritis. This was the time when successful kidney transplants from identical twins were first reported from Europe. I offered to give my sister a kidney, but it was not accepted because of the lack of success with non-identical twins at the time. She was given salt infusions which today we know are fatal — they were barking up the wrong tree. She died; she was twenty-two.

'Later I typed up lithium experiments done on humans. They used to give large doses, and one patient, a chemist, developed liver complications. I asked my boss, "How can you give him such lethal dosages?" He said, "It's better to die from lithium than die as a manic-depressive." I said nothing, but I thought it was a bit presumptuous of him to decide who should die of an overdose of lithium. I think it was because of my experiences that I had the nerve, as a secretary, to question "Who are you to play the role of deciding who should live and who should die?" This was also the time when the link between smoking and lung cancer was discovered. I asked why they did not publish the results? I was told because the tobacco companies provided the money for the kidney research. At such a time you did not think that you had the means to protest.'

'Did you find it paradoxical to work in a place of medical experiments?'

'I did not consider animals dying a tragedy, and I thought that the experiments were constructive. But when we had fatal human cases, the analogy occurred to me. I worked hard, through Christmas holidays, because the work was important. I continued working there till I was pregnant.

'I wanted to have a lot of children, but I started with three miscarriages. My doctor was horrified at my lack of vitamins, and I was given injections. After the third miscarriage, at six months, I had a nervous breakdown. I must mention here that whenever I am in a dentist's chair, or even a hairdresser's, I go straight into concentration camp. I just have to lie back and I am there. Anaesthetics are the worst experiences of my life. People's eyes looking down at me are Nazi eyes. I am told that when I come out of anaesthetics I say things like "I am willing to work. Don't kill me!" I also feel guilty in hospitals — for lying in such luxury, when the others were killed so miserably. Anyhow, after my third miscarriage I woke from the anaesthetic, and I was alone, without the baby. I had not seen it, it was just taken from me. I looked for my baby in fridges which to me were ovens. I just saw ovens in that labour ward. I was convinced that I had had a hysterectomy, because a nun assured me that I could adopt a baby. Then I tried to run away. That was the first time in my life that I went to pieces. I withdrew and cried all day, for many weeks. I had no treatment.

'From the moment I left camp, I wanted to rebuild. I loved the challenge of children, and I do have five, aged thirty-one to thirty-eight. I made a vow after my first son was born, that when he grew up, we would give him to Israel. He did not know of this vow, but when he grew up he went there. I have two children in Israel. I always felt that I was building, rebuilding what we lost. I have succeeded to rebuild, it was not easy. I also wanted to ensure future survival. In camp I decided that I would learn typing, because you could save your life doing that. I also considered that knowing how to drive could allow me to escape. So at seventeen I could drive a car.' I asked about knitting. 'When I was pregnant and had to stay in bed, I knitted two angora jumpers, of similar colours to those in Sered. I had to get them out of my system, prove that I could do it in an emergency. I have not knitted since.

'I am still really good in emergencies. I immediately put on my concentration camp hat. Also I can do anything when I tell myself that the Germans are chasing me. So I say if I don't return the ball in tennis ten times, they'll get me. So I get the ten returns. Or I say to myself that I do this on command. So I overcome my angina, which I have had about ten years.

'The things which are important to me and what I live for are my family, all of them, and Israel, Israel, Israel. I had to be there for the children during the Gulf War. I wanted to protect them and the future, and share their fate. I had to put gas masks on my grand-children. The notion of gas just made me see the camp. But I put my camp hat on and was very supportive, and organised everything. My stomach became terribly knotted up and since then I have stayed knotted up. And yet it was not like camp, because this time we could defend ourselves and this time I had the opportunity to assert myself. I told my daughter, "We are lucky, this time we can defend ourselves. We can hide, we can bomb them in retaliation, we have a chance to survive. And at worst, we can die with dignity."

'I made a great effort not to burden my children with my past. I stopped myself making them leave their plates empty. But I made sure that they learnt judo so they could defend themselves, that they could swim, and that they could run.

'The first child had most illnesses, including asthma. I did not handle the second child well. I gave him less attention, he is the softest. Perhaps there is something special between us. My family think that I am overprotective of him, but I don't think so.

I asked about love. Eva took time to answer.

'I can care. But I think I am a bit numb, perhaps even more so since my father passed away. My children think I am not warm and demonstrative enough. I am a great helper but do not dish out warmth. I do not have patience for small things such as babysitting. I do not embrace, cuddle, dote or smooch — it annoys me. My daughter said, "Mum, you are a very good mother. You are always there when I need you. But you are not here when I do not need you." I am always busy. I work in our factory (manufacturing underwear) more than I need to. I do not like people fussing over me, nor can I accept affection easily.

'My own mother is a very intelligent woman who has endured a lot. She has also been very caring but very busy. There was never time to talk. My parents never asked me, and I never told them about my camp experiences. After the war my teachers in Slovakia were anti-Semitic. Also, I could not sit my exams because they were on Satur-days. But I did not tell my parents about such matters. I felt they were so hurt and wounded, and their son had died. I was just a lost sheep, wandering the streets and writing poetry on my brother's grave, because I had no one who understood me, talked to me. But I was also busy, having responsibilities of a second mother. After the war I brought up my two little sisters. There was no time to talk.

'My father was caring but very dogmatic, regimented and domineering. Don't get me wrong, he was an extremely charitable and good man, and devoted to his religion. Had I needed money, he would have given it generously. But he was not perceptive of little needs. Though he could afford it, he did not accord us the right to study; rather he placed us where he needed us. I now see that as a tremendous injustice, as we were all talented. I feel I have missed out. But it did not affect my love for him. He had gone through a lot and I would have given my life for him.

'My marriage is good. We are sexually compatible. My husband does not cope well with illness and death and the Holocaust. We married because we were religiously compatible. I have no regrets, because he is intelligent and caring too.'

'What place has religion played in your life?'

'My parents had a very deep religious commitment. They ate kosher throughout the war. I also did not eat horse salami which they gave us at times in camp. And I lost a lot of weight on the boat coming to Australia because I did not eat anything not kosher.

'We stayed religious, we believed it, till liberation. But when that woman in Poprad said that my parents were dead, something happened. My whole drive for survival was in order to reunite with my parents. I ate *sholet* with ham. That was my rebellion.'

'How could you reconcile Auschwitz and God?'

'I wasn't such a deep thinker then. I didn't think of God. I kept things automatically because that is how I was brought up. Later in life . . . since then . . .' Eva was reluctant, sheepish, 'I often rebel. I still keep things because I am used to them. But I cannot go to *shule* [synagogue] without remembering *Yom Kippur* [Day of Atonement the most sacred religious day] in the *shule* in the old people's home in the ghetto. The Germans barged in during prayers and they slaughtered a pig. It jumped to the ceiling in agony. They drank its hot blood. The people cried and prayed, and beseeched the Almighty, but the Germans said, "God does not listen to dogs' barking." Then in camp I saw all those people being taken to the gas chambers. That is what I see in *shule* today. It is agony.

'I read on *Yom Kippur* this year about the torture and execution of the ten famous sages during the Inquisition. They were called before the king and were asked, "What punishment would you mete out for kidnapping someone?" "That person should die," they answered. "So you will die, because your ancestors sold their brother Joseph to the Egyptians." One of the rabbis went into a state of transcendence and asked the angels of God, "Did God really decree for us to die?" And they said "Yes." And the rabbi asked angrily, "Why, we are innocent. Why are we responsible for Joseph's kidnapping?" The answer was, "If you ask any more questions, your whole nation will be annihilated. Just do as you are told!" So he told the sages to accept death and not ask. Is this what God did with us in the Holocaust? I don't know, I can't think of a reason. Are we worse than all other nations, for such a decree to be placed on us? Were those innocent children who were slaughtered and murdered and experimented on . . . I saw a group of sixteen year old girls laid out on a concrete path in Auschwitz and sterilised with bicycle pumps. Many died in great agony because of infection. Were they guilty parties? Did I do anything so bad when I was thirteen, to deserve such a decree? I don't understand. Sometimes I rebel. I am so angry sometimes that I put the light on on the Sabbath.' Eva laughed. 'That is the worst I have done, when I am very angry. At other times I just can't go on with prayers in which God seems to be so hungry for flattery. I would not demean myself by asking a rabbi why we need to praise Him so much? So I don't.'

'Have you ever been openly angry with your parents?'

'Never. I was too disciplined for that. I had debates with God when my father was in intensive care. I begged Him, offered Him years of my life. He accepted my offering and my father improved. There is a God, but I don't believe the rabbis' trimmings.'

I asked Eva about something which puzzled me. 'Considering how precocious you were in everything else, how come you seemed to be so naive on sexual matters?'

'I'll explain with an example. Neomi was fifteen months younger than I, and we were very close in the ghetto. With all the other problems, we had another one. When Neomi went to Budapest, how were we going to communicate to each other the major event of getting our periods? We decided to use the code 'The red aunt from America has come.' In time I got a letter from her with the code. My parents burst into tears, understanding that she had been taken to concentration camp. They wept for weeks for her. The topic in the house was so taboo that I did not dare to tell them the truth. When my parents found out what the code meant, my father chased and hit me. But not for letting them worry so much, but for having such a dirty mind.'

'In what other ways are you still affected by your experiences?'

'I still have nightmares that my children or my parents have been taken away. But the biggest trauma is to make choices. I always have to make a choice. Whenever I come into a room, I feel I have to decide who is to live. Even at the dinner table with my children, I think, "My God, whom would I choose if I had to?" I try to blot it out, but I can't. I find it extremely difficult to sack people, or even to tell them off. To my dismay I preface it, "Don't make me tell you off, and put me in the role of the Gestapo." And when I look at my undressed body, I tell myself, "You wouldn't pass Mengele."

'Looking back, my own worst persecutions were the experiments, and standing at roll calls mornings and evenings. But the humiliation was equally bad. I found it most offensive to be kicked, be pushed off trams, to be demeaned. It has left me still feeling inferior. But during the day, and socially, I lead a very normal life. Nobody knows what is going on in my mind. And I take a Valium every night to sleep.'

'What made you start to talk in recent years?'

'Though Marta and I have stayed very protective of each other over the years, we have not talked about our pasts. I could not tell my children of my experiences face to face either, but I made a tape for them, not as full as this one. I started to think of speaking out already in 1967 during the Six Day War when an Israeli said to me, "In Auschwitz you were cowards. Here we are heroes." I thought, "You do not know what you are talking about. You need to be educated."

'And lately some people say the Holocaust did not happen. I felt it was my duty to keep the memories of those people who died around me alive. I owe it to the little boy, and those who said as they were dying, "Tell the world what happened to us." I get great satisfaction speaking to Jewish schools, because I see tangible evidence that we have made it. And I have gone to the Holocaust Centre for the first time. It is time for me to tell the truth now, the whole truth.

Comment

Eva's story is the individual side of the history of the Holocaust. She tells us what it was like to experience the progressive marginalisation, dehumanisation, persecution, exploitation and finally attempted annihilation of a people. Eva's story is also a story of survival of the remnant of that Jewish group and its struggle for meaning, morality and love.

How did the six year old child survive a world whose might decreed her existence a capital offence? A child who experienced in reality what is reserved for the most horrific imagination, such as being alone and helpless in a world of wicked witches and monsters who torture children, scoop out their organs and tear them apart?

Eva herself said that one way was to keep busy. Even in increasing hellishness, there were periods of adjustment, of eking out whatever security was possible for self and others. Busyness kept terror and other emotions at bay. And keeping emotions at bay was another prerequisite for survival. For instance, there could be no grief for the disappearing and dying relatives and friends.

The child became a survival expert, honing all skills and courage to various strategies required at particular moments. Often decisions had to be made on the spot, the instincts had to be right. It is amazing how a child could appraise the world with such skill. Eva herself expressed wonder at being such an expert 'adult or animal'.

While Auschwitz, with its death factory Birkenau, was the ultimate hellhole on hearth, Mengele's experiments on children and their murders were perhaps the ultimate evil in that hell. The face of evil was not only the physical torture and dismemberment. It was also a cynical attack on basic human bonds, on the basic fabric of human morality and values. Perhaps Mengele's cruellest act was to make children play games in which they believed it was their choice as to who would die. He perversely exploited the natural tendency to survival guilt when one survives and another close to one dies. It gives us pause when we try to understand the roots of morality, that innocents can be made to feel guilt while the evil like Mengele may avoid guilt through ideology and dehumanization of their victims.

Eva was also the victim of other apparent choices where it seemed to her that her survival meant others' death. Thus she felt guilty for the doctor who operated on her tonsils, the boy in Sered, for the girl who was raped instead of her, and most of all when she was momentarily willing to abandon her sister in order to live. Eva is still tortured about what choices she might make each day she lives.

Eva is testimony to the human capacity for the preservation of morality in most extreme situations. Even in this hell, while the Nazis tortured and killed children, Eva was concerned with the replacement of life in the future. She helped other children when she could, tortured herself if she put herself ahead of others, and tried to maintain her feelings and humanity, which she valued as much as life itself.

What personal values guided Eva and enabled her to keep going? Perhaps her own desire to survive would have carried her through. But she was greatly helped by the image of her father who played a godlike role. This father himself placed paramount value on surviving, even beyond religion and care for the old. Adherence to his image allowed Eva to face death and survive. This happened, for instance, when Eva denied her Jewishness even at gunpoint. Eva's father was with her throughout her trials. She talked to him through the stars. The hope of physically reuniting with him and the rest of the family sustained Eva through her suffering.

So Eva cared for her sister and for others. She wanted to undo the death around her, to give eternal life to the boy whose *kaddish* number she still carries; and through her own body to give life to children. Eva survived through a strong physical and mental constitution, a sense of meaningful connection with her godlike father, and luck. She succeeded replacing dead children with live ones.

Did religion help or not? In terms of survival it was a danger which had to be disavowed. It often did not help (it did not help Kurti after the war), though it gave comfort when departing for death. For instance, one could believe that one's soul and memory would live in the *kaddish* prayer. But religion for Eva was a strong symbol of father and his values, it was a symbol of belonging and continuity. At times this was more valuable than life, for instance when she did not eat horseflesh in Auschwitz. But religion did not reach the core survival moral dilemmas. Nor could Eva ultimately reconcile the fate of the innocent Jews around her and a praiseworthy God.

The Holocaust is fertile ground for consideration of moral dilemmas. As if Eva had not been plagued enough by them already, another reared its head. Its manifestation was in Eva's obvious reluctance to mention the hurts inflicted by 'our own people'. It was only her fidelity to 'the whole truth' which allowed her to mention the Jews who gave away her hiding place, spied on her, wanted to exploit her sexually, took milk away from children in camp, cast her out after the war, and wanted to rob her. The threat here was the inability to draw clear lines between victims and perpetrators, between good and bad. It can give us further pause to consider how the drive to survive can sometimes make perpetrators of victims.

A further dilemma has been the normal anger of a child to her father who was not sensitive to her needs of love and fulfilment. Such normal anger seemed like hurting the wounded. It also seemed like ingratitude to this remarkable father who was able to save six of his children and to replace the two who died. Again there was a threat of breakdown of the clear demarcation between good and bad. How could Eva be angry with her father? She could express her anger only symbolically and in secret, rebelling against father and God by breaking minor religious laws.

Another difficult moral dilemma to resolve was Eva's own participation (albeit relatively peripheral) in medical experiments whose morality she questioned. Some may say that she identified with her captors as hostages sometimes do in the so-called Stockholm syndrome. Others may say that she now had the upper hand in a situation where she had been helpless. But the answer may be more difficult yet. Eva believed in the importance of the experiments to do good, and in the prestige and goodwill of the people who performed them. She did not feel that killing experimental animals was bad, as good came out of it. And lastly she did not feel that she had status to question seriously what her superiors were doing.

Maybe we are confronted with the fact of how difficult it is to draw moral lines, yet how important it is to do so. It is too easy to move from the lives of animals being dispensable, it even being kind to kill them, to certain groups of humans being dehumanised and treated as such animals. It is also too easy to trust and be intimidated by those whom we respect. Moral confusions arise in relation to these tendencies. Eva herself is still confused about the morality of her superiors' work. What is clear is that we need to understand how morals can be staunchly maintained and yet at other times easily breached, even by the same person.

Eva has rebuilt her life although she is still plagued by the Holocaust. Eva still has difficulties sleeping and she is vulnerable to reminders which can plunge her into the Holocaust world. In some ways she is pervaded by the past, such as when she needs to make choices all the time.

Eva has repaired the past as much as she could. She has given lives to children as she wanted to and has preserved her children. More than anything, she has rebuilt her and her family's security which she guards jealously.

The passionate protection and preservation of Israel may symbolise love for a collective new generation, as well as making sure that the new infant state was not a helpless victim like Eva had been. Israel may also stand for an expression of love and grief for Kurti, and gratitude to the Jewish Brigade soldiers who offered kindness and protection among so many who did not.

Thus Eva's story not only paints a personal view of the history of the Holocaust, but also of more recent Jewish history. In it the Holocaust past still reverberates vividly, but so does the message of the Jewish Brigade soldiers, 'Never again will they do this to you. You will never be alone again.'

Maintaining a survivor mode after the war carried costs in love and fulfilment of life. Both Eva and her father found it hard to be involved in the everyday needs of normal children. They continued to express love through protection and preservation.

Eva has decided to tell her story fully now in order to be a living monument and testimony to those who perished and to those who may be threatened by the past being distorted or forgotten. Perhaps through the telling she will also allow the child in her to touch and be touched with affection. She deserves it.

Bernadette

—•—

'MY MEMORIES ARE

FULL OF HOLES: MY

MIND IS FULL OF HOLES'

*B*ERNADETTE'S STORY IS *a* struggle for memories, to reconnect with her past, and thus with herself. Bernadette has been an enthusiastic member of the Child Survivors group since its foundation. When we decided to document our stories in the group, she was the first volunteer. She spoke for twenty minutes that time, two years before this interview.

She said at the time, 'When I accepted last month to talk here tonight, I accepted quite easily, without any thought. I said "Why not? Yes, I will speak." But when I got home I realised what I had to do. I had to talk about myself. There seemed to be so little of myself, just some images, like some stills in a movie. The real story is probably between the images.' Bernadette paused. She spoke in a simple childlike manner, with a lilting French accent. She was a little shorter and plumper than average. Bernadette was an appealing and vivacious person. However, this time she spoke seriously.

$\mathcal{S}$HE TOLD THE GROUP, 'My name is Bernadette Gore. My maiden name was Szkop and my parents came to France from Poland at a very early age. They grew up in France and married there. I was born in 1938 in Paris, I am told. I have also found out that the events which I will relate to you occurred in 1944, when I was five and three quarter years old. But rather than tell you what I was told, I want to tell you what I actually remember. My images, my feelings at that time.

'So my very first memory and my first picture is in the little village where we were "hidden". I didn't feel I was hidden, but rather that I was a normal child living in a house in the village. But my first memory is when the Gestapo came and took my parents away. I remember being so afraid when I saw them hit my mother. I don't know whether they told me to get out, or if I ran out of my own volition, because my two sisters remained. But I found myself outside the house, I found myself running, I felt for such a long time. But going back to the village twenty-five years later, I found that I had only run across the road. I ran to my friend's place. When I came out again everyone was gone. That lady kept me and she made me two dresses — that's what I remember. One with little blue flowers, and one with little red flowers, and I remember the style. Then I remember nothing.'

The group was spellbound. Bernadette was the small girl whom she depicted. How could she cope with the sudden brutality and wrenching from family? Why did she run? How could she have escaped? As Bernadette said, it was like a gripping movie of stills. Bernadette's face gave away nothing. She continued.

'Then my next image is a place with lots of children. I remember boasting to them that I could make handbags and, I don't know why, sunglasses. By the way, my father was a handbag maker. But then I always had a fascination for sunglasses. I made sunglasses with wire and cellophane paper for those children. I have no other recollections from that place.

'In my next image I am in another place. It's somewhere in the country, on a farm obviously, because I remember there were animals and cherry trees which I climbed for cherries. And I have a memory of a woman, whose face I can't visualise, but whose voice I remember. I used to pray every night to God to bring my parents back. And this woman said, "Don't bother praying, your parents are dead." And I never believed her because I was so sure in my mind that my parents were alive.

'I also remember wetting the bed there, because I was terrified of having to come downstairs in the dark. So we must have been upstairs. I remember coming down in the morning and a whole lot of people laughing at me and calling me *"pisseuse"*. I had never been so humiliated.

'Oh yes — another memory. I could read at that time, and I remember a woman, probably the same woman, asking me to teach another little boy to read. She told me to slap him across the face if he did not read a word properly, and so I did. I must tell you by the way that I am a teacher of languages now, but I don't use that method!' The group laughed.

'I also remember lots of bombings and running down to cellars in the middle of the night. Maybe that is why the dark has always terrified me. And I remember a very funny incident. One night I was in the cellar with this little boy and I was wearing his clothes, and he was wearing mine. These are my only memories of that time. I do not know how long I was there, but my mother told me once that it was four to five months. [Actually it was two and a half months.]

'One day a truck came, with some people dressed in uniforms. That memory is very clear, because they said to me, "Come with us, because we are taking you back to your mother." And I remember fighting them and wanting to get away because I thought they were Germans. I screamed at them, "But you are Germans, and you took my parents away, and my sisters, and I don't want to go with you."

They just picked me up. Actually they were Red Cross people. I remember the truck ride though I did not know where we were going. The truck was constantly being stopped and checked by the Germans, I knew them by their uniforms. So I made myself very small because I was convinced that they would take me away if they found out that I was Jewish.

Bernadette's voice became emphatic. 'That's another thing that was imprinted on my mind. My name was Bernadette Laurent. I'll never forget that name. And I was not to tell anyone I was Jewish. And so I was taken back to my mother.' Bernadette's voice became choked for a moment. 'And so, by some miracle, I found my mother. I also found my father later, but the first thing I noticed when I was reunited with my mother was that she was not wearing any lipstick. That seemed very important. She did not look the way I remembered her. As for me, she told me later that I was in good health but full of lice, and we spent hours getting rid of them.

'I cannot recount the events after the war, because my memory is mainly blank. I had to be separated from my family again. I was told later that this was because my parents had lost everything and they had to look for an apartment. So my sister and I were again put in someone's place in the country. These times were perhaps as bad as the wartime ones. But fortunately for me, Frankie, my eighteen months older sister, was with me now, and she became my mother. I am still very close to her. Frankie has an excellent memory for all the bad things during this horrific time. For instance, that we were hungry for much of the time. I do remember stealing food to eat, and to this day I still feel how unfair it was that we had to be separated once again from our parents. But really I can only remember the good times from those two years.

'These are my only memories,' Bernadette concluded. 'What upsets me is that I have no memories other than these images. I should have memories from before the age of six, I just should have more memories. But my memories are full of holes. My mind is full of holes. Even the memories I have are difficult to associate with myself. I could not feel emotion for that little girl, because it felt as though these things happened to someone else altogether. Thinking about it for the last month and talking tonight has made me look at it as really my story.'

She was asked how had the war affected her? 'I haven't had time to think about it. But it has affected my life. I have always felt that life had been unfair to me, depriving me of something. I am still terrified of the dark, I am afraid of being by myself, but (with a smile) I don't wet the bed any more. I am afraid of violence and uniforms still. The fear never leaves you. In Israel I stayed near an army base. When I heard some shots I found myself under the bed, screaming, "The war has started." On the positive side it has made me a stronger person. I feel I can cope with difficult situations. It has made me more understanding of people's problems. I think that's about it.'

Bernadette's last comment in the ensuing discussion was, 'Twenty-five years ago it was too early to revisit these places. I just thought, "Oh, isn't it interesting, this is the house where we lived. That is the neighbour I ran to," as if all this had happened to someone else. But now I am thinking of going back to try to find out where actually I had been. Do these people remember the child Bernadette Laurent in the orphanage at Limoges? But I don't know if I'll ever have the courage to do it.'

Over the next two years Bernadette always encouraged others to express emotions about their stories. She stayed a very devoted and active member in the Child Survivor group. Then she told her story again at a joint meeting of Child Survivors and Adult Survivors.

In the introduction she said, 'I have looked over the first recording of my story before this talk. After not looking at it for two years, I watched it eight times. I couldn't believe that it was me talking, that it was my story. I realised that I had not expressed any feelings at the time.'

Again she mentioned that her images were the only things she had. But this time she added 'and feelings' after the word 'images'. Again she sketched out the limited scenes from her past. Her words were almost the same as last time, as if etched images could only be conveyed with a limited array of words. However, there were significant additions associated with the thawing of Bernadette's emotions. Recalling her first memory, she said, 'When I came out of the house [of the lady she ran to], there was no one there. And what I did not mention last time, was that I felt very abandoned. I felt very alone.' She also elaborated certain events, such as eating masses of cherries from the cherry trees. 'Even today, I eat cherries when they are in season and put on weight.' And she elaborated, 'It was very much impressed on me to not say that I was Jewish. It obviously meant that I was different. I was afraid of that difference, and I had to be very, very careful of that difference . . . I also connected my Jewishness with being taken away.' Bernadette was also more expressive about reunion with her mother. '. . . unbelievable happiness to see my mother (and sisters). I remember being held.' Bernadette wiped away tears.

The great difference in her expressiveness since her previous presentation was reflected in the audience. As she owned her story more, people warmed to the child in her. The older survivors shed tears. One man said, 'I did not cry when my parents were taken to the crematoria, and I have not cried since. But that one, she made me cry tonight.'

A further half a year elapsed. Bernadette had recently returned from France. I entered her beautiful, light, modern house for our interview. We were surrounded by many tasteful objects, including two delicate female statuettes made by her blind mother. 'Everything I own has a story. I am very attached to all these objects.' Bernadette indicated.

When we began, she said, 'I might start differently this time. I might explain where we actually were during the war.' Bernadette was more open again, perhaps more self-assured. She explained where Les Vignes was, fourteen kilometres from Limoges.

'And we lived there in a house, and my father worked making handbags, and no one knew that we were Jewish. My father also worked for the Free French underground. For instance, he forged documents for them.

She went on to '. . . the trauma to which I always return'. She seemed to have more mental control of the context in which it occurred. And she described the scene again.

'My first memory is when those men, the Gestapo, came into the house, and started being very rough with my parents. And I was very frightened. My mother apparently became cheeky and said "What right do you have to be here?" but I don't remember the actual words. What I remember is someone slapping my mother and then someone standing with a gun at my father's head. I remember running in terror. The first feeling of my life was terror.'

According to her oldest sister and cousin, the Gestapo had said to her, 'You go, we don't want you. You're too little.' Bernadette did not remember this nor did she remember anything of the twelve year old cousin whom mother had passed off as a visiting village girl and who escaped with Bernadette. As happened in Bernadette's mind throughout her life, we kept returning to this scene during the interview.

Next time we did so, Bernadette was puzzled that she imagined the Gestapo in uniform, when in fact they had worn civilian clothes. However, she had no doubt about this. Also, 'They had terrible authority, and power, because I can recall my father's face.' And yet it took much effort to recall, 'A very white face. Frightened . . . I recall more than anything the tension in this incredible situation. All I knew was that I was so terrified I ran and ran and ran. I saw my father's face opposite me. I felt rather than saw them hitting my mother. I felt terror. Terror is the only word to describe it . . . I have a feeling that I was on the road and there was no one there. My sister told me since that she saw me staring down the middle of the road after the car which drove her and my parents away. I remember simply that there was no one. I was by myself.'

The next time we returned to the first memory, she said, softly, almost reverently, 'The very, very first bit is my father's face. Something I have never mentioned before. Yes, my father's white face. A gun at his head. The face is still clear in my mind. My father's face was the image of terror, my mother being hit was the feeling. The feeling of these men with so much power and the terror of my parents being hit . . . I just wanted to be out of there. I ran. I had no thoughts but to run.'

Bernadette seemed more alive as she fleshed out the skeletons of her memories. The figures in her slides too, were alive and human now. Bernadette described how her recent trip to France helped this process.

'I wanted to remember. I tried to remember. I was desperate to remember. Because I feel that with memories I could put that story to rest, put it where it belongs. I have to a certain extent, I feel much better since coming back. But I still have some holes and I think I will always have them.

'I look upon my trip to retrieve those memories as the most unbelievable time, like magic. I was like Sleeping Beauty and it felt as if everything had just been waiting for me, and I arrived at just the right time, and saw everything I had to see.

'When I visited in 1970 everyone was nice, and reminisced about my brave father, they delighted in the grown-up Szkop girls. But it wasn't my story. This time it was so different.'

Bernadette and Morrie, her husband, were driving back from Oradour, a museum village preserved to commemorate its extermination by the SS just before liberation. The next day Bernadette was to see her *Assistance Publique* (State Ward) file.

'Suddenly I see a facade of a house, with a sign "La Bouteille". "Stop the car," I said. "This is near to where I lived." Without thinking, I walked over to the house opposite. Once again Messr Des Moulins's son talked to us about my father, but this time I was listening.'

'"Where is Les Vignes?" I asked against my will. I did not really want to go there. "Why, just down the road."

'The house was there. Someone was leaning on the balustrade . . . And I went into the room where it all happened. They have transformed it, it's a glorious little cottage now. But I couldn't wait to get out of that room. I couldn't stay in that house. It had a terrible feeling. I didn't feel right . . . safe in there. I hated it. I know now why I did not want to go back to Les Vignes. I had to pretend, say how lovely the renovations were, but everything in me just wanted to get out . . . Let me out of here, let me out! And I asked, "Is Mme Carreau still alive?" "Yes, across the road."

'I had visualised where I had been, and also my father's white face. I wanted to run to Mme Carreau again. I understood that my feelings related to the past, but nevertheless, I left to see Mme Carreau as soon as I could.

'I felt really bad that I had not wanted to see her again, because she was so happy to see me. She was very emotional . . . This time I asked her questions. She showed me exactly where I had run to her. She told me that she had gone over to my parents' house, but the Gestapo chased her away. They called for reinforcements by shooting in the air. My mother had turned to Mme Carreau and said "We are going away for a few days."

'I said to her, "Why didn't you keep me?" She said "We kept you a week. But we were frightened to keep you longer. We realised that your parents had been denounced and the Gestapo could come back for you at any time. In fact, three days after your parents were taken away this stranger, possibly a collaborator, came looking for a Bernadette. So we took you to the next village." So I think she was very pleased that she got rid of me.'

'Did you feel that she got rid of you?'

'Hmm, it's funny that you picked it up. Well, I suppose yes, in a way. It was dangerous for her. I would have rather stayed with her, wouldn't I? She was a lovely lady, she still is. I had such a warm feeling for her, like for a grandmother. I felt such warmth. How on earth could I have not wanted to see her?!'

'So I reconnected Mme Carreau with the two dresses she had made for me, the symbols of care and warmth. Mme Carreau had handed me over to the mayor of the next village, and he took me to the *Assistance Publique*.'

'The next day I had to wait till four-thirty to see my *Assistance Publique* file. I have no recollection for that morning. I was in great turmoil. My stomach was twisting in knots. God knows what I was going to find out. I was afraid. And yet this was mixed with a funny type of excitement. I walked around like a robot. I did ordinary things automatically.

'She came out with an old brown paper file. Written on it in the most magnificent writing was, "Szkop" and then "Bernadette". I look at this file, and that's me. Tiny, I mean hardly anything in it. My God, there is my life. She looked at me, and took us to a small room. I opened my file and on the first line it says "Bernadette Szkop, put in the *Assistance Publique* on the 19th of May 1944." I turned to Morrie, and said "Hey, Morrie, what is the date today?" and he said, "19th of May." So I opened the file exactly forty-eight years after I had been taken to the *Assistance Publique*. It was so eerie. And I see on the second line "19th of June put into the care of Mme Catherine Porcher . . ." The moment I saw the name, it did something to me, I went "Aaah, I've got that name somewhere." All at once the memory of that name was there! In my head! And then it said on the line '. . . née Laurent'. And the clerk said, "They did not change your name at the orphanage. She gave you her maiden name." So the name Laurent, which was in my mind all these years, was this woman's maiden name. So I had spent a month in the orphanage, obviously that must have been the place with the lots of children which I remembered.

'From the office, we immediately drove to Mme Porcher's address as listed in the file. I was looking, I was going to recognise something, my memory would be jogged, I would recognise it. I will know it! We arrived at En Bazac Crossac, a hamlet like Les Vignes. I approached the old woman standing outside the address. She retorted, "Ha, Mme Porcher died in 1964 . . . But I am her cousin. We were going to Limoges in fifteen minutes." After telling them my story, her daughter said, "*Mon Dieu, mon Dieu*, what a story. Come in, we are renovating, but the main room is still the same, maybe you will remember something."

'I was in a dream by then. I was walking through the house but I remembered nothing. Nothing. I looked for the cherry trees, nothing. I remembered a country farm. It wasn't a farm but from a child's viewpoint the garden, chickens, trees would have been like a farm . . . I asked, "Excuse me, this is hard, but was there a staircase?" "Look there is the staircase. We are ripping it down next week." I looked at the famous staircase, and the room downstairs, no bigger than a pocket handkerchief. The staircase barely one foot wide. Everything was there, all right, but in miniature . . . And the cellar was there too. Barely room for three or four people, tiny! They were offering drinks, and I am going through hell. I am trying desperately to remember. I must find the cherry trees, I must find the cherry trees! I walked out to the garden and I started to cry. They thought I was sad, but I was crying from frustration. "Where are the cherry trees, the cherry trees?" The old woman tried to console me and said how lovely Mme Porcher had been and how she helped many children from the *Assistance Publique*. And I just cried out, "Where are the cherry trees?" and she said, "There are no cherry trees here." And then I saw the toilet. "That's the toilet outside and I was scared to come out, that's why I wet the bed!" I went upstairs to the bedroom. There were two beds in the bedroom. "That was my cousin's bed," the woman said. So there was the big bed I slept in. Well, small bed now.

'I felt better now, because at least I knew that I had not invented my memories. In fact I had authenticated them. The cousin and her daughter said that this was like a fairytale. Later they sent me a photo of Mme Porcher. I still could not remember her. Nothing. Nothing. And she still looks like a witch like I felt her to be. And yet they said what a lovely woman she was. I don't remember affection from her. She was paid to look after me. But she did save my life.

'Part of me was frustrated. I thought that I had to reevaluate my memories now. I had to relook at all this from a different perspective. First of all, it must have been she who said, "Your name is Bernadette Laurent, and you must not tell anyone that you are Jewish, and your parents are dead." And I think she told me that because at that time there was such heavy fighting around there, the Germans were berserk doing things like Oradour. If they had come to her and I had given the game away, they would have shot her. So I suppose she had to be very severe with me, and she had to efface from my mind anything to do with my past. Her cousin and her daughter were such wonderful people, they could not do enough for us.

'I was confused. This was the place of the witch who tried to kill my past and my parents, and where I had this incredibly strong feeling, a strong faith, that my parents were alive. No doubt in my mind that my parents would come back for me.

'But this is where I also prayed to a Roman Catholic God for my parents and looked forward to Christmas. And this is where I did not want to enter the Red Cross truck, screaming that they had already taken and killed my parents.

'The woman who could have reconciled these opposites was dead.

'Coming out of there I was very frustrated. I wanted to ask Mme Porcher these questions. Who was I? What was I like? Why did she say these things to me? Now I will have to answer them myself because there is no one who can answer. I decided to find the orphanage.

'The next day this nun in the convent next to the gutted orphanage of Limoges took me by the hand. It's hard to explain how someone's face can do things to you. She had a face like . . . an angel. An old face with such serenity. I was no longer a fifty-four year old woman,

I was a five year old child. The nun asked me whether I remembered ladies with white head coverings and black skirts while in the orphanage. "Little children remember such things," she said. "No," I replied. "Then you could not have been hidden here." She reminisced, "We had so many children, they were up to here," she indicated above her head. She tried to remember where they placed some children. "There was that small orphanage . . ." The young nun broke in, "But she remembers many children," and I interposed, "I have learnt in the last few days that size is relative." The old nun continued. "What was it called? That small orphanage?" she mused. "Villa Robert," the young nun helped out. "Yes. Villa Robert. That could be it," said the angel nun. And I heard Villa Robert, and I thought of my son. He is called Robert.

'So we found Villa Robert. It was still an orphanage. I felt stupid. How could I explain why I was there? Of course they had no record of me. Eventually I left my name in case anyone ever remembered a Bernadette Szkop from 1944. But I was invited to look around anyway.

'So I walked outside. I was sick and tired. But then, all of a sudden, I turn to my left, and on my left I see . . . three . . . enormous . . . cherry trees. Filled with cherries! I would not have known they were cherry trees without the cherries on them. And I started to scream, "The cherry trees! The cherry trees!" and I rushed over to the cherry trees, and as I reached to pick them I just imagined as if I was that high (a five year old). I stuffed them in my mouth. They were unusual cherries, they were yellow with a bit of pink in them, but the taste . . . the taste was like yesterday. I said to Morrie, "This is where I was." The cherry trees were not at Mme Porcher's place, they were at the orphanage before I went to her . . . And I went to the orphanage at exactly the same time, as when I was there as a child. The cherries were ripe exactly as they were then. And why did I call my son Robert? So you see, it was all there, it was all waiting, except Mme Porcher. And the man who placed me with her. He was also dead.'

Bernadette exulted at finding her links. In this orphanage she had made handbags and glasses.

'I could always understand me boasting about my ability to make handbags, as my father made handbags. I found it very hard to understand why I boasted I could make glasses. I always had a feel about glasses. I always wanted to wear glasses. I made glasses. That seemed to be a happy memory, it was fun.'

'Did either parent wear glasses?'

'My mother, I found out, wore wire-rimmed glasses. Obviously I wanted something to link me. That is how I understand it today. I only worked that out recently — the glasses.'

Bernadette returned with open emotion to the Red Cross truck ride.

'And then, after a long, long, long, time, the truck finally stopped. And I was taken out of the truck. It was incredible. I couldn't believe it. Finally . . . finally . . . there was my mother.' Bernadette cried. 'I don't recall seeing my sisters. They did not seem important at that time. My father was not important. It was just my mother. And I remember asking her why she was not wearing lipstick? She told me recently, not only did I ask that, but I kept on pinching her face, and saying, "But they told me you were dead! And you are alive!" She was not wearing lipstick . . . that was important because she had changed. And I remember the great happiness. I never left her side after that. I clung to her.

'Yes. I can say it now. I can say it now. Because by going through all this work I can now say my mother has always been the most important person in my life . . . Strange, I never said it before. I am crying now — I never used to cry. I've never cried before. I used to tell my story as if it happened to someone else . . . I prepared myself to have no emotions.

'I visited the place of the reunion too. The courtyard was there but it all meant nothing. The only memory that mattered was that of my mother. And that I remembered.

'But . . . you would think that everything would be wonderful then. But it wasn't . . . My parents had nowhere to live, and we were sent away again. For two years. A new separation. They were very, very bad years. But this time I had my older sister with me. They thought the country air would be good for us. We stayed with a Polish Catholic peasant woman. It was a very bad time but my sister suffered more than I did because she became my mother. She acts as my memory because I don't have any memories for that time myself. I remember the nice things and my sister remembers every horrific thing that happened. The peasant woman's husband was an alcoholic who was

brutal to us and beat us regularly. We were always hungry. I do remember stealing food, but I remember it as fun. I remember eating
soggy lettuce, but I still like it like that. So I developed the ability to
shut out of my mind all the things I did not want to remember.
Every time my mother visited at weekends, I could not concentrate
the following week at school and was slapped by the teacher. When
she did not come weekends I was very angry that she did not come,
even though my father would come.'

'Were you angry with your mother?'

'In a way. In my child's mind I was never angry with my mother
because she could not help it and I had seen what happened with
the Gestapo. But after the war I felt that she could have kept me . . .
I don't talk to her about that. She knows. Because whenever we
broach the subject my older sister gets quite vicious about this. I always kick her under the table, because my mother gets very upset.'

Bernadette's dog sidled up to her at this stage, as if seeking and
giving comfort. 'She feels my feelings, she comes to me when I am
sad. She is demanding and spoilt like a child. She knows when I am
unhappy.' Bernadette gave her food.

I asked Bernadette how much she had been able to talk with her
family.

'I've always been able to talk with my mother. Not so much about
my feelings, but I was always interested in her story. Since being in
the group, and talking about my story it has been difficult because
my mother becomes quite defensive. She obviously feels bad about
the time that we were first separated. She couldn't help me because
she was in prison but there is that feeling about it, especially in
these past two years. But I don't want to upset her. That was the last
thing I wanted to do.

'My father was strong and authoritarian. He never talked about
the separation. He never asked me, "Was it very hard for you? Did
you miss us? I missed you." He never said anything!

'When I returned, for the first time we really talked . . . It was like a
miracle. We were so close. I asserted my own special past for the first
time, and the family took note. They filled in my experiences from
their own perspectives. How Anita [the oldest sister] summoned our
father when the Gestapo ordered her, how they saw me gazing

after the departing car, how they witnessed shootings in the prison, how they cared for mother when she had hysterical attacks at nights, how mother did not know whether to jump out of the window or run down the stairs to be reunited more quickly with me, how the Red Cross driver validated me trying to make myself small as a mouse in the truck at roadblocks, how I had no underpants and a red bottom when we remet, the exquisite joy and emotions of all the refugees in the home and the Red Cross driver when I was handed over into my mother's arms.

'It has brought us closer. I can now show affection to my mother. Because I finally admitted how important she was to me. My affection was frozen, because if you love someone you become vulnerable.'

'What can you tell me about your life apart from these three and a half months?'

Bernadette started when she realised at some deeper level that she really had no memories before she was almost six. In fact Bernadette's life started with the struggle between abandonment and a fragile hold on life. Her mother had jumped off the table trying to abort her when she realised that she was pregnant. At the time the family was in poverty and the oldest daughter was ill in a sanatorium. The day Bernadette was born her father was mobilised and her mother lost her milk. Yet she was a loved, thriving baby. She was even used in an advertisement for Nestle's condensed milk.

When she was two and a half the Germans captured her father. He escaped from the transit camp to Auschwitz. Her mother crossed with three children into Free France. A harrowing and dangerous journey during which mother fainted a number of times from carrying Bernadette. This was because each time she was handed to the guide, she cried, and this could have given the group away. Up to her separation from her family, she had been a quiet child. Similarly, she had two or three good years in France before leaving for Australia. The family had a luxurious flat, Bernadette was happy at school, and she had holidays with her parents.

'How did your experiences affect your later life?'

'I was never the same as everyone else. I tried to belong to different groups, but until the Child Survivor group I felt a fraud in all of them. I hid myself. I tried to be who I thought everybody wanted me to be.

I was the life of the party, while inside there was a scared little girl.'

Yet Bernadette did develop friendships which have lasted till today. Some were child survivors but they never talked about this.

Bernadette married Morrie when she was twenty-one.

'We've had many difficulties in our marriage. We've had marriage guidance. I am still seeing someone at the moment . . . When Morrie promised me the security which I did not have in the war, I developed this very strong link to him. When he said the magic words, "Look, leave it to me. I'll look after you," the key to me was his. I remained a little girl throughout my marriage. He became Mummy, Daddy, older sister, everything . . . I had no notion that I was a woman . . . I had to grow up through a very long painful process . . . I don't know if even today I'm a woman . . . I can't tell you the terror I feel when I am at home alone in the dark. I fear someone will break in and attack me. I'm just frightened. Just frightened.'

Bernadette repeated this as she had repeated earlier, 'I was frightened. I just ran.' On the last trip Bernadette faced her terrors. Morrie was by her side as a devoted husband.

'I fear separation. I can't tolerate it. I could never separate from Morrie. Even now, I just can't let people go.'

Bernadette always felt that she needed people more than they needed her. She expressed bitterness that somehow people did not return her offers of intense trust and lasting loyalty. The closest she came to it was with her children.

'Motherhood was the best thing ever in my life. I was happiest with babies. I never tired of looking after them. I was never too hemmed in by them . . . Hmm, my daughter stuck to me like glue, like me with my mother . . . It changed when she was thirteen to fourteen, she grew away. There came a wall, a barrier, I found it difficult to display affection then.'

Bernadette described how her daughter had nearly died at the age of two and a half [the age when Bernadette crossed the border to Free France]. She was told that her daughter was in the last stages of crisis of coeliac disease.

'For three months we did not know whether she would live or die. I was with her three months, fighting for her life. They had all given up hope for her. But I felt as certain that my daughter was going to survive as I had been that my parents would return. I willed her to survive. And she did.'

'How else had the war affected you?'

'Well, I sucked my thumb intensely until the age of thirteen or fourteen. Also, I overate and was overweight till recently, due to depressive moods. My father used to call me *"Birri"* [piggy]. Now I have control over my weight in spite of the moods. I am still scared of the dark and of separations. I still feel revulsion of things German, and I avoid buying German goods. I am terrified of the war in Yugoslavia, and I am deeply upset at what people are doing to the children there.'

'Why do you constantly return to these three and a half months, when other periods were equally dangerous?'

'Maybe because that short period was the only one when I was truly on my own, and I have never had anyone to confirm that experience. It has affected my whole life as a person. All my fears, everything about my life originated from that time.'

However, Bernadette has struggled and grown. A time in Israel allowed her to come to better terms with being Jewish. Her therapy gave her knowledge of who she was, and she came to like herself. The Child Survivor group gave her an even greater sense of identity and belonging and opportunity for self-expression. The return to France gave her memories validity and substantiated her own sense of self. Bernadette and others about her feel that she has grown, matured and relaxed.

'Now I am not always somebody's wife, mother, daughter, sister. I run a language school, I do it well . . . We even teach German. I may even have coffee with the German teacher one day.

'I see things clearer. For the first time I can relate in depth. All the warmth comes out of me. And the best of all is the capacity to help others. I have a deep feeling for the other members of our group. I feel I have the strength to help others. I am glad that I survived. I am one of the lucky ones.'

Comment

What did Bernadette want to remember, why was she desperate to remember, and why couldn't she remember? There is little doubt that it was the three and a half months which Bernadette spent away from her family which she felt emotionally driven to retrieve. This was the most traumatic time of separation, felt as abandonment to hostile forces which threatened her existence. Other periods of danger were not as threatening because Bernadette felt firmly attached to mother or a mother figure.

The three and a half months were different. Here nobody knew, or even wanted to know, about her sufferings. Here she was alone and no amount of subsequent clinging could resolve her terrors and anxieties from that period. Neither her symbols of her parents, in the handbags and glasses, nor her fervent faith were sufficient to soothe the terror which originated in the original traumatic episode and in subsequent events during her separation.

Why could Bernadette not remember? Perhaps the clue is in the process of her regaining her memories. As she became stronger and more confident in other areas, she delved deeper into the emotions and meanings of the trauma to which she always returned. Ultimately she was able to remember and feel (in the original room) the sheer terror and helplessness of her parents, especially as reflected in her father's face. Her own terror reflected their powerlessness and the situation of incipient annihilation. Remembering this scene in its entirety would have emphasised for Bernadette her parents' vulnerability and their incapacity to protect themselves or her. In situations where the small Bernadette felt abandoned, threatened by a witch and humiliated by her environment, she needed an image of her parents as powerful and protective, to keep her alive with hope. To remember the whole trauma would have negated this requirement for her survival.

So why has Bernadette been so desperate to retrace and retrieve these memories to the full? Some of the retrieval was an unconscious process which seemed uncanny to her. Thus she retraced her steps in the order of her previous life, even to the time of year. And she was very frustrated when this order could not be achieved, as happened for a time with the missing orphanage and cherry trees. This was replaced with great relief and joy when order, sense and meaning were restored to Bernadette's memories. Perhaps a person needs a validated thread of memories to achieve a sense of identity and a meaningful life.

The quest for memories carried a cost for Bernadette. She had to reface the terror of her traumas. But this time Bernadette had the advantages of her current safety, maturity and her husband. Thus the fifty-four year old could understand with compassion the five year old's terror in the house in Les Vignes. And after she ran once more to Mme Carreau, this time she could ask on behalf of the little girl the unmentionable question, 'Why did you send me away?' And the frozen abyss of the doubly abandoned child was this time filled with love and care as Mme Carreau explained with anguish that to send Bernadette away had been a great act of love which saved Bernadette's life. This new meaning released Bernadette's gratitude and love for her rescuer. Similarly, the understanding of the mutual joy at reuniting with her mother released Bernadette's love for her mother. Even Mme Porcher, the witch, developed a more human dimension as a person who had risked her life for Bernadette. Bernadette came to see herself as a much loved precious person for whom people risked their lives and for whom people yearned.

This new meaning reestablished a more confident identity which had been shattered by the child's sense of rejection and worthlessness. Perhaps this is what Bernadette meant when she said that she had to know the details and the links of this period, so that they could be put into context, 'to put it behind me, and get on with my life'. Without an enlivened memory, Bernadette's life could not make good sense.

And yet, some things were still unthawed and unvalidated. Mme Porcher could not validate that Bernadette was valuable to her, or that at the time Bernadette was a precious child in need of comforting. Nor was there an acceptable emotional meaning to the fact that the clinging postwar Bernadette, who never wanted to lose her mother ever again, was sent away for two years to cruel Polish peasants. This time the frozen abyss held not only fear, but also resentment, anger, and an unspoken sense of betrayal.

Bernadette could not confront her mother with a similar question to the one she asked of Mme Carreau. She felt that her mother became defensive and hurt whenever the matter was approached. So Bernadette learnt to avoid hurting her mother with such questions. Bernadette knew intellectually that her mother had been very sapped and ill after the war. She could surmise that her mother could not admit that for the second time she needed to be lightened of the burden which Bernadette imposed on her. But so far anger, guilt and need to not hurt the one you love most has prevented an emotional *rapproachement* in this area between the two women. So perhaps much of the remaining insecurity and resentment have been expressed elsewhere.

How else have the unprocessed memories expressed themselves? There have been the night-time terrors, the inability to stay at home alone, the thumbsucking, the overeating due to seeking comfort. Feeling different, fraudulent, pretending to be like others, seemed to repeat feeling different in the orphanage, with Mme Porcher, and the Polish peasants. The difficulties about accepting a Jewish identity seem to stem from the times when it was emphasised to Bernadette that to be Jewish was to be different, and to be in danger. To this day Bernadette feels more comfortable in a church than a synagogue.

And then there may be more subtle links to the past. Was it more than a coincidence that Bernadette named her son Robert? What about the coincidence of names all denoting pig? Her father called her *Birri* [piggy]; Mme Porcher's name meant pig keeper; the surname which Bernadette took on after marriage was Gore which Bernadette associated with *goret* (i.e.: little pig). Can these coincidences be symbolic links between her unthawed images? And can these hidden memories be unwittingly replayed with others, such as her husband and daughter? There was an uncanny similarity between the daughter's illness and the threats to Bernadette's life at a similar age. There was a similar blind faith which sustained survival of the child though in the later reedited version, Bernadette the mother never left her daughter's side. Nevertheless, could it be, that without remembering and understanding history, we are bound to repeat it?

So Bernadette was desperate to remember because her missing memories denied her her self and her progression in life. Even though their retrieval meant much pain, achieving a true thread enabled Bernadette to 'put her memories behind', not to forget them, but to put them in context and not to repeat them.

We may ask, how important were other aspects of Bernadette's background, outside these three months? Of course they were very important. For instance, it was important that her father was a brave underground worker during the war, and that he was generally an honest and virtuous man devoted to his children. It was important that her mother was also brave and devoted, a person of many gifts, even in adversity. No doubt Bernadette's generosity, creativity, devotion to her children and students was in great part a carryover of features of her background.

However, Bernadette teaches us that even with loving parents and a favourable survival outcome, a relatively circumscribed trauma early in life can result in lasting and pervasive negative effects for the rest of one's life. We can also glean that separation from the mother can be a core component of such traumas. Though Bernadette was affected by the bombings and shootings around her it was the separation from mother which cut most deeply into her.

Bernadette is right. Objectively speaking she is one of the lucky ones. Her tragedies were not as great as those which befell others. But perhaps it is a reflection on the Holocaust that Bernadette's traumas may be seen as relatively small. They were large enough to cause pervasive suffering and for the integration of her memories to be a long painful process. In fact, the little child suffered major disturbances to her vulnerable self. When we see the true nature of that child's distress, yes, even the hardiest may cry.

Frankie

— • —

'I FELT LIKE

MY MOTHER

MUST HAVE FELT'

fRANKIE PAPER WAS EIGHTEEN
months older than her sister Bernadette. The two women had similar French
accents and facial features. However, Frankie looked a little older, and more
taut than Bernadette. Though comparisons between the sisters were inevitable,
there was no problem in discerning Frankie's own individual story. Actually
it was surprising how different the two stories were.

Frankie was anxious because she had never exposed her story. We talked
in her home, a Melbourne suburban house, on the outskirts of Caulfield.

I WAS BORN IN Paris, on the 24th of February 1937. I was the middle child of three sisters.

'I have a sense of a good life in Paris before the war. My very first memory is of Bernadette sobbing, but actually, even earlier, when my mother left me with an uncle to have Bernadette, I remember going down two steps in his place, opening a door, and it was magical, there were rabbits in a hutch and lots of toys. I was one and a half then.

'My very first experience of something not being right was when I was three years old when in the middle of the nights we had to suddenly run into the cellar of our block of flats. I could not understand this. I was conscious of the noise of the footsteps on the stairs — boom, boom, boom. I was also aware that my mother was fed up with these repeated wakings and scurryings down with three little children. I did not know that my father was in the army at the time, nor that he had warned my mother to get out of Paris, as the Germans would bring blood and fire when they occupied it.

'My mother did heed his warning, and we became part of the exodus of women and children from Paris. I was told that a woman offered my overladen mother to mind me on the train. I do not remember that when we arrived at the station I got lost in the pandemonium. My mother screamed, "I lost my child." A policeman assured her that they would find me the next day. "You can imagine how I slept that night," Mother always said, when recounting this story. But my memory of this is only seeing a familiar figure walking toward me from the distance, on a country road. It had green and yellow on the head, like some clothing my mother had. My mother confirmed recently that she had worn that colour cloth when she came to fetch me from a farm where I had been found. The farmer said, "Had you not come for this child I would have kept her, she was so quiet and good."

'Paris was not being destroyed, the peasants were disgruntled with their city billets, and Bernadette had whooping cough. My mother had had enough and we returned to Paris. Many things happened, such as changing flats, but what sticks out in my mind is that one day a boy came to tell us that my father was arrested. He brought my father's bike. I did not understand, except that my father was not only not there, but he was not coming back.

'One day my mother dressed us up, put great big white bows, which we used to hate, in our hair and she took us to what I remember as a large square surrounded by blocks of flats. This must have been Drancy [a transit camp]. My mother said, "Look up there. That man is your father. Wave to him." I saw little figures in the windows, and we waved. As a child, being submerged among a lot of legs I wondered how my father could see us. I became absorbed in water between my feet, which came from a woman making pee pee in public. I was fascinated by the strangeness of it. Then there was a lot of whistle blowing and we all ran in panic. My mother explained that we had not been allowed to be there. Later my father told me that he did see us, recognising us by the big bows.

'Kids did not ask questions about these frightening happenings. This was simply the way life was. But while my father was away my growth was stunted and I do remember having terrible and frequent nose bleeds, even requiring hospitalisation. I improved once they took my tonsils out. They did it without anaesthetic and I still remember the sound of the cutting.

'One day I saw my dad at my mother's mother's place. Hearing adults talk, I learnt that dad's mother had died of diabetes in hospital. They did not treat Jews well, and they let them die. My mother had taken the three of us to Drancy, and told the commandant . . . She had *guts*! . . . that he must let my father out to bury his mother. There was simply no one else to do it. The commandant gave my father a twenty-four hour pass and my mother had to give her word of honour to return him to camp. Perhaps he was allowed out because he had been arrested for his papers not being in order, not because he was a Jew. In the flat my mother said, "That's it! You don't go to the funeral, you just go!" My uncle Sam cried like a child, the way I cried! My father just sat stunned. And then he disappeared again. My mother impressed on us to say to everyone, "Papa has gone back to camp."

'And then problems started. People banged on the door day and night. One night three men came in. One frightened the daylights out of me, because he was dressed totally in black. He had a cigarette hanging from his lips. To this day I can't stand people with cigarettes hanging from their lips. They turned the place upside down. I couldn't believe it. Adults were doing the very opposite to what I was brought up to do. And he said "If we ever see him, we'll shoot him on sight!"

'One day Bernadette and I were alone in the apartment. A woman asked where my father was, and I said in camp. The woman said, "No, you are mistaken. Mummy and Daddy have gone shopping." But I kept saying what had been impressed on me. Another day a woman (Anita insisted it was a man) pressed money in her hand, then called her a thief, and came to the flat to tell her father to punish her. So they kept trying to trick us. I was upset to see Anita cry. My mother yelled at the woman and sent her away.

'After nine months we had word that my father was in the Free Zone, and he wanted us to join him. And then one day we left! We left with nothing, pretending we were just going to the park. I didn't even see my grandmother to say goodbye to her. I never saw her again. On the train I remember being patted on the head by German soldiers. I did not know that our guide was in the carriage too, laughing with the Germans. I don't remember getting a bus from Tours. My next memory is just walking in the dark.

'I remember a shadowy group of people and the "*passeur*", and my mother carrying Bernadette.' In a soft, tense voice Frankie punctuated each word as if it were a step. 'Each time someone tried to relieve mother of Bernadette, she started to cry, so mother had to keep carrying her. It was incredibly dark.' Then Frankie spoke with passionate hope. 'I wanted the clouds to open up, and there be a door, and once we passed through the door, all would be okay. Instead we had to lie flat each time we heard dogs, because they belonged to border patrols. I went to sleep each time we lay down, and woke when I was placed vertically. At one time the *passeur* disappeared. Everyone was frightened, therefore I was too. When he reappeared, my mother said sternly, "Put your bike away, and walk with us, we paid you to be with us." And he did. He said that Anita and I walked like little soldiers — for ten kilometres across the fields.

'Then the *passeur* indicated that he was staying behind, and that we had to run fifty metres towards some trees, which were safety. My mother started to run. Suddenly she realised that she could not see me. And I was back there, with my pants down, having a pee! My mother couldn't call me, she just had to wait. When I finished, I ran to her, and we ran on together. My mother just could not believe that this was possible, me peeing just then!

'Then I remember drinking water in an inn, and then a station, and a man with his back to us . . .' Frankie's voice was breaking with emotion, 'and I knew that was father! I don't remember kissing him, nothing. The next thing I remember is being in Les Vignes. We lived in this little hamlet in two rooms.

'We were told that we were not Jewish, to forget all about Yiddish, and to say that we were refugees. We went to church like Catholics, and sang songs to the Virgin Mary. My father made handbags. Other children and I made umbrellas out of tree branches, we pretended to ride bikes on sticks, and played houses with broken crockery. I had no special toy. So life was different, but peaceful, and we settled down to country routine.

'Things which stood out from this period were my father occasionally slitting the throat of a pig which was then eaten by the whole village. He also carved stamps for forged identity cards for the Resistance. They allowed young Frenchmen not to be taken to Germany for forced labour. One day he brought the press home. My mother shrieked at him in anger for endangering her family. I remember my father then removing the box out of the sideboard.

'My aunt Alice came to stay near us after her husband, uncle Bernard was caught. We had to call her Roni. My mother's cousin Helene also stayed with us now and then. She was only a few years older than Anita.

'My father made me a school bag, and I walked with the other children to the school in the next village. We hid under desks during bomb alerts, and we were taught how to hide in the nearby forest. To me it was just an exciting aspect of schoolwork. I was not aware of the German occupation of the Free Zone, except that we had to be more careful.

'The teacher did not notice me on my first day at school. At lunchtime I hid in some bushes near home so as to avoid going back. By evening I was hungry and scared, but I was also scared that my father would beat me to death. You see, if you hurt yourself, my father would give you a hiding so you would learn to not do it again. Eventually I came out in the dark, sobbing. I could not believe that he put his arm around me and asked me what was wrong. He told the teacher she needed to give me something to do. She then gave me a pencil and a book to draw in, and then I came to enjoy school.

'We usually returned from school avoiding the road with forest on both sides because boys had warned us that a man with an axe would get us. But one day we walked that road, and saw a stranger, a woman on a bicycle who rode past us to Les Vignes, and then back again. In Les Vignes she rode past my mother and back, looking at her intently each time.

'Two days later came a dark car. Only the doctor had a car. I was playing on the road. One of the men from the car went to my mother, and said, "Madame Szkop?" My mother felt that something was wrong, and said, "She lives next door." He patted her on the shoulder and said, "You're Madame Szkop. Come with us!" The woman on the bicycle had identified my mother.'

Frankie's voice was awed and anguished. 'So she and two men walked into our place. Helene and Anita were there. I came in to have a look. The strangers were frightening. Perhaps because they wore black, like the man in Paris. The first thing the man did was to pull things out of the sideboard. As a child I wondered what would have happened to us if they had found the box there. My mother screamed, "What right have you to do this? Who are you?" "This is the Gestapo." My mother just stood there then. "Where is your husband?" "He is working in the fields." He turned to Anita and said, "Go and get your father." My mother could not tell Anita in Yiddish not to bring her father. My mother pointed to Helene, and said, "This girl is from the village. She came to do her homework." And she said to Helene, "Go! Go!" and Helene ran. She understood.

'I just stood there and waited. I can see in front of my eyes even now the way my father walked back with Anita.' Frankie's voice broke again. 'They looked at his identification paper and said, "Why did you cross out J [for Jewish]?" He said, "I am French." And the German said, "Drop your pants!" I was shocked. My father should take his pants off in front of me! Adults did not do these things in front of children! My father turned to the Gestapo and said, "In front of the children?" Anita remembered the man suggesting the other bedroom. He virtually admitted that he was Jewish and Father did not have to drop his pants.

'They ordered, "Parcel up your clothes! You're coming with us!" My mother said "You won't get me out of here alive!" The German turned and gave her such a whack across the face. My father went for him, but he took out his gun, put it to my father's neck and said, "Don't be stupid!" I thought, "It's not happening, it's a game, a horrible game." ' Frankie's breathing was shallow and panting. 'The signal would come to stop the game. I wanted to give the signal "Stop!"

'We heard a shot outside. I found out later that the driver fired the gun, because the lady, Madame Pomerans, who was in the car outside, tried to escape. She asked to be allowed to relieve herself behind a rosebush, and then she ran.

'Anita was marvellous. She asked, "Will I take my schoolbooks?" "Don't worry, we'll get you books," the man said. But she took a book, and tied up a bedspread with many clothes, because my mother just stood there after being hit. I also just stood there. The man said, "We are leaving! Take your baggage!" I thought I saw my mother going to Bernadette in the middle of the road. The Gestapo man said to my mother, "She is too young," and took my mother to the car. I remember getting into the car, sitting on a seat facing the rear. I saw Bernadette in the middle of the road. And that was that.

'My father's face was the colour of this [white] wall. I can't remember my mother. When we arrived at the jail, they separated us. My father just went. He could not talk. I remember his face. I didn't realise then that we were in Limoges jail. We went up the metal stairs, they made a lot of noise. We were put in a cell. The walls were brown and very rough. There was a table, some mattresses on the floor, and a little window with bars. In the corner there was a bucket, and Madame Pom[erans] said it was a toilet. She put the only chair in front of it. She told us to not use the bucket before the morning when they took the bucket away. Otherwise we would have this awful smell. So Anita and I developed strong sphincter control. The German woman guard had thick lips, and wore a dark pleated skirt, and a soft angora cardigan. To this day I cannot stand angora wool and black pleated skirts.

'That night I could not go to sleep. The blankets were so prickly. But the minute Madame Pom said, "Go to sleep. I'll look after your Mummy," I fell asleep. I looked up to that woman, because she was so big and strong. She had a big bosom and black wavy hair. She was so nice.

'We were taken downstairs for interrogation. Each woman coming out of the interrogation room was crying. We walked in. I remember a man behind a table who pushed a box full of photographs to my mother saying, "I want names and addresses". My mother pushed the box back. She said, "They are not mine. And even if I knew them, do you think I would tell you?" When I think what they did to people for less than that! My mother said later that she did not know what possessed her. Either she was a fool, or someone looked after her to say this. Maybe because we were there the commandant did nothing.

'I heard of a woman who did not identify photographs having her head pushed under water. As a child, I could not bear the thought of my head being pushed into a bucket of water, not being able to breathe. To this day I keep my head away from water when I have a shower. When I have to wash my hair, I make sure water does not touch my mouth or nose. I can't swim.

'The newspaper which they gave us as toilet paper had pictures of Jesus Christ. I stuck them with spit on the wall, and I prayed to Jesus, asking him to let me see again my father, Bernadette, my grand-mother, and the aunts, uncles and cousins who had been taken away.

'One day an old woman was put in our cell. She shrieked and bashed her head against the wall every night. She always rushed for the bread and felt to see which pieces were the softest and biggest.

But Madame Pom used to excuse her, saying she was old. Madame Pom was so kind. She lifted me up to the window, so I could see the blue sky and a red roof. Our neighbour repainted his roof and Louis [Frankie's husband] said it was too red, but for me it was just beautiful, wonderful.

'One day a soldier said he was taking Anita and me to the courtyard for fresh air, but he took us to another cell. We sensed that there was something wrong. Two women asked us various questions, but we said we knew nothing. The next day my mother refused to let us go with the German soldier. Somehow, they respected her. She never let on that she understood German. She was French, and they could jump, was her attitude.

'Another day the soldier promised emphatically that he would take us outside, and he did. I saw pieces of glass on the wall and I could imagine (with anguish) how much it would hurt to climb over them. I thought the Germans put the glass there specially for me, because they did not like me, because we were Jewish. I could not understand why that was bad. The German guarding Anita and me had a huge gun, a knife, and something I imagined was used to hit people over the head. I could imagine how much that would hurt me.

'Another time, there was this magnificent soldier in the courtyard. I hated him, but he was incredibly handsome in his blue-grey uniform with amazingly thin pleats in the trousers. I felt guilty for admiring him.

'Most of the time Anita and I had nothing to do. Anita was very bored. We made dice out of bread. Anita pulled hairs out of the toilet brush, and used them to knit the threads which she pulled out of the blanket. There were squares carved into the table, and Madame Pom told us to use paper and play drafts. But I did not want to because they were not proper pieces. And I was dying to have a doll. Madame Pom fashioned a shawl, and said, "Cuddle it. It is a doll". But I was not fooled, I wanted a real doll.

'One time I had terrible stomach pains. My mother banged on the door, and the woman came. "My child is sick, but I am not letting her out of here." The woman gave her a tablet. The pains passed.

'And then my mother started to get sick. Every night she started walking up and down the cell, up and down, fanning herself with a cloth. And we knew what was coming.' Frankie's voice held anguish and a degree of anger. 'It was an almighty nervous attack. She had hysterics every night. The first time it happened, Madame Pom called for help. A German soldier came, but he just thumped the door shut, he couldn't care less. And every night my mother would cry, sob, shake, belch a lot, and go completely hysterical.

'One night there was an almighty bombardment. The jail shook, it was unbelievable. The dark cell lit up with flames from the sky. We knew the Allies had landed. My mother said, "They are running like poisoned rats." But for me, the Allies just meant heavy bombing, and thinking we would die if a bomb fell on us. That is why during bombardments my body shook and my teeth chattered with fright like castanets.

'Not long after this, a short German soldier took Anita and me to see my father. I could not bear the soldier carrying me. It was like the response I saw in one of the hostage boys when Saddam Hussein picked him up and touched him on the head. And yet that man took us to see my father.

'There were a lot of other men in the cell. Papa kept on asking how Maman was, saying we had to look after her. I had never seen my father so thin, nor his skin so yellow. He did not smile. He just had this look of fear, fright.' Frankie had tears in her eyes. 'But I remembered that my father had said some time "I'll get him, that one," meaning the German who had hit my mother and held a gun at his head. He wrote a note for my mother with shoe polish.

'Madame Pom and my father were in groups of prisoners taken to find unexploded bombs. Then she was shifted and replaced by a mother and her son. The food was dreadful. One day we were served black pudding, but my mother stopped us eating it. But the mother and son ate it, and fluid and stench poured out of them from top and bottom. We called the guard who said, "The Jews can stay in the shit," and shut the door. The next day it was obvious that all who had eaten the food were very sick.

'They opened the door and said to us, "You are going out." My mother said, "That's it." We used to hear gunshots in jail — ratata-tatata. And then hammering. I understood that sequence. I used to imagine what it would be like to be dead in a box. So I thought that this time we were going to die. I did not know what dying was like, but it was very, very frightening. I had this warm feeling come up, I thought I would vomit. We walked out into sunshine. The courtyard was filled with people.

'The German woman said, "You're going . . . home." We didn't believe it. She laughed. "They don't believe that they are going home." They opened this huge door, and we were out in the street on the footpath. There was a big black car standing there, and Anita, like a good girl, went straight to it, and put her hand on the handle to go in. But the soldier in the car said, "Go, go home." We stood there, my mother like a drunk. The German woman said, "Don't stand around. Go!" My mother said, "Where? How? What time is it? I don't know if there is a tram." We just stood there. She pointed to the Red Cross, and we went to the building. The woman there said, "What would you like?" and she gave me some chocolate! I hadn't eaten something like that for an eternity, though it was only two and a half months.

'My mother said that she could not go home without Bernadette. She gave Bernadette's details, and we were sent to this women's shelter. The bombing was incessant.

'And one day a man came to say he had news of Charles Szkop. He said that he was unearthing bombs, guarded by the French police. The next day my mother took us to where he worked. She always took us with her.'

Frankie's tone changed to amazement and excitement.

'They finally brought Bernadette — that was a sight! We saw the big truck arrive in front of our place, and my mother did not know whether to fly down the stairs or through the window. When we saw her, she was putrid, filthy, fat. She had no pants on and her bottom was all red and sore. My mother immediately washed her. She was full of lice. Do you know? While I was in jail, I did not think about Bernadette. I had just accepted that she was not there. Now I was just amazed that we had found her. I just watched her on Maman's knees, touching Maman's face. I don't remember if I hugged or kissed her. I just watched. And once we had Bernadette, we went back to Les Vignes.

'Our place was shut up. The flowers had grown and died. I saw our cat Kiki on the road. Apparently she had not been seen since the day we had left. My mother pushed the door open. It was full of mice. The detergent had changed clothes into jelly in the pan. The food in the cupboard was gone.

'My mother asked the neighbour whether she had taken our rations. "Well, yes," she admitted. My mother said, "You took the food, but you couldn't take the washing out for when we came back?" "Oh, we thought the Gestapo put a bomb behind the door."

'The people across the road took me in and asked me how it had been for me, all the details. And they gave me a lolly, and the kind lady put an arm around me.

'I went back to school. I was upset to have forgotten how to read. The teacher said, "How terrible to do such things to children!"

'Then my father came back. He had a black Mauser gun. And he told us that he did get the Germans who arrested us. He killed the man who held the gun to him.' Frankie spoke with satisfaction. 'I thought it was wonderful, because I had wanted to do something horrible to the Germans. I imagined doing the worst things to them, like make them walk on safety pins which I'd stick in their feet. I wanted revenge for them hurting my parents. My father used to give the hidings, and he used to protect us. And there he could not protect us because this fellow had a gun at his head. He could not do anything! That man hit my mother and my father could not do anything! I mean that was bad. It was so unfair! I have this childlike feeling that a bad person should not get away with it. So it was right that my father had his revenge! I was terrified of that big gun, but my father got his own back!

'I don't know if the body does it to itself, but I became sick after the war. They found a stain on my lung, so I had to rest a lot. Recently I started to wonder at how come those three months in jail affected my whole life so much. It was a short time, and I had not been in concentration camps. But you can't measure time like that, for me the time was like two years. Sometimes I wonder if I dreamt it? Did I really feel that way? But then, the feelings have stayed with me all my life.

'Adults spoke in front of children, as if they did not realise that children listened. When my father returned to Les Vignes, he told the peasants that the Maquis was everywhere in the forests, wiping out remaining resistance. And we had to walk past these forests with the frightening Maquis in them. I went through hell, sure that they would get me. When I told my mother of this later, she said, "Why did you not ask?" But you couldn't. Children just didn't mix in with adult talk.'

How much could a child distinguish between realistic and fantasy fears? I asked, 'How did the Maquis fear compare to the earlier fear of a man with an axe in the forest?'

'With the man with the axe, we were in a group, and we believed and did not believe. We knew the boys in the village always teased us. This time I was on my own, and you know I don't remember going through the forest and back, but I did. But I know I was absolutely petrified.

'My father kept getting his own back too well, this time with the *collaborateurs*, so the French sent him to train rookie soldiers. During that time he used to visit us on a big black motorcycle. But my mother said, "That's enough, you can't keep playing soldiers forever, you have a family." And we went back to Paris.

'There I felt betrayed again. In my mind, if you pray and you are good, things turn out okay. But I had prayed to Jesus Christ,' Frankie blew out air in pain, 'and my grandmother did not come back. None of the people for whom I prayed made it.

'We stayed in what had been my grandmother's one-bedroom apartment with Aunt Elise. She and her girlfriend slept in the double bed, and my mother and we children slept on mattresses on the floor. My father slept at his uncle's place. One day a man came through the door while my mother was washing dishes. He was very gaunt and wore khaki. "Uncle Genot," I cried. He was a friend of Aunt Betty's. He was not Jewish but he was wonderful. My mother told him Betty had not come back. She gave him a photo of Betty and he put it in his pocket without looking at it.

'Aunt Elise had an American man friend. One day she became sick. We children had to sit outside while she was so sick. My father couldn't swallow this any more. There were arguments, and Bernadette and I were taken to Angervillers.

'Neither I nor Maman remember how we arrived there. Bernadette and I stayed at Madame Stozek's. Anita stayed in Paris in order to go to school, and my parents lived and worked in a rented room.

'Madame Stozek had her own two daughters, a good-for-nothing soldier son, and a few other children who came and went. This woman was a horse — she worked in the fields, milked cows, and looked after us. But we were neglected, dirty, and the food was bad. We had to wash piles of dishes in dirty greasy water, and dry them with wet towels. I hated it. But for some strange reason, Madame Stozek insisted that our feet had to be clean when we went to bed. So every night everybody had to wash their feet in this bucket of water.

'In the second year there, when I was nine, I refused to wash my feet. So her husband whacked me with his belt. I could have taken it from my father, but to take it from a stranger, an alcoholic, I went bananas inside. The next Sunday I told my father, and he told Mr Stozek, "If you lay one hand on this child again, I don't pay you." This was the worst threat. But for good measure he added, "And I'll break your neck." I felt so good that there was someone who protected me.

'I used to protect Bernadette from that bitch Stozek and her daughter Paulette. I suppose it was hard for Paulette having all the other children there. But one freezing cold morning she just pushed Bernadette out and shut the door. I flew into a rage. I opened the door, but then she shut the door on both of us. I shrieked with even more rage, threatening to break down the door if she did not open it. She opened the door. She used to taunt us by taking the crusty part of the bread. It made me mad. To this day my family keep the end of the bread for me.' Frankie cried freely.

'Were you abused in any other way?'

'There was a cruel teacher who hit us with a ruler across the finger-nails if they were dirty. I used to be hit a lot, and it hurt especially in winter when my hands were cold. I bottled this up, you couldn't tell the Stozeks. He also slapped us. And yet, he had saved my cousin Cecile. He told her to hide when Germans came to search for Jewish children.

'I liked my mother's visits because she brought us goodies, and we were nicely dressed for the day. But my father used to fix up bad happenings. At times one or other of us was taken for the day to Paris. I was taken once to a classical play at the *Comedie Française*.

I understood nothing of it, but I boasted about it to the kids at Madame Stozek's when I returned. Once Bernadette was taken to *The Wizard of Oz*. She came back enchanted. I desired to see it too, and I was bitterly disappointed when my father took me to some awful film instead. When Michelle, my daughter, was three, I told her, "I am taking you to *The Wizard of Oz*", but it was I who wanted to see it.

'One night at Madame Stozek's we went to the movies. They told all children from fourteen to eighteen to leave the hall, and us younger children to turn around and face the audience. Being a child, the minute the lights were off, I looked at the screen. I couldn't believe what I saw. They were the most horrific films from concentration camps. It was the first time in my life that I saw naked people. I saw lamps made of human skin, soap made from human bones, chimneys, gas chambers. I couldn't believe that people could be put in ovens to burn. I had no one to talk to, to explain things to me. I have never been able to smell strong soap since. In Australia I nearly vomited when someone had strong smelling soap. When I gave my daughter Colette a lift to work, I could not approach her hospital, because there was a chimney there. "Colette, I can't take you there! It's like taking you to the camp." Isn't it stupid? I tell myself that I am mixing things up in my mind from the film and the present. But that movie was worse than anything I went through, it was absolutely terrible.

'Bernadette was with me. That would have been the most terrible experience for her at Madame Stozek's. What did it do to her, she was younger? I don't think she realised. We experienced the same things, but I felt strong looking after Bernadette. For instance, I was always scared of the dark, so I took Bernadette with me to get some milk at dusk. I was petrified of bats, they said once in your hair you couldn't get them out. Suddenly Bernadette shrieked, I don't know if it was a bat or a bird. She ran to me and plastered herself against me, and we both shrieked. I cannot remember what we did next.

'I seem to talk more about my father than my mother. My father was a great, big person in my life, even though there were things on which we did not agree. I never enjoyed a hiding with his leather strap. But he taught us to be honest and hard working. "If you get paid for a day's work, you do it and do it well," was his motto. He taught me punctuality to excess. Even now, if I am five minutes late,

I feel sick. He gave me the exact money needed to do his jobs. God help me if I needed a penny to go to the toilet. He was severe like that with himself too. When I worked for him, he expected more from me than a stranger. And yet he was the kindest gentlest grandfather. He never laid a hand on my children, and when they fell he comforted them. I pointed out how he had changed. He did not answer.

'My mother, it is strange. Sometimes I wonder if I had much to do with her. I certainly remember her visiting us at Madame Stozek's place with a big black shopping bag giving us bits of chocolate, biscuits and orange juice. She looked after me when I was sick. But . . . my mother was always sick! I had to look after my mother. For instance, after the war when she was sent away to have treatment for her hip problems and she was bed-ridden, it was I who was sent to look after her. I have always seen my mother as sick. When I have problems, I don't go to my mother, because she can't help me, and I don't want to add to her burdens. I have more feelings for Anita who is always there for me; Bernadette too. I feel very concerned for Anita since she lost her son Danny four years ago in a car accident. He was was nearly thirty.

'My mother also did very hurtful things to me, and what's worse, she denied them when I spoke to her about them later. She would just say, "No, it did not happen." So I was hurt twice — at the time, and when she denied it. And I cannot forgive that.

'For instance, our class adopted a godchild. I was in charge of the money which we raised in various ways. One day I was entrusted to buy a doll for this child, and I brought it home at lunchtime. My mother accused me of stealing money from her purse to buy the doll. I was so ashamed to have to ask my teacher to write a letter to my mother confirming that she had given me the money. I could only give the letter to my father, who said to her, "So, are you happy now?" I gave up my post as treasurer. To this day I have problems being near money, and I certainly cannot take money out of my mother's purse if she asks me to. And I am fifty-five years old! And she says, "It's not true. I don't remember anything like that!"'

'I came to Australia when I was fourteen years old. I left school at sixteen in Year Ten, and then I worked for my father until I married at twenty-one. I had problems assimilating. I joined *Habonim* [a Jewish youth group], but the children there were much freer than I was, and it caused a lot of problems.

'I started to have nervous fits. My first fit occurred in *Habonim* camp. My father visited and immediately said Bernadette would not be allowed to come to such a place. I was also a wreck in exam situations and failed them. I had fits whenever I was upset or could not cope. I had crying sessions, and felt that I could not breathe. I hyperventilated, and had the shakes, and then I could not move my arms or legs.' Frankie repeated the movements with which she had earlier described her mother's fits in jail.

'I saw a psychiatrist, who was very nice, and explained to me that even though I was mature in body, I was very immature in feelings. She asked my dad not to be so dogmatic about everything. Once I spilt dye over my father's carefully laid out leather. I thought he would kill me. I had a fit then. But he was so nice not saying anything, he just worked on the bags.

'Not until recently have I connected my fits with my mother's fits. I take after my mother having arthritis too.'

I asked about other illnesses.

'I have always had a weight problem. I eat when I am under stress. Also, from the age of fourteen till six years ago I suffered migraines associated with stomach aches and vomiting. I always used to clench my teeth and six years ago I had my bite readjusted. Now I only have headaches.'

Were these symptoms associated with suppressed anger? I asked, 'How have you dealt with intimidation over the years?'

'I used to *very quietly* just allow people to say or do things to me, and I just pushed my feelings away. I tried not to rock the boat or assert myself. But then I tend to get anxious and wrought up about things. I am anxious when I am alone. Then my stomach turns over and I feel sick when someone knocks on the door. Yet when my children were home I was not frightened. And when my kids needed help, I pushed for their welfare. I was President of the Mothers' Club, and this gave me confidence.'

Now Frankie waxed, unlike at any previous time in the interview. 'I became a kindergarten assistant. I like being with children, because they are so straight, wonderful, a source of wonder. You are able to talk to them, they want to know things, they are so open. You don't have to hide anything from children, you explain things to them in a few words, and they understand, in their own little way. It's an absolute pleasure, I really love being with children. I was so sad when I had to cut down my work because of the arthritis.

'To me children are not threatening, I feel protective toward them. I look at the sleeping children, and I say to myself, "Isn't it wonderful — all these Jewish children, in peace, in quiet." At one time we had a spate of bomb threats in the school. That made me feel, not panicky, but very aware and vigilant. One day a girl ran in and said, "Frankie, get them out, there is a bomb threat!" Well, I woke each one and said, "Come on, kids, it's sunny and we have to go outside to play, but it's a surprise, so we have to go very quickly, one, two . . ."' Frankie clapped a fast rhythm. 'So I held this child, dragged another, herded them quickly. When we got to the middle of the ground outside, I started like this . . .' Frankie indicated the beginnings of a fit. 'It was like during the war, but this time I was the adult. I felt like my mother must have felt.'

And how did Frankie get on over the years with Bernadette, the first child she had protected?

'We didn't get on well when we were younger. Being the middle child, I was always left out. In Paris, Anita and Bernadette slept in the bed, I on the couch. But since we got married, we get on very well, we can talk. Our husbands get on well too.

'My parents had a tumultuous relationship, always screaming with each other. I only found out in high school that theirs was not the only marriage like that. My father could not bear my mother being blind, using her white stick. He found it difficult to be near anyone who was sick.

'My mother poisoned us as young adults against our father. If she wanted anything from him, she rang us to push him to give it to her. Perhaps she searched for her godlike father whom she lost when she was eleven. But my mother also used to say to me, "Louis is like your father. You'll be left like I was." And I believed her, and had arguments with him. Then one day I said "What on earth am I doing? He is a wonderful person!" Then I saw that I had a good strong marriage. Louis is very strong and reliable. Yes he tends to be isolated, but so do I. And sexually, I am amazed how normal we are.

'And yet I have much guilt toward my mother, I don't know why. I feel it when I go out and I know she is sitting at home alone. But then I resent her, remembering how it used to kill me when she rang to complain that my father was working in the garden and she sat alone inside. After he died, by chance I saw a beautiful thermos at my mother's place. She commented nonchalantly, "Yes he put coffee in it when he used to take me to the park." And this after she implied that my father always neglected her! I do for my mother what needs to be done. But I can't go to her with problems like Bernadette. I have a certain amount of good feelings to her, and pity that she lives in the dark, but I also have . . .'

I tried to supply the forbidden word. 'Did you feel anger toward your mother?'

'The day I came back from Madame Stozek, I came up the stairs in my cast-off army clothes. And there was my mother looking absolutely resplendent, in a most magnificent dressing-gown. I looked at my pants, and I felt angry. Isn't it stupid? I don't think I felt angry with her over the years for sending me away. At the time I never thought about it. I just accepted it. As an adult I tried to understand.

'I tried to be quite different with my children. It's been good, good, with them.' Frankie spoke passionately. 'I have been a supportive, listening, explaining mother. I was always there, wanted to know their side of things. I gave them what I hadn't had. And they turned out to be very nice, kind people. I've been able to talk to my children over the years about my war experiences. It has been such a good feeling, to tell them and they asking and listening.'

'How were you and your children when they were the age when things happened to you — about seven?'

'I don't know. I didn't have time to think, because at the age of seven, Colette had a heart operation. She had not been growing well, she was little and thin. They discovered a heart murmur, which must have been present from birth. After the operation she started to be overweight. Both my daughters have had nose bleeds and had their noses cauterised when little.

'I was in a terrible state when Colette got married and Michelle went to Israel. I missed Michelle enormously. Yet I was never over-protective. As children I encouraged them to swim and go to camps. And now I wanted Michelle to experience what I had experienced in Israel — to feel Jewish and to be in the majority.

'I am still nervous about being Jewish outside Israel. "How will they accept me?" is the first question with non-Jews. There was a little girl whom I took to school in the mornings. She quite openly stole Colette's toys, but I was scared to tell the parents in case they called me a bloody Jew. Eventually the father rang himself, and I explained that the little girl took things to draw attention to her desire that he take her to school. In fact he was kind and understanding.

'We had a German caretaker at this Jewish school, would you believe it? She took a liking to me, though I just wanted to get away from her. One day she started to tell me, "You know, during the war I was sick, my mother did not have enough to eat . . ." And I thought, "Don't say anything but one day I'll explode and ask her whether she thought it was a piece of cake for me?" '

Frankie was angry quite overtly for the first time, and her hand indicated a feeling in her chest.

'What do you feel in the chest?' I asked.

'Anger, this is how I feel when I get angry. The fits were associated with helplessness, things I could not cope with. The stomach pains and warm rising nausea were associated with fear. Actually, I am seldom free of these things. When I wake in the night, my mind wakes to this never-ending war movie which does not leave me alone. I have not joined the Child Survivor group because I feel I might not cope in the group emotionally. And it takes me a long time to get over being stirred up, and then I am depressing to be with.'

Frankie was stirred up now. It would take her two days to settle.

I asked if there was anything of importance which Frankie had not mentioned.

'The only thing which I have not mentioned is that in Paris my father had a mate in his Communist group, who one day said he had tickets to a concert. My mother did not want to go. I said that I'd like to go. And my mother allowed me to go with this man! In the theatre he pulled up my skirt, but I pulled it down firmly. I was beside myself with anger and upset. No one had touched me like this. In the metro I told him to be ashamed of himself, "And you a Communist!" I said. I was thirteen years old. He tried to pacify me. He told me to say nothing to anyone. And I didn't, till recently to Louis. He was disgusting. The next day after this incident I got my periods. I thought I must have done something shameful. It affected me in that I did not like Louis to touch me like this man. And there was this little Jewish dentist in Australia who used to touch my boobs. I could not tell my parents about him either.'

'How did the sexual harassments compare with your war experiences?'

'The war affected me a lot more. I coped with those two guys, even though I was scared to open my mouth. Neither was big and powerful. The first man was my height. Some weeks ago I brought up the first incident in the family. My mother asked why I did not tell her. I asked her, "Why did you let me go with him?" And she said she could not remember the incident.

'Ultimately the war left me with its constant replay, but also with a determination to give my children a better life. I am still fearful for security, but I enjoy my children having it more than I did. And even more generally, I want to do to others as I would they did to me. I am not Christian, and I am not as tolerant as I would like to be sometimes. For instance, I cannot easily be nice to Germans, even if they are young.

'Perhaps I take after my parents too. They tried to rebuild their lives for us, and my mother, in spite of everything, has been strong and has maintained her family. And I am very grateful that they both survived.'

Comment

Indeed, Frankie was lucky that her parents and her sisters survived, though so many of her extended family perished. Again, it is a comment on the Holocaust about what is considered to be 'lucky'. Still,

Frankie's traumas do not include the deaths of those near to her. Her core traumatic period started with the arrest of her parents and herself and ended two and a half months after release from prison. This period engraved itself on Frankie's life. She herself has wondered why such a short period affected her life so much. Nevertheless, unlike her younger sister Bernadette, we can see with Frankie how pre-arrest and post war stresses also added to and interwove with the core traumatic period.

Some of the after-effects from the core traumatic situations include responses of fear to anything which reminded Frankie of threats in that period. Such things were angora wool, cigarettes slanting from the mouth, loud noises, the German language, and so on. It is also clear that similar fears arose from strong impressions gained from others, such as having one's head submerged under water, and from films of concentration camps. The anxieties arising from these direct and indirect impressions have pervaded Frankie's life to this day.

At the time the impressions were imbued with a child's view of events. For instance, that the traumatic events were like a game which could be stopped with a signal, or that they could be influenced by prayer or being good, or that bad people should be punished. Similarly, Frankie had a childhood horror of adults reversing recently learnt mores such as keeping things in order, and having sphincter control in public. There was also the child's attitude of not questioning major events which seemed to be adult business, and to leave to adults the business of protection and worry about the world. This worked while the adults could offer protection. It left an impression of lasting confusion and insecurity when they could not. Frankie also used concrete symbols as children might in fairytales to signify some core fears. For instance the superstitious fear of bats may have represented atavistic abandonment to predators fears.

Frankie was particularly affected by her parents' helplessness at the time of the arrest, and by her mother's helplessness and nervous fits in prison. The latter image of mother stayed the dominant one, overshadowing her coping in other situations. It was accentuated when Frankie had to look after her sick mother after the war. On the other hand, Frankie idealised her father as coping and protective and he partly cleansed himself of his powerlessness through his later revenge. At least she did not have to care for and protect him in the same way as she did her mother.

And yet, each parent carried opposite images too. Mother did protect her family, even father, in certain circumstances, and Frankie took after her in both protecting her own children, and having fits when she could not cope. On the other hand, father could be very demanding, punitive and could even be seen as dangerous. Frankie could have fits stimulated by fear of her father, as her mother had fits stimulated by fears in the prison. We may speculate that Frankie's later timidity and symptoms were influenced both by being suppressed by the Holocaust, and by her inability to express her anger toward either parent. She still feels unable to express anger for lack of care and injustices from childhood. This has hampered Frankie's feelings of love and gratitude.

Nevertheless, Frankie has been able to fulfil herself in her marriage, and especially with children. Perhaps this was not only a means of overcoming her trauma, by preventing it in other children, but it was also a means of identifying with her parents, who, after all, did what they could to preserve their children. Bernadette was the first such child whom Frankie protected.

The replication of symptoms and illnesses across the generations is striking. Is it just genes or coincidence that Frankie had fits and arthritis like her mother and that Colette had similar symptoms at the same age as Frankie?

Lastly, we note once again that, though her moral world was badly shaken, Frankie reconnected with the values and morals of her pre-war parents as they themselves attempted to do so. It was helpful that the trauma was avenged. Frankie could reestablish some faith in the correct order of things. Not completely, of course. Neither the Holocaust nor a depleted mother who could not care for Frankie could be placed in the order of a good world. Yet Frankie continues to provide security for children while she wrests love and meaning from her inner terrors. The struggle continues, in the right direction.

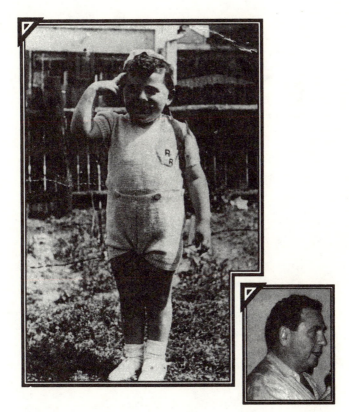

Richard

—•—

'AT THE TIME

IT WAS NORMAL'

$\mathcal{R}$ICHARD 'CAME OUT' three years ago. His story was sought after by the media at the New York Hidden Child Conference. There were two reasons for this. Firstly, the story of his first decade could fill volumes of adventures and human issues. Secondly, Richard could fit his story to the hearer's needs. He was the prize interviewee of Women's International Zionist Organisation (WIZO) ladies in an orphanage in France after the war. He traded his story for a supply of chocolates. Today there were no prizes.

Richard was a little short like so many older survivors, and carried a paunch around his stomach. He overtalked, describing events from slightly different angles in a flow of sentences, adding sardonic commentaries as he went.

Richard Rozencwajg (now Rozen) was born in Radom, Poland, on the 15th of April 1935.

*I*T STARTED QUITE okay, back in the thirties. I was fortunate to come from a well-to-do family. My father was a doctor and my mother was a mothercraft nurse. My father was distant and busy, used as a figure of threat by my mother. One day I broke something and he hit me on the bottom with the rubber part of his stethoscope. I was four. That is quite a vivid traumatic memory for me.

'But my first ever memory had to do with fussing. As a two year old my white socks always had to be up and clean, also my white shoes. I was my mother's possession, she exercised full control over me, and I had no rights whatever. If my mother was out, the domestic watched me. If I opened or closed the curtain slightly, or put a bit of dirt on my sterile self, I got a little smack. I was the only child born to a couple in their thirties, and I was to be brought up "properly". In a sense I was spoilt. I was overfed, and was overweight. I had a lot of toys, mainly educational, no guns. At three and a half I had a four-wheel cart from France, but the wheels had to be clean like my shoes.

'That car was my pride and joy. I rode it down the footpath and met my best friend, Helenka, who also had such a car. We played at getting petrol from a tree.'

Richard started to talk about the war.

'I was four and a half. There was panic in the air. My father spent more time at home. There was always news, people talking, they said the Germans were coming. There was a lot of packing. We were going somewhere. No one told me anything, as if I didn't understand. Eventually I heard explosions in the distance, noise. Suitcases were brought to the door now. Finally we put all our possessions on a cart. There were explosions, like continuous lightning. There was panic, but I was supposed not to worry, as my parents were taking care of everything. If I asked too many questions, I got smacks on the bottom. It must have been a fashion in those days.' Here started the sardonic comments. 'I have never smacked my children so much.

'We travelled with other carts toward Russia. We crossed a river called Bok, which separated the Russian and German sectors of Poland. We stayed in Lubolm, a town just on the other side of the river. Within days things became normal for me. My father was in charge of a hospital. The only differences were that there was no office I had to keep away from, there was more activity with people coming and going, and more people, strangers, lived in the house. I lost my cart of course, and other toys, and war games crept into my play. I was alone more. My mother was always busy, there were no nannies to force feed me, and I was fussed over less. This gave me a chance to have my own games. Overall, the changes seemed to me like previous holidays.

'After a few months my favourite aunt Dorka came with her fiancee. They had escaped from the ghetto in Radom. They told us how bad things were there. They brought photos (the last ones) of my grandparents. Grandmother seemed to have aged by twenty years. My father married my aunt and her fiance. This was the first wedding in which I had a role. That was very exciting for me.

'They moved on east. I remember them trying to convince my father to go too. They said that the Germans could not be trusted, it was only a matter of time before they invaded. My father said that there was nothing to worry about, the Germans and Russians had made a pact, and the Russian army was too powerful to be attacked. I saw them again only after the war.

'In July 1941 [after twenty-two months in Lubolm], the Germans suddenly invaded. There was a lot of noise. One day the Russian soldiers were there, the next day German soldiers. There was unrest again, like before the invasion earlier. But this time I saw from our window columns of tanks, cars, and German soldiers. No one could believe that there were so many of them. We shut the windows and started packing again. People came at night to discuss best ways of escape. We had no illusions as to how the Germans would treat us.

'Once again someone picked us up in a horse and cart, but this time we had a lot less to carry. Once again we travelled through the night, and heard shooting in the distance. After three hours we came to a village. It was all secretive. We never knew the name of the village or the names of the people who were to hide us, nor did they know our names. We went down to a cellar. There was a false cupboard, and a cupboard behind it. We went into the second cupboard. It was a metre tall, just taller than me, two metres long, and a metre wide. It was totally dark. And we stayed in that cupboard for the next thirteen months. This time life changed drastically' Richard gave a sardonic laugh, with the first overt emotion. And again, from a different angle, 'This was very very different to anything I had ever experienced.'

'No one came near us the whole time except the couple who brought us food and water once a night, and took the toilet bucket from us.

'The food consisted of bread, cold soup, vegetables and, very occasionally, meat. It was sufficient. They gave us what they ate themselves. We could tell day and night only by when food was brought, and by my father's luminous watch. We could hear loud sounds at times, like a car passing, or shooting. My parents could only lie and sit. We all slept packed next to each other. We changed clothes infrequently, and I had no toys.' How can humans spend thirteen months in these circumstances?

'At first I thought it was a novelty, a bit of fun, walking between my parents in the dark. Then routines developed quickly. First the food, then washing. My father was very insistent on washing, though my mother was less fussy than in the old days. We spent a long time over the ritual of washing every part of our bodies. Exercising each part of the body was also a ritual, taking up a lot of time.

'My parents whispered (we had to be silent) stories into my ear. My father taught me letters and numbers, to read and to write, by touch on my hand. I was very busy. Counting took a long time. First to ten, then twenty, thirty, one hundred. Days were too short for me. I was so busy trying to work out this, then that. I retold father's stories to myself, then extended, changed them so the boy did not get smacked. I extended the stories. I had a lot to do. I was not bored.

I was busy all the time. If someone had asked me to come out and go for a walk, I would not have had time.

'Certainly for my parents, life was no longer normal, but for me it was just different. I adjusted to it quite well. It is only when I look back, when people were sorry for me much later when I told them of this time, that I realised how this time was drastically wrong. But to me at the time it was just different. To me it seemed quite normal. I can honestly say it didn't seem to me that there was anything wrong with it. All my needs were well taken care of. I had my walks inside the cupboard, I played, I had my stories told, had my schooling, exercise, washing, eating, everything was normal.

'Darkness did not actually bother me. But I think I could see. At least the feeling was that I could see. That is my impression, because later on when I saw the letters I remembered that they felt like that — they got it right! Actually, for years if I saw a number or letter I could feel it on my hand. I could feel what I saw. I think there is a connection between feeling and seeing . . . Also I developed a good memory, I think because I had to memorise what I was taught.

'My father calculated that the war would last a year, and he had parcelled his gold coins and other valuables accordingly. After the year was up, we were told to go.

'My parents begged to be allowed to stay longer. Eventually they gave all their possessions, including my father's French shoes, for another month's shelter. This last month was quite unpleasant, because my mother was crying constantly (though she tried to hide it), and my father became very, very quiet. The routine continued, but my parents' mood was unhappy. They were constantly preoccupied. I was worried because I heard them whisper about the big trouble they were in. They were irritable if I asked questions. The world now was not normal.

'Then one night, it was August 1942, we were given more food than usual, in bundles. They did not bring a bucket. We put on a lot of clothes. My feet had grown, so parts of my shoes were cut and my feet wrapped. We were told to leave, and this time we left.

'We started wandering. I walked between my parents. It was dark, we could not distinguish anything. When there was a bit of light,

I saw that my parents walked like the monkeys in the Warsaw zoo. Of course they had not stood up for over a year.'

Richard's voice became excited. He said, 'Early in the morning suddenly something happened. Oooh, that was the most exciting time of my life. It was something phenomenal. It was seeing the light.' Richard was enraptured. 'In the distance just a little bit of light appeared as the sun was coming out. It was something extraordinary, something that I had forgotten. We were in the forest. My father said to cover our eyes for some minutes, otherwise we would go blind. I cheated of course, and I peered between my fingers. I was so curious, so fascinated. The whole process took, say, half an hour, but to me it seemed eternal. Then I saw my parents and they looked so different. My father had hair everywhere, he really did look like a monkey.' Richard's voice became choked. 'It was quite a scare.' He resumed in his normal voice, 'We decided to hide in the forest. After breakfast I must have gone to sleep, because I woke to my father talking in a foreign language [Ukrainian] to two men with guns but no uniform. I knew my father was pleading with them to let us go. He offered them his watch which the so and so's just took. Then they took us to a town. In a room, like an interrogation room I came close for the first time to a German officer. He looked so different to the Ukrainians. He was taller, his boots were shining, I was fascinated by all the buttons and medals and swastikas on his uniform.

'My father insisted that we had been hiding from the Russians, even though they had retreated long ago. He also kept on denying that we were Jewish. That discussion was resolved quickly. We were told to drop our trousers there and then. Only Jews in that part of the world are circumcised, so our worries were over, in a way. For my parents it was a kind of relief to have to accept the situation. We were put in a hold with other people. After two days we were marched to a train and we were transported to the Lublin ghetto.

'There were masses of people there. Life changed dramatically again. People were not just sick, they were thin, lying in the street. There were lots of guards, and Alsatian dogs. At times they chased me, but I managed not to be bitten. I developed a great dislike of them.

'My father went to work. There were eight or nine people in each room, everybody unhappy. Food was scarce. It was dangerous for me to go out, because they took children and the old away first. I was always hiding, often in a cupboard — again. I disobeyed and looked out the window. Each morning I saw what I thought at first to be sleeping people, but they were dead, always naked. I had never seen naked bodies before. They were naked because their clothes were traded for food. The old and young bodies were carted away in the mornings. And the day would start. It went on like that for three or four months.

'We all had to wear a star. I had not known what being Jewish meant, we were not religious. My father had been a Polish intellectual, Pole above all. So at first I thought the star was a kind of badge. But it came to mean being Jewish, and different. Being different now meant that you could be confined to a ghetto, be robbed, be shot. Being Jewish meant there was something wrong with my existence, with me.'

Uncharacteristically, Richard slowed down. 'I came to the conclusion that things were quite wrong. This was different to adapting to different lifestyles like the cupboard, which at times was even fun. This was no fun. We suffered permanent hunger. There was no schooling, no stories. I had to be quiet and just sit like a dummy. The days were very long. I hardly saw my father and he did not communicate. I was sad because everyone around me was always unhappy. People around us were always disappearing, dying.

'They disappeared to a camp called Treblinka, and they never came back. They were killed there. I was not supposed to hear, but I understood that all the children were already supposed to have been taken there. So there were no food rations for me, my parents gave me part of theirs.'

'Were you aware that there was a system which wanted you dead?'

'That was not exactly so. I did not understand death. I saw dead people and I knew nothing good can come of it. It was final. Treblinka was the end of the road.'

'Was that frightening?'

'Yes, it bothered me. I would have preferred to do other things than be put in a position like that. I found the whole set-up in the ghetto totally uninteresting, there was just no way of enjoying myself. People were crying, grieving, parting, dying. My parents were resigned, relieved in having no control. But that philosophy did not come to me. To me it seemed that I could not work anything out. I could not understand death. There was nothing right happening. There were no rights except to obey and be taken away. Sooner or later they would take you out of the cupboard and take you to Treblinka. It was hopeless.

'And sure enough, our turn came in December 1942. Our names were read out to go to a "labour camp". It was our turn to say goodbye. We were marched to a train and taken to a transit camp. My parents did a bit of work, but it was mainly waiting for the inevitable. Now we were in barracks, sleeping on bunks. Guards and barbed wire were constantly visible. People were always hit and bitten and mauled to death by dogs. We were permanently hungry.

'I don't know, what was worse? To worry about death, which seemed like something coming anyhow. Or, though I could not have put it into words then, to see it like the change of seasons. Like it was hot before and now it was cold, you are being taken to an end. Nothing good is happening, everything is getting worse since the cupboard.

'Then my father was offered a chance to escape. A couple of men, like the ones who captured us in the forest [Ukrainian guards] put us in a wagon under a lot of clothing. I understood that they would kill my father if he was not really a doctor. We travelled for ten hours to the forests to the partisans.

'The officer spoke beautiful Polish like my father, something I had not heard for a long time. He also had a nice uniform with things on it, though it was torn. The other partisans also spoke nice Polish, and they gave us our first good meal in six months. I was not used to people in uniform being nice. My mother was still in her resigned mood, but I was joking with the partisans. My father stayed with the partisans, and my mother and I were taken to a village. It was December 1942.

'Next morning I was bathed for the first time in two years. I thought my skin was coming off with the scrubbing. And I was dressed as a girl! I became Marisha, and our surnames were changed. My mother explained to me how as a girl I would not be asked to expose my penis and be caught as a Jew, as happened last time. My mother trained me to be a girl — to change my walk, and so on. Not even the children of the family with whom we stayed knew that I was a boy. I got used to sitting on the toilet to wee. The most difficult thing was to use the feminine gender while referring to myself. And I learnt Christian prayers, and that my father had perished, and my mother came from another town. And I understood that nothing good would come out of me making even a single mistake.

'As well, other children were told to keep away from me, and the reason was that I was retarded. After a while I became cunning, because I acted more retarded than I had to. I knew I was not retarded, but when they made fun of me, I decided to pull faces at them and look stupid, making fun of them in a way, that was my way of having revenge.'

Richard volunteered the following with anguish. 'My mother was unhappy throughout this time. One reason was that she did not see my father. But as well, though she was protected in the village in one way, men would come and they would abuse the women. Later I understood that they threatened to give the women away as partisan sympathisers if they did not comply. I could hear the happenings during the nights which made my mother very unhappy, and she would often cry at night. It bothered me a lot. I knew it was wrong. I didn't quite understand what it was. And I heard "Don't harm me, don't harm my child!" I didn't see the men, but I heard a lot. It happened regularly. I was never touched myself.

'Sometimes I made noises from my nearby mattress which stopped mother's abuse. At other times I pretended to be asleep.

'It was complicated, but in some ways it was funny, enjoyable to trick others into believing that I was retarded. It wasn't such a good thing for my mother.

'In the spring my mother explained to me that there were rumours about me, and that I had to join my father in the forest. So suddenly things were different. My ribbons were removed from my hair, my hair was cut, and in the morning I was reunited with my father for the first time in months. He had changed again, this time back to how he had looked before, with tie and shirt, white gown, and stethoscope around his neck. My father then returned to the hospital. The hospital itself was well guarded by concentric rings of partisans.

I stayed with the partisans in one of those rings till liberation eighteen months later.

'Life became quite normal once again [Richard was barely eight]. It was different, but acceptable. There was a certain degree of danger, but that in itself was challenging and fun. Actually, most of the time it was exciting and good fun. We had control now. Everyone had a gun. I had a gun. It was wedged in the tree in a dense pine forest. I learnt to climb trees quickly. I was allowed to shoot only if someone pointed a gun at me. I never shot. In the winter we hid in trees, in the summer we often hid for hours in marshes under water, only with my mouth above water, under a leaf.

'I was the only child there. Most partisans just ignored me, but our commander, Jurek, who wore the Polish officer's uniform, had a bit of time for me. He soon gave me a job, and I became known as the Feather Boy. The partisans attacked small groups of Germans. They slit their throats so skilfully that a German two metres away would not even know that his comrade was dead. My job was to put a feather under the nose of the person just killed, to count to one hundred (so my schooling in the cupboard came in very handy), and to call over the partisans if the feather moved. Then they would give another stab to finish the person off. That happened quite often. That was good, and I was a good Feather Boy. The Germans used to plead with me, they talked to me in German. Some showed me photographs of wives and children. But for me that had no meaning, because I had been schooled with so much hatred for the enemy. And I was so brainwashed that I totally believed it was either us or them; that the way they were dying they would do to you if they got you; and the more you kill of them the more likely it is that you stay alive.

'This part was not fun, it was very serious business. I had to be very conscientious. Because if I didn't do my job, he might get us later. And there wasn't one of the dozens and dozens that I used my feather on that survived. I counted slowly to make sure. It wasn't so much hatred or revenge at this stage, but just that I was part of the machinery of survival. Now I wonder if my job was so important, they would have died anyway. Perhaps they just jollied me along. But I had other partisan duties as well, such as carrying boots from the ambush, and standing guard in camp.'

'How did you feel about dead Germans?'

'No feeling at all. It bothered me a little bit to see dead Jews in the ghetto, because it was wrong. But here it was perfectly right and absolutely necessary to survive, because if the partisans did not kill their enemies, they would kill us. That became quite normal, and I had absolutely no feeling toward the people. To me they had no meaning at all. I was already nine years old now, I understood clearly, and I was hardened by the previous sequence of events. I would have had no emotional problems shooting Germans from the tree because it was self-defence.

'Early on I saw two of our group have their throats slit, because they came from a foraging expedition empty-handed and drunk. I was very surprised, because they were people I knew, friends. But it was explained that if we don't have food, we all die, and being drunk they could have exposed us. But it was exciting to keep on staying alive. So many enemies were dying and many of our own fellows too.

'And then I had one of the most exciting moments of my existence. It was the present I got from the partisans for my ninth birthday, on 15th of April 1944. It was a whole loaf of bread. It was more sawdust than flour, but it was the most treasured possession of my life. Normally it would have been shared between twenty partisans. And they made a bit of fuss giving it to me, too. For me it meant security. As long as I had that bread under my shirt, I knew I would eat. Just the thought that I could scratch a few crumbs at any time was a wonderful thought and gave me the feeling of a full stomach. Though we did not starve with the partisans, food was at a premium. I was still scratching morsels from it in June when we were liberated. To this day I cannot stand it if bread is not eaten to the last crumb. With my children, unfinished steak didn't bother me, but unfinished bread was not negotiable.

'One night there was very heavy bombing. There were terrible explosions right around me as I was sitting in the tree. When I came down at dawn, there were many bodies, and bits of bodies. Everyone was sad. No one cried. Partisans don't cry. And I found a leg, and it was a good leg, boot and all. I decided that leg would be useful to my father. It took me four laborious hours and all my ingenuity to wade through deep snow to the hospital.

'My father was very excited to see me. However, it took him some time to get my meaning about the leg. I explained that this was the best leg there was. He took the leg and said he was very grateful, and he started crying and muttering, "What sort of a world did I bring you into!" I was ashamed of my dad. I said, "Look we are among partisans, and partisans don't cry." "Yes, yes," he apologised. As we parted, he forgot the leg. And I looked at him and I just shook my head. Partisans don't cry, and they don't forget. You get shot for being so careless. Unfortunately that was the last time I saw my father.' Richard was sad briefly, and he did not cry.

After a brief pause he went on. 'After a few days the retreating Germans passed over our dugouts. They killed all the wounded in the hospital, and they took away the six doctors. The Russians came and the partisans took me back to the village. That was liberation. Liberation for me was just another change, and I was suspicious of changes. There was no surge of joy. For one thing, I was hardened not to feel emotions except hatred for the enemy. For another thing, I was very sad that my father had disappeared, though that he was dead did not sink in till six years later. Liberation for the partisans was also sad, because now they reflected on all the dead.

'My mother made a fuss about me being reunited with her. I thought it was uncalled for. It was just another event when you live one day at a time. Yesterday I caught a rabbit. Today I am reunited with my mother. I don't acknowledge that I did not see my mother for one and a half years. I was a tough partisan. I let her cry. And she worried that I did not have a clean handkerchief, and that I would catch a cold. She thought that I was a nine and a half year old child. Well,' Richard laughed, 'I put the feather under one hundred noses, and I survived minus-40 degree winters. She lived in an unreal world.'

'She lived in an unreal world?' I queried.

'The abnormal world became normal, because I had no comparison. I know I was given this bizarre childhood, but I lived a day-to-day existence. I am still confused about what is normal. When I look at Vietnam, Cambodia, Bosnia, the normal and abnormal blend so much that for me it is normal that the world is abnormal.'

Richard and his mother never related to each other in any depth their experiences while they had been separated. Richard brushed me away a number of times: 'There was nothing to tell her.' 'It was boring.' 'She did not understand a man's world.' Then he referred to shame. 'I think it was shame, it started with the star in the ghetto.' Perhaps mother and son could not share shame.

'Perhaps it was a premonition that I was not excited at liberation. In June, Russian soldiers took us back to liberated Radom. My mother called on her closest friends, anticipating their joy that she was alive. They were doctors' wives. We looked neglected, and my mother was bent due to the cupboard, and she looked older than my grandmother before the war. The first friend said "You still exist! We thought that all the Jews were killed." She gave us some food and said "Here, go away, we don't want to have anything to do with Jews. My husband is a very important doctor." And she slammed the door. Her husband used to be subordinate to my dad.

'The bread was my happiest moment, the sun coming up the most exciting moment, what happened next was the saddest moment. Even for tough partisans . . . you look forward to . . . this was beyond acceptance. I wanted to meet again a friend and regain a sense of community. At the second place the door opened, and there was my closest friend, Helenka. I felt a surge of pleasure seeing her. And she called out, "Richard!" It did not last long. Her mother pulled her back, saying, "That's not Richard. All the Jews are dead." And she closed the door. And I was calling her name. It was so sad. You do all to survive. You go back to your own town, and your best friend is told you're dead. And my father died as a partisan for that country.' The nine year old partisan had tears in his eyes. 'My mother went to her third friend. She took us round the back, gave us some food, and said she couldn't have anything to do with us, because there were no more Jews, and her husband did not allow her to help Jews.

'My hatred of that country has not lessened to this day. It only increased when I learnt more of Polish (even partisan) atrocities against Jews.

'What was worth living for at this stage?'

'Staying alive was just so important. All the persecutions make you realise how precious life is. As a child you just want to see tomorrow, you are curious. Instead of a game you say, "I am still alive." The alternative seemed so bad. I just did not want to have my throat slit and have a feather under my nose. It's just no good.

'I started coughing and I had shadows on my lungs. A doctor suspected TB, and I went to a sanatorium for three months. By then separations and changes were the norm for me, so it was like for a kid today going to summer camp. But I ate twenty-three slices of bread when I arrived at the sanatorium — a record. I was very thin at the time.

'I rejoined my mother in Lodz, where she sought refuge from Poles who killed Jews. But one night two Polish bandits shot a Jewish jeweller in our house. We rushed to his room, and as he was sliding down I saw his brain and blood on the wall. My mother, the silly woman, tried to stop me looking. But in the previous two years I had seen as many dead as live people. Well, we didn't need a second opinion, or we already had two opinions, so we decided to leave Poland.

'End of 1945 we left Poland. The Poles gladly let Jews go, especially for money. Later we crossed the Czechoslovakian border into Germany. We were directed to a certain point, and then we got sprung by guards. It was all a trick. We were put in jail, and Americans came daily to ransom you. So one year after the war we were still currency. The Americans took us to a Displaced Persons camp in Stuttgart.

'We went to school there, and I learnt Yiddish. It was 1946 and I was eleven years old. I also learnt that only thirty-seven out of the thirty thousand children from Radom had survived.

'My uncle in Paris located us, and we joined him.' Richard paused with emotion. 'The second saddest episode occurred here. I always expected the unexpected, but here I was caught off guard.

'There was dinner for us and another family who had survived. My uncle presided as befitted a respected Parisian doctor, with his two nicely dressed and well-spoken daughters at the table. For years I was lucky to be in the right place at the right time, but not this time. My aunty placed steaming slices of roast next to me. While everyone was talking excitedly, I quietly put away slice after slice of the roast inside my shirt. I thought, "Today seemed all right, but you never know what tomorrow brings. With the roast under my shirt, I'll have some-thing to scratch on, just in case."

'But then as my aunty started to serve the roast, she noticed the juice dripping down my shirt. She and my uncle took me out by my ears. She screamed and kept hitting me. My mother was sent out. My uncle said weakly that she was a hard woman, but she kept on hitting. So after a while I told my uncle "Tell that silly woman she is just wasting her time. I spent one and a half years with the partisans, and I'll never cry." I felt bad, but couldn't understand — why do they put the roast next to me, if they don't want me to steal it? And I did a good job stealing. But I was tricked, and was caught. My pride was hurt by the hitting, but to be caught was worse. If you don't do things properly, you don't survive.

'But the sad and bizarre part was that the next day my aunt had me put in an orphanage, and I stayed there for four and a half years. My mother was too helpless to not go along with this. And what they did not know, was that just as I learnt to be a savage, I could have learnt not to steal food, and gone to school like a normal child. They forgot that my father put my uncle through three years of medicine. But I was not given a chance. Once again I was dealt a crook hand.

'But I didn't mind being in an orphanage. We got food each day, we did go to school. At school our uniforms identified us as Jewish. We were always outnumbered. In 1946, before we asserted ourselves, we lived like animals. We had to fight to gain respect. We only fought for survival and not to be insulted. And the best way to do that was with a blade. A sharp blade was highly respected by people who pointed fingers, called you names, threw stones at you. We formed a very tough gang to protect ourselves.' Richard pointed to some scars. 'This fellow hit me with a razor so hard that it stayed in my nose. I worked my knife in his stomach. We both finished in hospital. He was transferred.

'Having established that you were not a pushover, the defenceless target that you were before, you had to take control. Sometimes we even looked for trouble. It was a way of being on guard. We had to let them know, if they looked at you the wrong way. If we picked a fight deliberately, it was only because we were insulted, someone had got away, or we wanted revenge. If they left you alone, they were okay.

'One interesting feature in the orphanage were the WIZO ladies who gave you chocolates if you told them interesting wartime stories. I focused my ingenuity and innocent appeal on these ladies, and I had frequent interviews, some even came back to hear me again, and others came specifically to interview me. I became a businessman. I talked for ten minutes per piece of chocolate. And they cried and laughed, and they kept me supplied with chocolates.'

'In 1951 we were brought to Australia by my aunt Dorka and her husband Berek who had survived in Russia. This new country seemed to be a good one. But I was very careful when I had my first meal with them, breakfast this time. For the first time in my life I sat on my hands while the table was full of food. Turning away from excited talking, my aunt suddenly asked me why I was not eating? "What can I eat?" I asked politely. She said I could have anything. "Can I have some milk, please?" "Yes, of course. How much would you like?" "How much can I have?" I was not going to show my hand this time. "Why, you can have a whole glass." So I carefully filled the glass up to the brim. Then I licked the milk from the top like a cat. Everyone laughed. Since that full glass I realised I was in the right country.

'Well, then I caught up most of my grades, but my English stopped me going on to matriculation. I was determined not to do medicine, as my mother and uncle wanted me to. I felt that I could not meet the same challenge that my father met by doing medicine against all odds. I felt that I would fail, and to fail was worse than death. Because if you fail, you die. I did not want to try to follow in my father's footsteps and fail. I went to a technical school to do engineering.

'I left engineering because the prospect of working for Telecom for a wage was not enough for me. I became obsessed with making money. So I went into business, knitting for three years, then distributing confectionery and chocolates. I worked eighty to one hundred hours per week, seven days a week. And I achieved my aim of retiring by fifty.

'I married my first cousin at twenty-two, the daughter of my mother's other brother who survived in France. We had an unpleasant divorce because I insisted on having custody of my son, then seven months old. I did get custody, and he was looked after by my mother.

'I remarried in 1970 to Rysia and she has been very supportive and tolerant of me and my obsessions with my hobbies and the Holocaust. She had two children, but our daughter Sue died of a blood disease twelve years ago at the age of nineteen.

'I was obsessional with my hobbies — chess and bridge. In 1963 I was third in the Australian chess championships. In bridge I did better. I represented Australia at the 1982 Olympics in Biarritz, and the world championships the next year. In 1988 I became a grand master.' [Richard showed me the trophy from Biarritz, France.] 'When I was given that medallion when we finished sixth out of eighty-two countries, I was so proud . . .' Richard was more moved than at any other time in the interview. 'I was never happier in my life. It was not just the achievement, it was more that I, Richard Rozen, born in Radom in 1935, kicked around for so many years, and deprived, was able to finally do something worthwhile and represent my country, my new country. To finally be able to shake off being stateless, useless, being second-rate, being a Jew. It was also important that I gave something back to the country. It was a bonus to come sixth, it was pleasant to beat France, and I had great pleasure in beating Poland.

'But I really regret this. A German player mistook my AUS sign for Austria. "If I were Austrian, I'd hang myself." I said to him, and walked away. My reaction was uncalled for. But after all I had gone through, and I am here representing Australia, and he calls me Austrian!'

'What has given you your capacity in chess and bridge?'

'I think it started with my father teaching me in the cupboard. I was able to absorb, understand and remember. If something is important, I'll memorise it photographically. I can replay for you the last ten games between Spassky and Fischer. I could win blindfold chess. I could visualise the board and see moves in anticipation. I could do it in chess, bridge and conversation. Yet my memory is selective. I can't remember the registration number of my car. I can instantly forget names of people when I am introduced.

'I started to play chess in 1945 in the sanatorium Otwock. An older boy in the next bed taught me. I learned quickly, but when I was about to beat him, he changed the rules. He exulted in winning and I hated passionately being a loser, though of course I showed no emotion. Obsessively I memorised every trick of his. I won ten games in a row. From that time on I concluded that winning was much more fun than losing. I do not show my feelings of a bad loser. But it is not the game that matters, it is winning. Winner takes all.'

'How else have your experiences affected you?'

'That is difficult. The major effect is that I have lost trust. In humanity. I trust my friends in one-to-one situations, but in some ways I don't even trust my mother. When you get kicked around, separated, abandoned, deceived, tricked, put in orphanages by people who are close to you, how can you trust more removed people?

'I try to trust my wife, friends, mother, but in reality I check on them. No offence, but if I ask you to write a letter for me, I need to see the letter you wrote. I still need to know and to be in control.

'I have no doubt that living with me is very difficult. My wife Rysia is a very understanding person. I am not only a survivor, I am selfishly ambitious, and family has to fall in place with this.

'Love — I don't know what it means. I've read books about it. I like people, but the real meaning of love I lost somewhere early on, like trust. I never hug anybody, even my child, because unfortunately it goes through my mind "Today you have them, tomorrow you might not". I've lost a lot of members of my family. You feel the whole system has betrayal built into it, and close attachment means later hurt. So I control my emotions. I can trust and be sexual, but I must be in control, so it is a limited commitment. I trusted the partisans, the gang, to the degree that we needed each other for survival. I think my children trust me to the extent I help them to survive. I have always done things with them to help them achieve something. I could not just change nappies or take them for a walk in the park. Both my sons are successful professionals, one a solicitor and the other a chemical engineer.

'My mother — we do not have a good relationship. She delights in pointing out my faults — my marriage break-up, never becoming "somebody", meaning a doctor, like my father. That hurt her a lot, and she has never forgiven me for that. Being one of only one hundred and twelve bridge grand masters in the world could not make up for that. She used to throw my chess sets out the window when I didn't study. I didn't tell her I won the Victorian junior championship that year, in 1953.

'For me, providing security for my children, becoming bridge and chess champion, compensated for what may or may not have been a mistake. I finished up with a clear conscience.

'We had little in common, really. I could never confide in her, during or after the war.' Richard's mood saddened. 'Well, my mother did all she could. She had a hard time . . . I never discussed, asked her what she did for the eighteen months that I was away. We never discussed these things. She never talks about the war at all, she says she can't remember. I never told her about the circumstances when I last saw my father.'

'You both remember things, but you don't talk about them.'

'That's right.'

'Are you bitter that your mother allowed you to go to the orphanage?'

'No, no. She regrets that till today, but she had no control, like my father had no control over the German occupation. But [Richard had tears in his eyes], after what I had gone through, to be put into this dangerous jungle by my own people when it was not necessary — it was just unfair, it did not make sense.'

'What about your father's actions?'

'I feel very bitter about his wrong decisions. A great disappointment that my dad went wrong. Not so much for me, the danger and deprivation I could have been spared; but for him, who paid with his life for those decisions. I can't be angry with a dead man. But he was so intelligent that to misjudge a situation so much showed a shortcoming which was really shameful. He felt that Poland was his country, and he was a Pole so he stayed. He had plenty of time to leave as his brother and two brothers-in-law did, and he could have stayed alive.'

'Do you feel hatred for your parents?'

'No, they could not help what happened. But there is permanent hatred, it was more intense in the earlier years. I was disappointed with myself because I could not catch the man who killed my father. I imagined how I would torture him to death, frying him slowly in oil. I would still have no problem at all killing the German who killed my father. But I might not kill a war criminal, because I wouldn't want to be caught and suffer more because of that criminal.

'Over the years I came to hate those who dealt me a crook hand, a pair of two's while they sat with a pat hand. I hated the Germans, and the more I read, the more I hated all those who cooperated with the killing machine; the people who took us to the Germans for a pair of shoes or a bottle of vodka, the people who slammed the doors in our faces.'

'Richard, can you tell me about your sense of humour?'

'I already made fun of them when I was masquerading as a retarded girl. But I developed my sense of humour shortly after the war. I became cunning and deceitful, such as giving answers before the questions, anticipating with an animal instinct, being one step ahead. My way of speaking is part of my humour. It gives me control of the situation, and of emotion, for instance if I say "Things weren't that bad, sometimes we ate after all".

'With my background, if you don't have a sense of humour, you'd be so morbid and so sad that you'd look like Eli Wiesel permanently, or jump out the window like Primo Levi, or put a plastic bag over your head like Koczinsky, all child survivors. I prefer to crack a joke.

'It might be no joke when I have frequent nightmares about hiding or being chased by Germans. But in the morning I joke with Rysia "I escaped the Germans last night . . . We are safe, the Russians are here." She pays no attention. My commonest joke is when we go to our holiday house, and I say "It's a long way from Warsaw, isn't it?"

'Eating is a problem to me.' [Richard was still carrying extra provisions under his shirt.] 'It is difficult to tell myself not to eat, now that I can eat anything.'

'Have you ever fought or cheated in Australia?'

'Only at the very beginning, when some boys called us Jews. I set my own standard of morality in business. I never cheated at the expense of others. I tried to be fair, but I am a results merchant. So I maximised, legally, shortcomings of the system. Cheating an individual would be demeaning. So would cheating at chess or bridge. If I lost a chess game, or a business venture did not succeed, I would analyse and try to remedy this. If I couldn't I would ruminate and curse for long times. If anyone took advantage of me or tricked me, I would spend a lot of effort to get revenge. I have been victim enough.'

'What is valuable and meaningful to you now?'

'I have reached my goals now. I don't have to strive for necessities and security any more. I am aware of a certain lack of direction. There are things I can do with those around me, but I miss something.

'I don't fully know the meaning of happiness. A piece of bread, winning a medal, buying a house, a marriage which is working, that's happiness. But happiness that comes from inside, without external events and objects, or a basic happy mood, are foreign to me. For me, now there are more good events happening than bad. Over my life-time maybe there were six hundred good happenings and four hundred bad ones.

'My commitments to the Holocaust Centre and the Child Survivor group are worthwhile and I enjoy them, but I miss a goal, like my twenty-year plan to be a grand master. Will I get a medal at the end of twenty years at the Holocaust Centre?

'My friends and I had never talked about our experiences in the Holocaust. I have only started to talk of mine in the Child Survivor group. I am very serious about that group, as I am serious about this interview. This is not for chocolate. This is for the record, for the world to know what happened to us. I was ashamed for forty years. I thought it was shame to be deprived, to be different. People thought I had lice in my hair or that I was a savage, a delinquent, second-rate, when I told them where I had been in the war. Now I am not ashamed. I have not committed a crime, and I am not guilty of anything but having been screwed up and kicked around as part of Mr Hitler's final solution. If my crime is to have survived and to talk about it, I'll live with that crime.

'It is very important to me that my interviews and teaching have some use and historical value. My testimony may only be a grain of sand among many, but my life must make some sense and have meaning. If I can play even a small part in making people see, and remember, the destruction of six million Jews at this point of history, and ask why, I will feel rewarded. I also agreed to this interview in the hope and belief that it can be useful to people in some other ways. I would like to dedicate this interview to the one and a half million children who perished in the Holocaust, and to those who have sur-vived but for various reasons cannot tell their stories.

Comment

Richard's story is a testimony of what a child is capable of doing in order to survive. It is also a document of the cost of such an effort, and the continued struggle to love in spite of the costs.

Unlike some others in this book, Richard could remember the details of his struggles. Even before entry into the cupboard, he had reached the watershed age of six or seven following which children remember events akin to adults. Like adult survivors, they are subsequently haunted by their memories, and the reliving of past traumas in a fully conscious way.

Richard's story demonstrates the degree to which children can adapt to external necessities and parental injunctions. Richard even forgot to see. The most abnormal could become normal. Yet, as long as he felt secure with his parents, not only could Richard maintain an integral sense of his self, but he even developed it. In fact the year in the cupboard was a time of much learning.

It was only when his parents lost their sense of security that Richard's own life entered another dimension, of turmoil. His development then took two concurrent streams.

On the one hand, Richard was still a growing young child. He was enthralled by sight, was fascinated by the buttons on the Nazi's uniform, was extremely curious, and craved for fun and enjoyment even at the worst times. He was excited at the partisan adventures. He tried to emulate the adults around him, and to be like them. Yet the child was socially naive in the normal world even at the age of fifteen.

On the other hand, Richard was propelled into precocious adulthood. He could no longer rely on his parents for protection. He had to rely on himself to survive. He used adult manoeuvres to do so.

Thus he took on the equivalent of an adult's mantle as a member of a forest tribe in a hostile environment. Richard, like the group, concentrated on day-to-day goals of survival involving hunting for food and obtaining shelter from predators and the elements.

The group was also at war and the warriors had to hunt down enemies. If they did not do so, the enemy would hunt them down. This was another law of the jungle — kill or be killed. The enemy had to be killed, without mercy or sympathy, otherwise he would kill Richard and his comrades. In this sense Richard was a good warrior as he did his Feather Boy job conscientiously and with pride.

To survive, Richard, like the other partisans, had to develop great physical skills, and the ability to recognise threats, make quick correct decisions, and be a faithful cog in the machinery of the group. These were the elements of 'doing a good job'. He had to live one day at a time in order not to be overwhelmed by the enormity and cost of the task. Apart from hatred of the Germans, he had to contain his emotions, especially tears and grief which would weaken his resolve. Keeping the mind and the body busy, like in the cupboard, helped to control feelings and thoughts. Lastly, there had to be fervent hope of being able to recover and reconnect with the past. That is why the rupture with Helenka and being sent to the orphanage were such bitter pills, making the whole struggle for survival appear senseless.

It is not only the naked fears of being chased and fighting enemies which have pursued Richard in his later life. He was also subject to compulsions to continue the methods of survival which had served him so well. Thus he has been obliged to keep on meeting survival goals and be busy in both body and mind.

Survival modes have pervaded Richard's life from instinctive levels such as not being able to throw away a crumb of bread to the levels of morality and world views. As well, aspects of survival such as busyness, vigilance, protection, hiding and anticipation came to be incorporated into aspects of himself, such as speech and sense of humour.

One has to admire the creative means Richard used to triumph over past hardships. For instance, Richard overcame hunger not only by having permanent 'food' under his shirt, but by being a confectionery wholesaler. Richard overcame not seeing by 'seeing' through touch and developing a powerful photographic memory. Competition for life was channelled into more benign games. From being powerless, Richard became a champion chess player. Similarly, he overcame being dealt a bad hand by becoming a bridge champion.

But there were costs. His survival modes did not allow for the 'luxuries' of intimacy, trust, love and happiness. A block interposed itself in the wrenched heart of the little boy. Angry questions of his protectors came to the boy's confused mind. 'Why was his father not a better "survival merchant"?' There arose a deeper anger with his father for dying and his mother for not understanding what he had gone through. Yet it was impossible to fight a killed father, and Richard also recognised that his mother had done her best. He felt an intense protectiveness of her grief, shame and pain, in spite of her resentment that he was not more like his father.

But there was good reason for this. Life had taught Richard that he could not model himself on his father, because his father committed the ultimate crime of not surviving. Being a doctor had not saved him. But had he had more money, they might all have been saved. So Richard had to make money, and divert from his father's path. And yet Richard has identified with his father through his devotion to the survival of his children, and of other frail children like his fellow child survivors. He gives himself to the memory of the children who did not survive, and to the live children who may find his story useful. Underneath the tough survivor, Richard's wrenched heart craves and connects, whether to a new family, new country, or other hurt children.

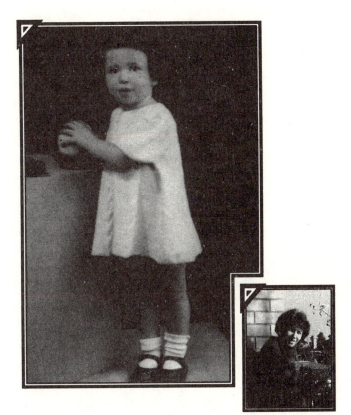

Juliette

—•—

'MY FEELINGS AND

MY SELF BECAME LEVEL'

I ARRIVED AT *Juliette's one-bedroom flat in a respectable, non-Jewish suburb in Melbourne. She was at the time negotiating to buy the flat. There were relatively few artifacts scattered around the living-room. Her violin rested on a chair. Juliette was neatly and demurely dressed, and her bearing was upright. She was appropriately hospitable.*

There was something ephemeral about Juliette, and yet she was also kind and earthy, even naughty at times. She was most alive and endearing when she laughed unexpectedly, whether a chuckle at some irony, or a hearty laugh as she related a perhaps inadvertent non-compliance with an irritating rule.

I AM JULIETTE ZEELANDER, and I was born in October 1938 in Amsterdam. My very first memory, from around the age of two, relates to a scene in Diemen, a suburb of Amsterdam. It is a street scene, looking toward the fence at the end of the street, with paddocks beyond it. The sun was shining, and there was a sense of openness.

'My next memories are set in the headquarters of the Jewish Council in central Amsterdam. The Council was set up to mediate between the Germans and the Jewish community. My father worked for the Council as an electrical mechanic. We moved to the premises in 1941, as my parents thought that they would be more protected living there.

'My own memories are playing with my blue three-wheeler bike and my red scooter in the corridor with offices on either side. I must have been three and a half to four years old then.

'I remember the flat and the kitchen and my mother cutting vegetables at the sink while I sat on a stool. That is my only memory of my mother.' Juliette repeated wistfully, 'That is the only memory of my mother . . . I remember the living-room, which also served as my parents' bedroom, but I remember only a single bed. I remember playing peek-a-boo with my father in that room, with me hiding behind the curtain. He also taught me to whistle. Much effort went into this tuition.' Juliette burst into happy laughter. 'Though I do not see my mother in my memory, I remember that she was not very pleased about this.

'My next memory is going to a kindergarten or school. I must have been four to four and a half. I remember that instead of going up into the building as usual, I went down into a cellar. I knew that school was not to be spoken about. It was somehow illegal, "underground", and I had a sense of hiding while there. I now know that it was probably a clandestine Jewish school. I have no overt memory of ever being told not to speak of certain things, but I have a sense that this was a difficult, fearful, hiding period for us. However, looking back, the tone of my memories is kind of level, not particularly happy, nor sad.

'My final memory of the time with my parents was seeing my father in a kind of sentry box in the foyer where he probably checked visitors. But what shocked me was that he had no teeth. Just before he died, my father verified that he had all his teeth taken out, but he did not think it was at that particular time. But this is how I remember it. And this was my life until the Jewish Council building was raided, and my parents were taken away.

'My only memory of this episode is being in my bedroom, actually a kind of cupboard with glass on one side, and my bed was a cot with sides. It was early one morning and I was sitting up in bed banging my head against the head of the bed as usual prior to my parents paying me attention. An acquaintance came in, but he was out of place in my room early in the morning. He sat me on my chest of drawers and dressed me. I had a sense of "What's happening?" — a very very clear memory. I remember details like his beige suit, though no memory of his face. It was like a film . . .

'My next memory is of a place called "The Jewish Invalid", which I now know was a home for old and disabled Jews. That is where that man took me in March 1942. I remember I still had my three-wheeler and scooter, and I rode them in a foyer. That is my only memory of the place. Again my feeling tone was level, neither happy nor unhappy.

'My next memory is being taken by a large woman I did not know, and me screaming as she was about to take me on a tram. "I am not allowed to go on the tram!" I remember I felt that I was in mortal danger. So it must have been instilled into me that as a Jew I was not allowed to go on trams, and other places.' Juliette laughed. 'It must have been a dreadful episode for this lady. It was certainly a dreadful episode for me. But then I remember sitting on the tram with her.

'My next memory is of being in the living-room of this lady's house. There was a double door going out on to a patio, and I was told to join a group of children playing in the room near the window. I think I remember wearing a bright yellow jumper . . . and a brown skirt, and we played ring-a-ring-a-rosy. I had a very strong feeling that I was being asked to accept, to be accepted, and to stay with the children in this circle. And this feeling is not particularly peaceful. It was a question, more than anything else. That is all I can say. Perhaps the question had to do with "Who is this?" in regard to the large lady. This was symbolised in the question of what I was to call her. I did not call her "Mother". I called her "Mama Mien". Her name was Mina.

'I have a generally good feeling about this woman.' Juliette changed to the present tense. 'She is a large woman, she is a motherly type, and she is warm.' Juliette was quite definite about the latter characteristic. Her speech accelerated. 'And she evoked safety. And I have pleasant memories, actually feelings, of being accepted by the children. I was the seventh and youngest child. The girl next to me was one and a half years older. The oldest were two boys aged thirteen and fourteen. I stayed with this family till after the war. I was . . . I became a member of the family.

'I have a general sense of the children playing with me and scaring me. I remember them locking me up in the coal cellar. I suppose I was a sitting duck for the normal games where children make others scared. I know I was fearful of water, of having my head held under. I was fearful when we were given baths. I don't know whether I was made fearful. I must have been a scared little child, but I do not have actual memories of a scared little child.

'I have very clear memories of the house. It was in what was an outer suburb in 1942. Again it was a dead end street with barbed wire separating us from the market gardens. I have memories of playing hide-and-seek under the table. I remember the youngest boy, three years older than myself, being very musical and singing us all to sleep. Many of us slept in the same bed to keep ourselves warm at that stage. I remember banging my head and singing to the rhythm of his music. This is my first musical memory. It was a happy one.

'I remember that we ate potato peels and a very watery soup, and a kind of bean which we ate every day for months. It was monotonous. I remember being outside in a very snowy winter, perhaps in 1944. We built a snowman facing the gardens, and we had a fun time.

'And yet, even as I was getting accustomed to and accepting my new family, I remember searching for my mother, and expecting to see her in a crowd of people. She had to be alive somewhere, and I believed that she would come back, even after the war. Perhaps this expectation was prolonged by my father coming back, I don't know. But my efforts faded only some years after the war, after I saw the papers relating to her death. Then I realised that she would not come back.

'I had a sense of both separation and being at home. I cannot explain it . . . it was not a total belonging, it was a separation as well. But not an unhappy not belonging. That is all I can say about it. When I think back to my childhood I do not remember it as unhappy. It was turbulent, but not unhappy. And I think it is because that family, the children, really did accept me. And it was novel for me to mix with children my age.

'I had to change my surname to theirs, mine was a Jewish name. I knew I had to hide my identity. It was instilled into me what my new name was. But one day, I must have been about five and a half years old, I went shopping with the lady of the house [Juliette still found it hard to call her even Mama Mien]. I see myself clearly in front of a display cabinet, with a lady in black, me looking up, and the lady asking me in a friendly tone, "Dear, what is your name?" And I said quite cheerfully . . .' Juliette started to laugh. '"My name is Juliette van Tijn, but my real name is Juliette Zeelander."' Juliette laughed now without restraint. 'Neither adult responded, but I realised that I had said something not right.' Juliette said seriously, 'I think as a little child I put this lady's life in danger several times. I mean real danger.'

'To what extent did you know that there was a war going on, with threat to lives?'

'I was not aware of the danger of being denounced as not a child of the family, nor that the children could inadvertently give me away. I was not aware that the children's father had been taken away before I arrived because he was Jewish, and that the children themselves were half Jewish. I was aware that many adults came and went all the time, but I did not understand that the lady of the house did underground work.

'The nearest I experienced of the actual war was in that cold 1944 winter. We children were trying to scavenge fuel, which was illegal. We went to a dyke and collected this sort of coal material. We were moved off this dyke, either with the threat of being shot, or with shots actually being fired. I do not remember the sounds of actual shots. But I sensed that there was real danger of death. That was when real fear was born in me. This was different to the imaginary fears, like going on trams. This was tangible, potentially paralysing fear, a large constricting fear, and it impelled me to run.

'Yet apart from this, there were cues which gave me a sense that there was something dangerous going on. The lady of the house was put in prison at one time, and we were dispersed to different places. I have two memories of this. One was being placed somewhere next door, I think it was only for a short time. I was on my own there and I was unhappy. Then I was parcelled out somewhere to the southern part of the country, with the youngest girl, for some weeks. I rememember her being very homesick. I was not. Homesickness has never been part of my life, even after the war. I have always put it down to being shifted at four and a half. Even before that we shifted to the Jewish Council, so I was used to being shifted. So with this latest shift I was not unhappy, but I knew that there was unhappiness. It was not like an emptiness of feelings, but for me there was just that level tone, not feeling happy or sad . . . Perhaps I could have felt those feelings, but I just did not. If I had to label any feeling, it was being fearful.

'I have just remembered that I was very joyful once. It was when I recovered my lost teddy bear, which I had had as a little child. I don't know how it came to be returned, but when I saw Teddy, I was really, really joyful, like I opened up, something opened. I was told that I said, "Oh, my Teddy from before." So I had somehow distinguished between my current and previous life. I remember being very angry and sad, when the chidren took this toy and played keepings-off with me, with me running and trying to retrieve it. In the process it lost an arm and an eye, and I was very, very upset and sad. Even now I feel the joy and the sadness thinking about this toy. And I kept it till quite recently. He had always been a part of my life, even when stowed away in a cupboard. But it was okay to part from him in the end. Teddy had been my only comfort toy. My bike and scooter were not as important.

'I went to school. I remember my teacher as a nice and good person. I remember her hair in a bun at the back. I played ball games. I was not an antisocial child, the family socialised me.

'I must mention at this stage that soon after I arrived in the family, I developed frequent and severe attacks of asthma. Soon after arrival I also became a very bad eater. I was scolded and left at the table to finish my meals for long times. I was diagnosed as having tonsillitis, and I had an absolutely traumatic operation. I saw the big scissors coming toward me, and the blood gushing out. But it solved the eating problem. I also had boils on my legs — eight of them, I still have scars from them.

'I also started to wet the bed when I was with the family, and I continued to bang my head. I kept rhythm with the boy when we sang together. This motion of my head was necessary for me to relax and sleep.

'The end of the war had not much meaning for me personally, but I remember this incredible sense of elation in the streets when we were liberated. People in uniforms, cars or tanks, I don't remember which, threw out sweets and chocolates. I do not know whether I was happy myself.

'I remember clearly when my father returned in 1945. I was asked to open the door for him. I was introduced, "Juliette, this is your father." I had no feeling of elation or any other feeling, more like "Here is another person." The words that this was my father did not connect. I was told that I was not very kind to him, but I cannot remember. And who knows why, but apparently I gave him a kick.' Juliette chuckled with delight.

'I remember visiting him in his flat. I was fascinated by his billiards table, and he taught me to play billiards. But it was not a joyful experience for me to go there, I did not want to go. Again, it was a level tone experience. I don't remember my father ever being joyful to see me. I don't remember sweet foods from him.

'The father of the house did not return, and there was some violence between the lady of the house and the eldest son . . .' Juliette sighed and was silent for a long time. 'I had happy memories of a normal family life, playing with the children, digging up potatoes. Then my father met up with my step-mother. Like my father, who had finished up in Auschwitz, she had survived concentration camps. I had learnt that my own mother had died in Sobibor concentration camp soon after she arrived there. My mother had worked for my step-mother's father as a book-keeper. My step-mother was fifteen years younger than my father.

'I was introduced to my step-mother. "She will be your new mother." After they married, I left Mrs van Tijn, and came to live with my "new parents", in 1948.

'I don't recall any trauma about the move. I remember the youngest girl being upset at losing her playmate, but I don't remember being upset myself or being sorry to leave. It was another shift for me. And it was not like when my parents were taken away from one moment to the next.'

At this moment, Juliette allowed herself to note, 'Looking back on it, the asthma was a manifestation of that trauma.

'But I liked my step-mother immediately. There was a good, familiar feeling about her. I accepted her easily, and we have always had a good, friendly, and trusting relationship. So the shift was also a good one.'

'Did your step-mother remind you of your mother?'

'She did not remind me of my mother. She was a different person. But I had real difficulty finding a name for her. I could not call her mother, I had already had two. I remember thinking totally clearly "I can't accept three mothers". So I have always called her aunty Margaret. But in the initial years she really was a mother to me. Later she developed into a really good friend.

'I saw little of my father because he worked evening shifts. I was brought up by my mother [!], father being a shadow in the background, just meting out punishment when I was naughty.

'I had a kind of normal childhood then. We lived in a new district and I went to a new school. I was average at academic achievement. I was restless and always in trouble for being too talkative. I made friends, played marbles, skipping and football in the street, and I was quite vocal. Also, I was happy learning music. Both my father and step-mother loved classical music, they always played it on the radio. My step-mother loved to sing melodies from symphonies and concertos, and asked me to guess what she was singing. That is a happy memory.

'I still wet the bed initially. My father stopped it by waking me and taking me to the toilet before he went to sleep. I kicked and screamed, but it stopped the habit. The asthma persisted. The head banging changed to rhythmical movement of the head back and forth on the pillow. Together with singing I have retained it into my adulthood as a means of going to sleep. I use them even now on the rare occasions when I cannot sleep.

'I kept contact with the van Tijn family. I do not remember, but I was told that the youngest girl visited me frequently, and I also visited them. I just accepted that this was how things were now.

'Then my parents decided that they would . . . shift!' Juliette placed an angry contemptuous emphasis on the last word. 'There was political unrest in Europe with the erection of the Berlin wall. My father especially wanted to get out of Europe.

'I was thirteen by the time we set out for Australia. It was hard for me to leave a familiar way of life, school, the kids in the street, my friends, and especially a boy I was attached to and fond of in an innocent boy-girl sort of way. But I also had a sense of adventure. The word Melbourne still retains a feeling of excitement, of something new. I had no feelings about leaving the van Tijns.

'I was seasick on the journey, and was struck by the heat when we docked in Perth. We joined my father, who had preceded us by nine months, in Melbourne. The three of us lived in a rented room with a Russian family. That was a hard time, with my mother cooking on two jets in the hallway, and I hated the smelly outside toilet. I set up a pattern of withholding stools since that time.' Juliette laughed unexpectedly. She recalled, 'Once my mother saw me in agony outside the toilet, but I refused to go in. I was very determined, and the pattern set in. But I also remember vividly the smell of a basket of tropical fruit, and I still enjoy the aroma of pineapples.

'School was strange and I felt lost not speaking the language. But I picked it up quickly, and I was happy learning music . . . and learning about the variety of lollies in the milkbar! I liked learning generally at school. Again I made friends, and had a happy time at school.

'But things changed dramatically in the family. Till now I had known my parents to be old-fashioned, and father autocratic. He was always very clear about what was the right thing to do. Rebellion was never acceptable, and I had not felt rebellious as a child. I tended to go with things.

'But what changed was that from being a background figure, at work when I was at home, my father was now always there. And my dad kept long periods of silence which I did not understand, and with which I could not cope. The silences were very destructive, full of anger and accusations. He blew up the smallest misdemeanours into major ones, and then followed them up with a long silence. Or you would be told only after the silence what it had been about. I always felt that I had done something very wrong, but I did not know what could have warranted a three months' silence. This is when I started to feel rebellious.

'The worst of it was, too, that I just could not ask him any questions, even simple everyday ones. He simply turned the questions back at me, saying, "Don't you know that? Why don't you know that?" It made me feel guilty for not knowing.

'I could not express my frustrations openly, so I only rebelled inside. But you know, at the same time, and quite early on, I was utterly convinced, without any doubt, that things were unhappy because of difficulties my father had had during the war. That was just a strong intuitive feeling, not explained to me by anyone. It made it possible for me to put up with these silences.

'So I was thrown that much closer on my mother. I talked to her about my frustrations. As my father did not talk to her either, we became friends and confidantes.

'So I was a teenager with really major problems at home, and I could not do anything about them. Outside I always had really good, even bosom friends, in whom I could confide. But the war came to overshadow my life.'

Juliette said emphatically, 'I always related the bad relationships at home to the war. Though I hated my father for what he was doing to us, in a very deep sense I did not totally reject him. On a very deep level I was aware that it was not the person who was bad, but the experiences he had which he could not resolve.'

'What gave you the knowledge that he was not like that, but was made like that?'

'I could see that he was not a bad man. I could see that when I first came to know him at the age of nine. I could see that he was bitter about life. Though he never talked about the war, I just knew it was related to it. I don't know how I knew.

'I had a good relationship with my father when he taught me to whistle. I liked him, and I have a very strong feeling that I was close to him, that we were normal father-daughter very early on. So those are good memories. When he was good . . . he was not a demonstrative person . . . but I always felt that I understood him in some way, all the time from the age of nine on. I can't explain it, it is just a normal daughter-father relationship. I understood him, all through the difficult times, I can't tell you why. I understood his teasing sense of humour. I had this firm conviction that had circumstances been different . . . I understood him, but I hated his bitterness and its poison on him and us.

'My step-mother was affected differently by the war. Apart from one sister, she lost her whole family, and this included five brothers and sisters. She did not talk about the war because it gave her nightmares. But she was not bitter. Maybe because she was twenty-five against my father's forty when the war ended. My father also had a surviving sister, and he lost his father, wife and two sisters. Two of my real mother's brothers survived intact with their families.

'In my family Jewishness was a big thing. Definitely, "We are Jewish" but,' Juliette whispered, ' "We cannot say that we are Jewish." This reflected the fact that many Jews were denounced during the war. So my parents, especially my father, stayed terribly suspicious. When we came to Australia, it is as if my father had said, "We are going to a new country, we will establish a new life, and we are not Jewish."

'But how can you be Jewish in the house and not Jewish outside? All three of us felt very Jewish, I don't know why. Why did I feel so Jewish emotionally? It was not religion, we kept nothing. We did not even have anything Jewish in the house. The only connection was a record of religious chants, of which my father was very, very fond. Perhaps we kept our Jewish feeling alive in them. We all loved the chants, they were emotionally rich, and I think they nourished my father.

'I never felt right about denying my Jewishness in our new country. When I was thirteen, I made a very good friend, who was Jewish. We had made close contact, we felt akin. She asked me point blank, "Are you Jewish?" There was no question for me, I had to tell her. For me that decision was a turning point in my life. It opened up something worthwhile in my life, and till today it has enabled me to be straight.

'I have not had contact with the Jewish community. My parents kept away from it. I had to draw the line somewhere. It was at the point that if someone asked me if I was Jewish, I told them. If they did not ask, I did not talk about it.

'So I just stayed at home. On the one hand I felt insecure about the outside world. On the other, I felt protective of my mother, making sure she survived, and had someone to talk to during the silences.

'Then my father's remaining sister visited from England. After confiding in her, she validated my feelings of feeling imprisoned, and she made me see that the situation at home was abnormal, false and untenable. So I left home in my mid-twenties. I had a secure job by then as violinist in the Melbourne Symphony Orchestra.

'My home situation had made it difficult to establish relationships with males. For instance, when I went out with a man I was fond of I had to be home by twelve. And in the end he was refused permission to visit me because of some imaginary badness.

'Even after I left home my relationships with men were difficult. As I see it now, it was because I grew up with this feeling of rejection, which stemmed from my father's rejections of my questions, and his silences. I could not trust my father to be in a stable relationship with me, and my mother had her own difficulties. So each relationship proved to be untrustworthy. I could not trust people enough to become deeply involved with them. I always got involved with a man who proved to be unsuitable, so my mistrust was vindicated. Unfortunately this became a pattern, and even now it is hard for me to break it.

'I always wanted a relationship with a man, and missed not having it. I do have these natural inclinations, but somehow they never came to fruition. But it was only in my late thirties that I realised that if I did not have a relationship I would not be able to have children. But you know, these feelings also became "level", and my personality became "level" too.'

Juliette placed her hand and arm horizontally in front of the upper part of her chest, indicating both the levelness of her feelings (as before), and an invisible plane which separated feelings below from the head above.

Juliette suddenly lost her levelness and became more alive. 'I decided that I did not want this level life any longer. I wanted out of it, and to find out "Why?" And why could I not make the relationships I needed?'

Juliette became diffident, shy. 'The war became a constructive experience now, because through it I started to ask deeper questions. I started searching libraries for books on the larger aspects of life, in psychology, philosophy, spirituality if you like. My world had been so small, angry, frustrated. I felt that there had to be something bigger which subsumed my world, and other people's worlds. I started to read about why people get into ruts and patterns.

'I kept searching for a long time . . . Maybe I can put it this way. I was searching for roots which were not there for me. Though my father rebelled and never went to a synagogue after his *bar mitzvah*, both my parents had gone to Jewish schools and they knew where they came from. I could not communicate with them about my problem. I only had this terribly strong Jewish identification. I wanted to know the whys and wherefores of it.

'Going to synagogue with Jewish friends made no meaningful connection for me. I read a bit about religion, but again it meant nothing. Then one day I was invited to a demonstration of dancing exercises for body coordination. When I saw these exercises, my eyes opened wide . . . so did my mouth. They were done by a group, in uniform. I was utterly fascinated by the coordination, I thought that if you could coordinate like that, to make your head go in one direction, your arms in another direction, your feet in another direction again, be able to hold that, and then put it all back in a totally different kind of whole, that to me was totally fascinating. I knew that if I could do this kind of coordination, I would have something very valuable.

'Playing the violin was also a coordinating exercise, but this was physical coordination with a different fascination. But I had to join a group. The emotional problems at home somehow stopped me being attracted to groups. I was never at home in them, though I did belong to school and orchestra groups.

'But this group was doing something extraordinary, and what is more, my friends were part of it. It turned out to be a Gurdjieff group. Gurdjieff was an Armenian philosopher and a professed master of dancing, who was interested in human self-development. So I became part of this group, I really made a connection and it turned my whole life around.

'It turned out to be a self-help group which worked with psychological ideas to develop one's self. I attended it once a week for some years. It touched on all the questions for which till then I had no answers. My emotional problems from home, my own responses, stopped me making a whole life for myself. My parents and I, and the world never made any sense till then.

'I discovered that there were similar groups around the world, making up a system. Then I learnt that there was a nine months course of deeper exploration in America, living in a community under the guidance of a person who worked with Gurdjieff himself. But the orchestra refused to give me leave, so I had a major dilemma. I had been with the orchestra for fifteen years. I liked music and I knew it was good for me to be part of that group. I was leading an externally good life, secure, with job, house, car, and superannuation. What more did I want?

'But it was always the same. The same music, and the worst of it was, I was always the same. Something had to change. And it was 1978 now, I was thirty-nine, and I had been with the group for two years.

'I had to pursue my questions on a deeper level, and I decided to go. I gave up the security, which was ingrained in me by my parents as the most important thing in life. But I had found something which was more important than my security. I knew at my age, it was now or never.

'I will always be bonded to people who have done a major Gurdjieff course like I did. We did dances, meditation, retreats where one concentrated on one's own reactions, but the major emphasis was always on the group. I no longer attend the group, but I cannot say that I am not part of it. In a larger sense I will always be part of it. It changed my life, it improved it.

'Over the years my quest has been, if you like, a search for God, for that which is bigger than I am. There has to be some sense to this world, even to war. One has to be able to put it into context. Otherwise I would have to say that my father was right. But he was not right, because he could not live with himself nor us.

'Why do we fight each other? Why is there fight inside ourselves? You have to ask, where do the inhumanities in war come from? From humans who, like us, contain the ingredients for war. The war in me — that is the question I have to come to terms with. Killing, greed, hatred, anger, envy, all these elements are within us. That is the only place where the search can be. And that provides not only a greater understanding of why life and why am I here . . . but also of God.

'My family used to say, "God and war makes no sense." But then you realise that that there are so many religions and spiritual groups, all relating to the same spirituality which must include God. There is a central hub, and many spokes to the wheel. The wheel needs spokes and a hub.

'Through the group I have come into much closer contact with people generally. I came to realise that there are people outside myself, and that I am part of the human condition. That has been an incredible realisation for me. It enabled me to put my father in a broader context, as someone who needed help.

'Currently I am studying Chinese medicine. It is an attempt by me to get in touch with people in a larger sense than a secretary, or even a musician. It is good to work in this larger sense, and yet have physical contact as well.

'I have thought about what music has been in my life. Music can give highs occasionally, when you have a wonderful conductor it can raise the roof, and it is a wonderful thing to be part of a team. I love music, but it has always stopped — somewhere. I could not study beyond a certain level. It has been disturbing to me that it could not go deeper. The violin has been an emotional outlet for me to an extent, but it has been a disturbing aspect of my life, because it has been a substitute for the emotional life which I could not lead.

'My parents were very angry at my going to America. They did not trust or understand, nor did they want to understand anything about the group. The nine months in America turned out to be five and a half years, and it made our family relationships very rocky, but our bond was strong enough to withstand it.

'Then my father started to become an invalid. The reconciliation with my father came in the last period of his life, quite recently. He talked to me only a few times, but for the first time, about some of his wartime experiences. Once he told me how his life had been saved by a workmate.

'It was a period when he talked to me in depth for the first time altogether.' Juliette's voice slowed. 'And then he confided in me his eternal regret about how he had neglected to send my mother and me to his sister in England, who had offered to take us. He said, "I have never been able to forgive myself for not sending you." ' Juliette almost whispered, 'And he was almost in tears when he spoke to me. That was the first time in my life that I saw my father emotional. He was very emotional. This was normal, and it had always been there. I realised immediately that this man had been wanting to cry for years. He had tears in his eyes now but he still could not cry. And I had a sudden realisation that this had coloured his whole life. The guilt which he carried for his wife's death, and the regret for mine and his own suffering, which he could have saved had we all fled to the safety of England.

'Suddenly everything totally changed. I saw this man as a very emotional person, one who never really rejected me. And I realised that I as a person had never been rejected. But, it took me a while to realise, I had made it hard for him to live! I was the spitting image of my mother! So I was a constant reminder of his guilt. He asked me, "What do you think of me doing such a thing?" For me all the years of misery and resentment had ended. So I said to him, "Okay, you did the best you could. How could you have predicted the future? Whom do you know who could?"

'He still could not stand physical touch, but I needed it, and he let me kiss him each time I visited. Perhaps it was necessary for him too. He did not change much, he just was not a communicative person. He had a couple of mild strokes, and he shut himself away from the world.

'But the last moment of my father's conscious life was an active, loving, taking leave of me. There was no mistaking the feel of it. I had never seen his face like that, toward anyone. There was a total transformation of his features. He did not have his teeth in, so it made it a bit difficult, but the whole face transformed, and my mother witnessed this too. It was totally obvious to both of us that there was simply all this love pouring out toward me. And he allowed me to touch him, and really touch him. This was a touch where I stayed and stroked his face, in a way that could not have happened at any other time. I talked to him, but he left, he was in some mental stress. It was a very special moment, one of incredible closeness and love. It was definite. It was a leavetaking. He was at peace with me and I was at peace with him. It has remained like that too. And the past is really gone. There is nothing in me which has connection to the bad feelings and frustrations of all those years. It was a very important moment. He died that night.'

Mijntje

—•—

'SHE IS ALWAYS SO LEVEL'

Maartje (Mijntje) van Tijn, Juliette's wartime foster-sister, was five and a half years older than Juliette. I had the opportunity to visit her in the village of Wormer, one and a half hour's drive outside Amsterdam. She lived in a modest Dutch house. She gave me a book she had written, Ik heb niet de Jodenster gedragen *[I did not wear the Jewish star]. The book was dedicated to Jet and Antonio, who had taken her to a Holocaust memorial. After attending it, Mijntje felt that she had to speak out about her wartime experiences, and she wrote the book. It starts thus.*

'What happened in my early childhood years,
That has retained for me the smell of dead wood
Just dragged out by the roots
It has of course a colour,
A depressingly lifeless colour.

'It was summer of 1942. Her father, a Jew, had disappeared into hiding. Mrs Berkemeier, the teacher, drew a dyke and a wavy line indicating water. She explained how the water was making a hole in the dyke, but no one noticed it. The dyke appeared solid and trustworthy, and had withstood all weathers, but one day it collapsed. The day before no one suspected that the dyke would collapse. Bang, splash, gone. A disaster. The waves of water engulfed the whole land, putting all in danger. "And this is called," said the friendly Mrs Berkemeier, "the caving in of the dyke."

'The child now knew what it was called, this painful bruising, nagging pulling at the heart. Within the chest, that is where it was. Always, nagging. The dyke was this heart. It seemed to be strong and solid, but it was undermined by this pain. One day the heart would break with the immense pain. "And this," the little girl told herself, "this is called the caving in of the heart."'

'In the middle of the war I got a little sister four years old, though she corrected my mother proudly and said, "Four and a half." She had a round wondering little face, surprised eyes, and she was breathing hoarsely. She wore a home-knitted yellow jumper and brown skirt. My mother said, "Look, children, this is Julietje, she is coming to live with us for a while." And so it was.

'My mother had hidden Jews, of all ages, and they stayed from hours to weeks, and even years. *Tante* Joke had stayed for years, and she told my mother one day furiously, "They have rounded up my little great-niece! They need not have done that!" The Dutch police missed Julietje in her little cupboard, and the Jewish Council bureaucrats handed her over to the Jewish Invalid building where orphaned children were waiting for deportation and death. My mother could not bear this. She strode out to rescue Julietje.

'We children loved the story. My mother went to the Jewish Invalid. She told us how she walked into the building confidently, giving the German guard a haughty nod. She found Julietje and said to her, "You better come with me." And surprised, but willingly, as a well brought up little girl, she gave my mother her hand, did not cry, and they went. Past the German guard with the same small nod, and to the tram.

'But Julietje said, in a whining voice, "I am not allowed on the tram." This was a definite highlight of the story. We would laugh at the idiotic situation. My mother said, "You are not allowed on a tram with your Mummy, but with me you are allowed." And so they arrived home.

'Julietje tried hard to fit in, to belong. But to my searing shame, which I feel to this very day, we four youngest children kept her out. As the five of us lay in bed together, we said, "Sujetje (that is what we nicknamed her) is gone! Sujetje is gone!" And in word games we would ignore her as if she was not there. We could not be nastier.

'But one day as we ignored her like that, she suddenly had a wheezing attack. She coughed, cried, screeched and yelled. We were shocked. My mother and *tante* Joke ran in. We never played like that again.

'Julietje began to fit in. She played games on her own, like hiding behind curtains and under the table, calling out in a high child's voice, "Don't look behind the curtain; or under the table." My mother looked on disdainfully.

'I will never forget how on her fifth birthday Julietje came downstairs with anticipation. Among other gifts, there was an ugly worn teddy. Sujetje grabbed it joyfully in her arms, and yelled, "Oh, my Tommy, my Tommy from before!" Julietje's parents had carefully packed the teddy in their rucksacks, in preparation for when they might be caught. But as Julietje was not caught with them, they asked people in Westerbork (transit camp) to send the teddy to Julietje, and through untraceable channels it had arrived — her only contact with her past.

'At this moment of joy, I realised how *tante* Joke hated Julietje. Her own two children whom she had carefully put in hiding were denounced and killed. Julietje, for whom no arrangements had been made, was alive.

'Our food was abominable, mixed with bark and clay. Julietje lost a lot of weight, had bronchitis, and she refused to eat. But she was forced to, in spite of crying and nearly vomiting each time.

'We searched for small pieces of coal on a dyke which had been a shunting yard. We five youngest children went as usual one day. Everyone had left already. As we started our search, a German soldier in uniform shooed us away with his gun. We started to run back in panic. We heard shots, and as we looked back, we saw that the German was motioning us to descend on the wrong side of the dyke, into a stream. We clambered out wet and muddy, and I lost a shoe.

'My mother did not want to keep Sujetje after the war. She was going to go to her aunt in England if her parents did not return. But one day when I came back from school there sat Julietje's father at the head of the table. He was a thin, small, nervous man with a grating laugh. Before that I had not believed in the existence of Julietje's father.

'My mother asked him about his experiences in concentration camps, but he did not want to talk about them. My mother expressed regret at his wife's death. But *ome* Jules (as we came to call him) waved his hand in a tired gesture. "So many died, so few returned," he said.

'Then Sujetje came home and stared at her father. He rose from his chair and looked nervously at his daughter. She had been with us for years, and had grown. She was stunned and stood without a word. And suddenly she kicked him. No one expected this from our shy Sujetje. Then she turned and ran upstairs, and we could hear her agonised sobbing. My mother said, "Leave her, she is a bit confused." And *ome* Jules repeated, "Yes, leave her. She will get used to me."

'I visited them often in their home. *Ome* Jules was very skilful with his hands. *Tante* Deetje made a wonderful home. She adored classical music, and she regulated her life according to music on radio. When she listened to music, she was in a different world, a world free of concentration camps. When my mother visited, Julietje still called my mother "Mama", and *tante* Deetje "*tante* Deetje".

'At the outbreak of the Cold War, the three of them emigrated to Australia. *Ome* Jules said, "It will never happen to me again; that I safeguard my furniture (he got all his furniture back in immaculate order), but not my family." They did not tell the immigration officials that they were Jews. *Ome* Jules said, "We've been on Jewish lists before, we don't need that any more." People always prepare themselves for the last war.'

Mijntje was quite emotional talking about Juliette. She pointed to all the books she had written, and said, 'As soon as I finish a book, I forget it. But I remember every word of my book about Juliette.'

She recalled Juliette with affection, and shame. 'I still cannot forgive myself for the way we treated her initially.'

Mijntje (and the younger sister) and Juliette have kept up a correspondence. 'But we never discuss the war. I am waiting for Juliette to bring it up. I hope she will.' And regretfully, Mijntje added, 'It has always been difficult to get really close to Julietje. There is always some . . . barrier. She is always so level.'

Juliette concurred with the accuracy of Mijntje's book. As to her own importance in it: 'I never considered that I meant so much to her. I was a little girl between four and a half and nine, a part of the memories she had to write about from within her own life.'

The barrier, the levelness was still there.

Comment

There is obviously more to Julietje and the later Juliette than the emotionally level person. However, it may be that at the age of four, when the strange man came to dress her after her parents were captured, Juliette had finally learned to suppress her emotions. Her parents would already have given Juliette the example of hiding feelings of loss, fear and insecurity as part of the way to survive. But now she distanced herself from the threats to herself and saw them as if they were a film. Such responses are common in traumatic situations. But for Juliette it meant that she became 'level', distant from dangers, from separation, and distant from herself. Juliette continued to suppress her feelings when she was taken to the Jewish Invalid, was picked up by her rescuer, and became an orphan in a strange family.

What is it to become level? It means that feelings are flattened and suppressed, and so are acknowledgements of situations which may evoke them. So Juliette lived in an unnatural calmness in which she repressed the meanings of situations, and thus she was neither devastated nor euphoric. She was not terrified by her loneliness, but she was also disconnected from enjoyment of life, and from herself.

However, that Juliette had a subterranean world of suppressed feelings became plain in the occasional eruption of those feelings, such as when she felt fearful beside the tram and on the dyke, and joyful at her teddy's return. Some of Juliette's behaviour also betrayed latent feelings, such as her head banging, bedwetting and kicking her father. Her chuckles at having been 'naughty' perhaps reflect some hidden rebellion relating to those times. Then again, it appears that Juliette channelled some of her feelings into physical symptoms, such as asthma (its precursor may already have been present in the 'hoarse breathing' when Juliette arrived at the van Tijns), not eating and constipation. It is interesting that the explosion of asthma in the setting of rejection helped to reverse the rejection.

The suppression of feeling had a pervasive effect on Juliette throughout her life. For instance, Juliette could never hate openly, nor grieve for her mother. She could not fall in love for long. There was certainly always a sense of a genuine, nice, deep person in Juliette, but this person could be hard to reach. In this way she resembled her father.

Yet Juliette always maintained a sense of continuity with the good 'time before'. She reconnected with her teddy. Juliette's immature individual games behind the curtains and under the table seemed to be reenactments of earlier games with her father. She always retained the memory of her father teaching her whistling. Perhaps that musical activity connected with the van Tijn boy's singing which, together with the rhythmic movement of her head (also from before), combined to soothe her at nights. Perhaps music became a thread representing good times. This was enhanced by Juliette's step-mother's love for music. Juliette's conviction and faith that her current father hid 'a father from before' were steeped in a yearned-for memory. Juliette and her father were in fact able to reconnect with each other and with that memory as father was dying.

Juliette demonstrates how a child's feelings can become subject not only to tangible external situations, but also to the unfathomable secrets in others. The little girl could not know why her parents had disappeared, why she had to conceal her identity, what being Jewish meant. She could not know that her second cousin was envious of her existence, that Mama Mien never planned to keep her, that she looked like and reminded father of her mother, or that she evoked a deep secret guilt in him. She could not easily gauge that the music which symbolised early love and fun was also a distraction from the evils of concentration camps. Thus Juliette did not have the knowledge with which to extract meaning for some deep influences on her life. From this perspective she was like a second generation child, dominated by the shadow of the Holocaust, without ever understanding the original contexts.

Juliette illustrates how post-war fallout can be as important for a child as the direct turmoil of war. Thus Juliette's resilience was severely tested with another uprooting to Australia, and her father's moodiness which became obvious there. Juliette became captive to the family dynamics, which were themselves captive to the Holocaust.

Juliette made a break with the mould provided her by her parents and tried to find her own life. It is a testimony to Juliette's spirit that she undertook the long journey to find her roots and the meaning of her life. She found a philosophy which to a large degree explained and rectified her sense of disjointedness and aloneness in the world.

Mijntje reminds us that there were non-Jewish child survivors of the Second World War. Though half Jewish, she lived the life of many ordinary Dutch children with an absent father. Non-Jewish children also had it tough during the Nazi occupation. It is possible that the van Tijn children treated Juliette cruelly because children make scapegoats of others to hide their own fears. Mijntje also demonstrates that hiding a Jewish child can have long-term effects on the rescuers and their families.

Mijntje also lost a parent and had difficulties with the remaining one. But she grew up to be a very emotional person. Perhaps the difference is that, for Mijntje, the expression of emotions was not life threatening, and that she was never wrenched away into strange families. The two foster-sisters still correspond. Only now have they started to communicate about the Holocaust, and a barrier is thawing between them. Mijntje has been able to confirm Juliette's memories and give them more sense. Perhaps both are secure enough now to acknowledge the pain of absent parents 'from before' which they unwittingly shared in their individual ways.

Juliette is opening herself more. She now carries a live connection with her father 'from before' and has a valuable tangible link with her step-mother. She also has a 'family' in her group. Juliette is thawing, but some levelness persists.

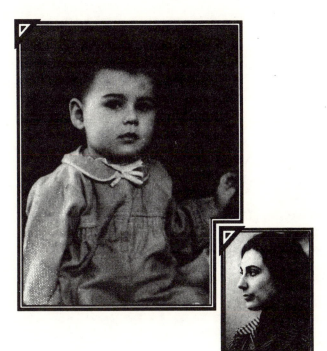

Eva G.

'SEPARATION, SEPARATION,

IS THE TRAUMA

OF MY LIFE'

$\mathcal{E}$VA CAME FROM *Sydney for a* child survivor conference in Melbourne. In a workshop she expressed passionately her opinion that children should be both heard and told the truth in their families. Eva told me that she had been a young child in Teresienstadt. She readily agreed to be interviewed.

Eva was tall, dark, and strikingly attractive. She had that deep sad beauty which comes of having surmounted much suffering.

I AM EVA GRANT, my maiden name is Steiner and my Hebrew name is Rachel. I was born in December 1940 in Turčiansky Svätý Martin, which is a village in Czechoslovakia.

'It is hard to know where to start. Maybe I should start with my parents. My mother was born in Stará Ďala near the Hungarian border and she spoke Hungarian. She came from a well-to-do family of five children, of whom three survived. My father was born in Bolešov, a small central Slovak village, and Slovak and German were his main languages. He graduated in Prague as a dentist. Later he specialised as a dental surgeon. His reputation was so high and he was generally so well-liked that he was even exempt from having to wear the yellow star. He came from a family of eight children of whom only two survived. The others were wiped out with their spouses and children. They were a beautiful family.

'The following is what I have been told. Because I was so young, dates and geography do not mean much to me. So perhaps it was in 1943 that my parents were forced to leave their homes and they went to live in my father's father's house in Bolešov. But then that house was attacked by hoodlums who threw stones in preparation to forcing entry into the house. My grandfather and two of his sons went out and were attacked. It is amazing, but my mother went out and threw sand in the hoodlums' eyes and they left. One point of this story is that we could not call anyone to protect the family. Neither the law nor the police protected Jews. The second point is that my family knew that they had to leave town.

'That night they pushed wardrobes against the windows. The next morning we all left for a place called Bánovce, where we shared a house with another Jewish family. It was more crowded, my parents and I lived in one room. My father was employed by another dentist. When that man retired he let my father take over the practice.

'People were always disappearing and you never knew who would disappear next. News kept filtering through to us that some member of the family had disappeared. It was too frequent. One day the Germans sought out my father. When they found him, they said, "Everyone we asked about you had only good things to say. It seems that your only fault is that you are Jewish." They let him be for the time being.

'Then one day my father's younger sister who had been staying with us was taken away. My grandfather just could not bear his children being taken away any more and he actually died of grief. My mother always broke down in pain when she reminisced about this.'

Eva struggled to search her memories and to make sense of this time of turmoil.

'I remember a playground next to our house on the corner of the street. I remember crouching at the fence looking in as I was not allowed to play inside the ground. Five years ago I made a sketch of this scene. I looked at my sketch for a long time in order to get it out of my head. The sketch was very tiny, perhaps indicating that I was still scared to express myself.' Eva showed me a small picture in which I could just discern a little figure looking through a fence.

'My only memory of my father from Bánovce is of him taking me for a walk. We were near a river when we were caught in a terrible downpour of rain. He picked me up. I can feel the large size of this tall, strong, nice-looking man and I remember feeling so small . . . my small size again. Unfortunately I do not remember my father's eyes or face. But I do remember the feeling of protection. Yes, of protection. And then it was not there any more. I felt the loss of this feeling many times, such as on the cattle trains. It felt devastating . . . Yes, it is the first time I have zeroed in on this feeling and given it words. I have felt this loss of protection throughout my life, right up to the present. I now think that I was attracted to my second husband because he had similar physical features to my father. He reawakened the psychological impact stemming from my father's nice high eyebrow and forehead.

'My mother had always been highly over protective. For instance she was crazy on making fruit and vegetable juices. And even in Bánovce, under these very difficult conditions, she walked to the country to get a few baby carrots which she would grate and squeeze for juice for me. She was an extremely devoted mother. Later, in Israel, she paid me to drink lemon juice.

'While my mother was devoted to her housekeeping, my mother's father looked after me. That was good. I was told by my mother that I used to sit on his lap. One day I chewed a box with staples in it. That caused a lot of drama, but Grandfather was a solid protector through this too.

'In Bánovce there was another Jewish family with a little boy called Peter. I used to play with him. I do not remember any toys from this period. Though I had dolls after the war, I still have a wish to have a doll now, which perhaps comes from an unfulfilled need from these earlier times. Anyhow, one day Peter and I went shopping for grapes. I must have been three and a half by then. We sat down and just ate the bag of grapes. My mother panicked as we were late and I remember being in trouble.

'The predominant feeling from Bánovce was hardship. There was sadness and a strong feeling of being shut out, not being allowed in, clearly felt with regard to the playground. I would not be surprised if this left a strong mark because later on in school I had trouble mixing with others.

'There was a family very close to ours who were caught in the forest and they were burnt alive. I do not remember knowing about it then, but I associate Bánovce with this kind of knowledge.

'One night we put on as many clothes as possible, made up some bundles and walked to a farmer's house. We were to hide in his attic. My father had given our linen and other possessions to a banker friend of his. After the war his family returned some of these things to us, but not all. Still, it means a lot to me now to have my father's silver cigarette case and a few other lovely little things from before the war.

'In any case, our family went to this attic. There were my grandmother and my parents and me, and a single man who had been a colleague of my father's. I remember that he was a tall man with red hair. My grandfather had died by then, and all other family members had been taken away.

'But we could only spend one night in this attic because my grand-mother could not stop herself from pacing up and down on the floorboards. So in the middle of the second night, and I do remember this, the farmer took us to the forest in his horse and carriage. I remember the clip clop of the hooves in the dark. We had to be extremely quiet. I remember very vividly a typical blue farmer's pot with a flower painted on it. It was very important, probably because it contained food. I am very visually oriented. Maybe I should paint it to get rid of it from my head. I love painting. Even now I especially love to paint houses from different countries. I have a feel for where they belong.

'At first we joined other families who had dug deep long tunnels in the ground. But after two or three nights my mother's fear in the tunnels became too much for her so we went to a different part of the forest, dug a bunker which we covered with branches, and hid there. I remember my parents had to crawl into the bunker. We were there eight months. Here is the little figure with the big fir trees.' Eva showed another drawing.

'At about this time, unbeknown to us, Peter's mother had heard of a little girl found alone with a board hanging around her neck. There were many Jewish families hiding in the forest near Bánovce. Parents would hang little boards or tablets from their children's necks so that they could be identified in case the parents were caught. The mother said to her husband "That lost child must be Eva. We are going to adopt her." But it was not me.

'I had a little light-blue winter coat. One day I must have stood too close to the fire which was lit in the bunker and my coat caught fire. So to the end of the war I had this missing tail in my coat.

'My father's colleague developed frostbite. They cut off his legs and he died. I personally must have been shielded from the cold, as well as hunger, because I do not remember them. What I do remember from this time is the forest stillness, little hills and fir trees. I still love forests. I could stay away from people for six months. Once I was confronted by a wild boar. He looked like a frozen pig. We just looked at each other. I must have been separated from my parents at that moment.

'My father paid a man a lot of money to bring us food weekly. My mother begged him to take her to his home so that she could have a bath after months of not having had one. He took the two of us to town and we had this bath. I do not remember it.' Eva gave an ironic laugh. 'What I do remember is that on the way back we were caught in crossfire between partisans and probably White Russians. Bullets flew all around us, one whizzed right past my mother's ear. She picked me up and we fell into a ditch. Poor Mummy, it was terrible. We were very lucky to stay alive.

'I felt protected in the bunker. However, one afternoon as I was having my nap, a troop of about seventy White Russians marched by. After they passed my father climbed out to see who they were. Unfortunately two stragglers saw him and they called back the whole troop.

'The commander ordered everyone they discovered to be tied to the trees and be shot. I was still inside the bunker, but the noise woke me and I came crying to the entrance of the bunker. That must have been a sight! The commander asked my mother, "How old is she?" She answered "Three and a half" though I must have been almost four. He ordered my mother to be untied. He told her that he also had a dark little girl just like me, and he did not know where she was. Then he ordered everyone to be untied.

'I remember this episode. I cried as soon as I woke. At any other time I would not have cried with my parents not there but this time I think I sensed the danger in the air. I realised that things were drastically different when they did not answer my cry. It was distressing. I had a sense of trouble, fear, panic, it was like a climax, instinctively I knew that what I was told to be quiet about had suddenly materialised. It happened! Like you wait for a wedding and suddenly it happens! It was trauma! Tragedy! And then I saw this scene! Each of them against a tree. I knew those trees. And there were all these baddies! I think I stopped crying then, I was stunned. I knew life was at stake. I knew what shooting meant. I was frightened, I knew my parents would be shot by those soldiers in uniform.

'It was pointed out to me at the conference, "Do you realise that you saved your family's lives?" It had never occurred to me before. I have no illusions about my power to save people, but I developed a sense of being able to carry things through against great odds. For instance, my husband and I managed to have our profoundly deaf son graduate university. We were just determined to achieve the unachievable. I do not know if it relates, but the little girl then also did the impossible.

'They marched us to Sered, to a school used by the Germans as a hospital. We were taken to a large room full of soldiers with bandaged heads. To my child's mind they looked like corpses with no heads! But some were smoking! We were in this room for three days totally without food. We just sat in a corner, despondent, trying not to be noticed. It was quiet, only this puffing smoke . . . But my mother went hysterical at one stage and banged on the door, asking for food for me. As a result they brought half a cup of black coffee without milk or sugar, just for me.

'They walked us to the railway station. I identify with the photos in Holocaust books where Jewish families carry their meagre baggage being taken to their fates. We were going to the unknown and we were not going back. In any case, back was bad. I had a sense of having no home, no base.

'So we were at the railway station and they were separating the crowds. I remember the feel of the crowds and the darkness over me from bodies pushed together. Hollywood could not reproduce the atmosphere of desperation. The most desperate moment for me was the separation from my father. My memory for that event is border-line. My mother might have mentioned this scene briefly only two or three times in my life. But I think I remember it because I feel it so deeply.

'The feeling is that he moved, actually left. I wanted him there for protection and he had to leave. He had to. I feel the sensation that he was ordered to. I feel that he wanted to be with us but he could not. Because he was clinging to us. We were all clinging, but it was not possible. And that is the sensation which I relive whenever I go through the traumas of my life. Repeatedly. I am really very aware of it. I have had great problems with separations from my mother and others throughout my life. The doctor said that I had a symbiotic relationship with my son. I think I remember the danger of him going. My mother was desperately upset. Of course! And I remember being with my mother and grandmother. I remember being there.

'He was separated into a group of men. He broke away from them and came to my mother . . . I can't . . .

'This is when he came over to her to kiss her goodbye. He did that. And do you know what happened? They beat him up for it . . . He got beaten. That was the last time we saw him. I personally do not remember him being beaten up. Mummy said that.'

'Do you remember him kissing goodbye?'

'I think I am aware of him coming back because he must have kissed me. Now that you said it, there is no question about it.' Eva became more certain. Her mood brightened and she laughed. 'Thank you. I never thought about this episode in relation to me. There is no question about it. He must have kissed his mother and me too. Then I felt sadness, a deep sadness, being left by my father.

'Recently I discovered a note which my father managed to write at the railway station after the separation. He smuggled the note out through his uncle's acquaintance who worked at the station. It was addressed to the uncle's son, and that cousin in Bratislava let me have a copy of the note! My father promised his cousin that he would look after his father as much as he could. On the other hand, my father asked his cousin to look after his mother, wife and child. It was written in German so he mentions me as *'mein Kind'*. And he requested that a headstone be erected for his father. Imagine! He did not forget that the headstone had still not been erected. They did not have the opportunity to erect it.' Eva cried in pain.

'My father was taken to work in the mines, but at the time nobody knew where anyone was being taken. My mother, grandmother and I were put on a cattle train bound for Teresienstadt.

'The wagon was overcrowded with only room to stand. There was just this sense of overcloseness, lack of air, hunger and tiredness. Out of cruelty they shunted the train back and forth, let it stand on side rails, so that it took fourteen days to reach Teresienstadt. A kibbutz museum has the files of everyone who was transported on these trains to Teresienstadt. Our three cards were there too and here is my copy.' Eva showed me the copy of her card. 'Here is my name, birthdate, transport number 466, destination Teresin and date of departure, first of December 1944. These are German records, for those who say it never happened. My mother remembered that we arrived in Teresienstadt on Christmas Day, so actually the journey took us twenty-four days.

'I see very clearly in my memory mothers feeding their babies water from the bucket which they warmed on spoons with candles. There was a clean bucket of water, and a bucket for dirty things in the wagon. My mother confirmed this memory later. I did not soil or wet myself on the train because I would have remembered that. I spent my fourth birthday on the cattle train.

'Later on I saw the arrival of trains like ours. People unloaded the dead bodies, others were carried on stretchers. I do not remember getting off the train when we arrived, but I identify with the people I saw alight subsequently and I still identify with them. I cannot remember any people dying in our wagon but my mother probably protected me from knowing.

'The people who walked off the trains were very tired and desperate. They tried to stick together, and worried about the near and dear who were missing. You were together with a crowd of strangers like in a showground but you wanted to be close only to those whom you knew.

'When we arrived in Teresin, I was taken to a kind of child-minding room full of cots with children in it. I remember tall windows with bars inside them. The children clambered over each other when the trains pulled in. That is how I remember it. It is a strong memory, though no one has ever confirmed it.

'I remember the musty, muggy atmosphere in the room. I had to stay there during the days while my mother worked, though at nights I slept with her. I do not remember the actual process of being separated from her, but I know I was separated from her there. I see myself standing in one of those baby cots in the room, being alone, yelling, crying, desperately calling for my mother. I was interminably waiting for her to come. I kept looking toward the doors waiting for her to appear.

'I remember that terrible feeling extremely clearly because it has never stopped. It was with me throughout my childhood and I have relived it daily for years in various ways.

'It is a feeling of pathetically desperate longing. It is a crying which becomes an actual chest pain. It is an oppression, like a rock physically crushing my chest. I have it with separations and when my husband died. When I had it in Teresienstadt I cried "Mummy, Mummy." And when I was giving birth I screamed "Mummy, Mummy" too.

'I have to verbalise this somehow. I did not associate separation from my mother with the dead bodies which I saw being unloaded, nor with my father of whose long absence I must have been aware on some level. But I was aware that she was the most important thing in my life, that there was nobody and nothing else, and without her I would have nothing.

'They used to take us for walks, with no underpants and no shoes, and my half burnt coat. Of course I suffered from malnutrition. I got pneumonia and impetigo. Fleas got into the pustules and my whole body itched and was full of wounds. For years I constantly begged my mother to scratch my back at nights. For years there remained marks on my arms.

'I was put into a room which they called hospital. My mother took me there, I still remember the sound of walking on the wooden floors and walking past a pot-bellied stove. I have very clear memories of the hospital room, probably because I was so desperate there. I would stand by these memories no matter what.

'There were cots alongside the walls again. I was standing screaming at the top of my voice as loud as I could, crying for my mother. Then this woman took me to give me a permanganate bath. But before she undressed me she literally threw me at the wall. I still know the sound of bones ringing in my head. I was aware I was crying very loud, being separated from my mother.'

'Which hurt more, the pain in the head, or your mother not being there?'

'My mother not returning. I was desperate to have her back. Without her it was hopeless, I was helpless. But the pain in my head upset me very much too. The woman then put me in this pink steaming water in a tub in the middle of the room, with women around it. I remember sitting in it. Then they put me back in the cot where I continued screaming.

'Again I stood crying in the cot for hours, looking this time at the windows above my head because I knew my mother was out there somewhere. Nothing else interested me. From time to time my mother did come to see me. She told me later that she managed to bring me cubes of sugar which were served with the black coffee in the coffee shop in Teresienstadt.

'My mother had several jobs in Teresienstadt. Once she worked in the kitchen and she would smuggle out a potato. Another time she worked in a perspex factory for German aeroplanes. Once I went with her to the old people's home where she had to wash the steps. Another time she washed the old people and when they died she had to drag them out. Later she became obsessively clean, forever washing. I only understood the connection a few years ago. For a person born into an over protective family it was very hard for her.

'While I missed my mother terribly, I was less aware of my grand-mother's absence. She stayed with the older people, separated from us. I vaguely knew that she was there and I sort of missed her. We probably saw her sometimes.

'At this stage I did not sleep with my mother at nights, but I rejoined her in the barracks later. She worked night duty and she was terrified of the pitch dark. Her fear as she left must have trans-mitted itself to me. I was very aware of her leaving me and I was very fearful.

'I remember the wooden staircase, the wooden double bunks, and other mothers and children there. There was a peaceful atmosphere in the dormitories. I remember being with the other children and I think we must have played.

'About eight years ago I shared these memories with my mother as I realised that I needed her to substantiate them. She had taken it for granted that I could not remember so she was surprised how well I remembered even details. She even became excited herself at being able to share her memories with someone.'

Surprisingly, Eva now jumped forty-one years, without interruption to her speech, or the intensity of her subject matter.

'I had a very great need to meet other children from the dormitories and the other rooms where I had been. I had never met another child like myself. I needed to share and compare feelings and memories with other children. That is why I had an urge to go to the very first Holocaust meeting in Sydney in 1985.

'Yet it was so hard for me to go to this meeting. I could not even tell my husband about it, though I had shared everything with him till then and he would have understood. I entered the building and saw the names of the camps around the wall. I squirmed and tried to walk close to the wall. I did not know the people because I did not mix much in the Jewish community. So in a way I was a stranger. But,' Eva whispered with conviction, 'I wanted to be there.

'And when they announced that there would be a session on children, I was overwhelmed, I could not believe it. I was going to hear every word. No one had ever, never, never ever, spoken about the children. Never! Adults would ask where each other had been during the war, but they never asked the children.' Eva was quite vehement on this point. It was as if forty-one years later her day had come.

'And it was wonderful. Every child survivor needs to hear Sarah Moskovitz the way she spoke as if specially to me, that first time, with such warmth and kindness, like a mother. It was as if she was saying, "Yes, it did happen to you." Till then I had carried my world on my own, but now someone else knew about it. She validated my experience, she made it real. My husband and mother came the next day, that was fine.

'Near the end of the conference I finally took my courage in my hands and I asked Sarah whether she knew anyone else who had been in Teresienstadt. She said she would try to find someone for me. After two weeks Litzi rang up. We were both excited, we had found each other. We talked so much. We authenticated our memories. On a certain level I was desperate to know that my memories were correct. It was not just the externals such as the pot-bellied stove which my mother could not confirm. We needed to share and compare our feelings too, and yes, we had the same feelings. That was very good to know. We shared our world, just the two of us. No one else could share it who had not been there . . .' Eva seemed to be relieved, now having somehow conveyed her whole experience of that time. She seemed free to return to her chronological story.

'Well, when the Russians liberated us, they had chocolates and apples. I remember crying when encouraged to take them because I did not know what these strange things were. I cannot remember joy at liberation, but I felt relief. Just before my mother died two years ago she talked for the first time about how she felt at liberation. She said that there had been so many false hopes about liberation previously, that when it actually happened at first she could not believe it, then when it was really true she broke down and cried hysterically with relief. This must have transmitted itself to me.

'I felt happy and at peace on the train. This was not a cattle train, but a passenger train and it was taking my grandmother, mother and me back home. I had mumps on this journey.

'I remember that on the way home my mother was pathologically concerned about the cleanliness of her collapsible aluminium cup. She would not drink from anything else. For years she carried it around with her in her handbag, using it for drinking or to rinse her mouth.

'We went back to Stará Ďala, my mother's parents' place. It was desolate, empty. My mother took me to my grandfather's timber yard and sat me down on our bundle while she went to look around. She was full of anticipation but no one had returned. Soldiers had occupied and ruined what had been our sumptuous family home. We moved into one of the uncles' homes. Eventually people trickled back. I remember meeting them in the street. They would talk about who had come back and who had not. They mostly came back alone. No one came back from the uncle's family whose home we moved into temporarily, not one of his three beautiful daughters.

'My mother then took me to Trenčín to our own family home. There was no one anywhere.' Eva's voice quivered. 'The disappointment was terrible. I remember the loneliness of it. We just walked alone in the street. My mother must have felt so alone. She was twenty-nine.' Eva let out a full lung of air.

'We went back to Stará Ďala. We got ID papers and relief organisations gave me clothes which I liked. Then my mother's other brother came back. His wife died in Belsen, but his daughter survived in Budapest. I remember the day when my uncle brought my three year old cousin Anna from Budapest. My God, this was the first family. This is where dolls made their appearance, and we fought, and she scratched me. This was my first childhood fight. We have been together and played ever since. She lives in Sydney, my darling cousin.

'My mother kept searching for my father. But more than anything I remember her endless waiting for him. Her anticipation never stopped, I grew up with it. She eternally hoped for his return and that is why she did not remarry. What fuelled her hopes were reports of him having been seen after the war. But he still had not returned by the time we left for Israel in May 1949. In 1955 she heard of a man who returned to Czechoslovakia from Siberia and who reported that he had seen my father there. It was feasible because people had been just picked off the streets and deported to Siberia. As a dentist perhaps they needed him. In any case, the whole thing flared up again and my mother never settled down after that. She started searching again, in vain.

'It was one of those marriages. My mother loved him very much. We dealt with it by just hoping.' Eva wiped her tear-stained face. 'I always hoped and missed him. I just had hope that he was alive, like the man who was released from Siberia in 1964 and was reunited with his family in Sydney.

'Both my mother's surviving brothers remarried and established new families.

'But I had bad problems adjusting. Not so much in the home but I was petrified of going to school. School for me was the school in Sered, or the so-called schools in Teresienstadt. I simply did not want to go. I did not want to separate from my mother. Again I screamed.

'But on top of that there were anti-Semitic children at school. These local peasant children linked their hands across the road wanting to block me from going to their school. They sang songs about dirty Jews. I was the only Jewish child at school and I came home crying. My mother became desperate and she consulted the headmaster. I remember walking behind them. On his advice she hit my bottom with a stick, locked me up in a room with a potty, and she and everyone else left the house.

'Eventually I went to school but I did not learn well. Besides, I was constantly sick with colds, sore throats and bronchitis so I had legitimate reasons to stay at home. I did develop two friendships, with the stationmaster's and the butcher's daughters, and I did participate in dancing.

'My mother moved to Bratislava for a few years in order to train to be a cosmetician. During this time my cousin and I were left in the country in the care of a peasant servant. My cousin and I shared only recently our experiences of this woman giving each of us "sex education" by getting us to touch her private parts.

'Eventually I joined my mother in Bratislava and went to school there. Again the children were so anti-Semitic that my mother became aware of this and she transferred me to a convent school. But in whichever school I found myself, and I went to sixteen different schools, I felt different, the odd one out.

'And so in 1949 we went to Jerusalem and we lived there for seven years. I sat at the back of the class, still feeling different. Other children had two parents at home. I stayed with my aunty most of the week while my mother worked hard as a cosmetician. She was paid little and she lived in a single room with no bathroom, kitchen or amenities except for one burner. I only lived with her on Shabbat [Saturdays]. I sat at the window of her place looking down at the children playing. But I never played or talked to them.

'I can articulate it now, that it was sad, a tragedy that my mother had nothing to spare to mother me. She never gave me a birthday party. My mother was in her own trauma, she was trying to survive. So I could not overcome my isolation.

'My mother came daily to have lunch with us at my aunty's place. Each time she left I accompanied her for as long as I could. We parted in front of a particular shop which had a ledge from which I could follow her till she became very small, almost a point. I literally stood on the tip of my toes, absolutely every day.

'It was all right, safe, even good and warm at my aunty's place. And with my two cousins beside me there, I had no problems playing with other children. But I did not have my home.

'Being Jewish was okay in Israel, I even went to a religious school and I am grateful for knowing the Jewish Bible, I like it. In that sense I felt at home in Israel and I was definitely not the odd one out because I was a Jew. In Czechoslovakia my uncle had taught us religious songs but we had to sing them secretly. In Israel we could sing them out loud.' Eva's voice expanded with pride. 'But my being the odd one out overshadowed, overpowered my sense of belonging in the country.

'At school I always wanted to have one friend. It was a struggle, but I did always have someone. They never came to my home though, and there was always the disappointment of losing them whenever I changed classes.

'I never wanted to join youth groups and my mother certainly did not want me to join the army. I had a slight heart murmur without any disability, but my mother obtained a doctor's certificate stating that I had a heart problem. I did not even attend physical training at school. In the end, the reason my mother reluctantly accepted coming to Australia was to make sure that I would not join the army.

'My uncle had by now become my father image. But he developed diabetes and poor circulation, and life was just too tough for him in Israel. He wanted to go to Australia and as he felt responsible for his widowed sister and child he brought us with him.

'We came to Australia in 1956 and the isolation continued. Neither my mother nor my uncle found work in Melbourne so we moved to Sydney. That meant another uprooting, another change of schools.

'In Sydney we lived in a suburb with no Jewish population in a house on which we borrowed heavily. None of us spoke English properly and my younger cousin was deaf. We felt isolated in our struggles. Whom could we call to participate with us? We had no community network. Then six months after we arrived in the country, my uncle died of a heart attack. We were in a mess.

'My aunty and mother had to work shift work in factories. This was very hard for them. To supplement their income they took in boarders — German boarders. German, because they spoke German and thus they were able to draft an advertisement in the German paper. The boarders were provided with breakfast, so my mother had to rise at five in the morning to make it for them. It was not a pleasant life, just the best they could do. Yet these boarders became part of the household and became friends.

'There was a German woman among them who attempted suicide because she fell in love with one of the other boarders who was married. My mother stayed up all night with her and saved her life.

She was grateful to my mother ever after. Another man was an asthmatic whom we took to the doctors. These people became very good friends. Very good. They came to my engagement party and they have kept on visiting us till quite recently.

'Only one of them, Klaus, made anti-Semitic remarks once and my mother said "'Raus!" and she packed his things and put them out on the footpath, not caring about the consequences. That was the first time ... It must have taken guts! I mean, there were other Germans there, but they were our friends.

'I decided to become a kindergarten teacher when one day I picked up my little cousin Judy from kindergarten in Jerusalem. I saw the teacher sitting there on a stool with the little children against the wall. I thought, "This is what I want to do!"

'When I was about thirteen my older cousin and I always gathered all the little children on Shabbat or school holidays and minded them. We put them to sleep, packed their lunches. We had a proper kindergarten and we were paid. We continued to do this in Sydney too. I did become a professional preschool teacher and later I specialised in teaching deaf children.

'I love the creative aspects of the job and I love little children. When my children cry for their mothers I always hold them. I remember this little girl (she had a Jewish mother but I did not know this at the time) who was always upset and I always held her. I was told that she should be allowed to play with the others, but I knew this little girl was terrified of the blasts and noise coming from the next-door construction site. I knew this child needed me. I held her and she cuddled into me. Today she is a fine actress.

'But I was there for whoever was upset and I remember them. I could tell you even about children from my training years. One of them is a lawyer, and many still come to see me. Many parents appreciated what I had done for their children and some are my best friends now.

'Alongside this, I have looming, ever-present memories of the only kindergarten I went to, in Teresienstadt. It is possible that I was able to mother my kindergarten children because I had been mothered properly up to that point of my life myself. I was certainly not mothered after.

'As well as my work, my marriage was also wonderful. I met my husband in 1957 when I was sixteen and a half doing Year 10 at school. He was thirty. He had been brought unannounced one day to our home by a very distant relative. He was also from Slovakia and he had lost every relative in the war except for four siblings. So he had no parents or uncles or aunts who could have been a base for him. He would talk to my mother and aunty for hours. But they also needed him. My mother could talk to him, he could handle her problems, he could advise her. He was a source of solidity, stability, reliability.

'As soon as I saw him, I attached . . . I accepted . . . in my heart I wanted to be with him. He told me that I was too young. In a way he was closer to my mother's age than mine. He told me that I should go out with others first, but he promised he would come back one day if I wanted him to. You see what a wonderful and fair man he was. But I only wanted him! So I married him at nineteen and had my son at twenty while I was in my third year of teachers' college. But I contracted rubella while pregnant and our son was born deaf.

'I literally went from my mother's bed to my husband's. My mother could not cope with having a proper bedroom to herself. So the two of us lived and slept in the kitchen dining-room, the other rooms being let. The way I explain it to myself is that my mother had lost so much that she did not want to lose any more. She had lost her family homes, the home her father built her, the best furniture, the tailor-made clothes . . . Even what she salvaged from Czechoslovakia she lost in Israel. So I slept with my mother in a single bed all those years, until the day of my marriage.

'I had a very loving and happy marriage and my husband and I were emotionally and physically compatible. But I think that I repeated my mother's pattern with me with my son. For instance, when he was in America at school I was the only mother on campus. I put on jeans, wore a ponytail, and tried to blend in. I should not have done this. It was not normal! But I was not going to deprive him like I was deprived. I had the opportunity to be with him, unlike my mother with me. So I was always there. If he studied, I sat by him. He was never left alone. At times I slept in his dorm at Washington Uni when another student was away. When I could not do that I kept the elevator under observation, waiting for him to appear at last. I did this secretly because I did not want him to know that he had a *meshuggene* mother. But I simply could not take the pain of separation. I did not want him to have it, but it was mainly me.

'It was me who decided not to have more children. I felt we could not cope with more. We were emotionally and physically exhausted. I had always wanted two children, and with all the kindergarten theory, there always had to be at least two children. My son always asked me for another sister or brother. I did become pregnant once and I was very happy, but I lost it and then that was it. I gave him anything and everything except that.' Eva's voice suddenly dropped to an almost imperceptible whisper. 'And I said, "Johnny, no, darling." Occasionally I have pangs of conscience about it when I see that he is very alone especially with his deafness. He would like to have a family. He would like to replace the losses "because of what happened to our family".

'The time is nigh to let him go and I get panic attacks. At night especially, the thought of him living alone somewhere . . . So if he moved out, he knows that we would want bars on all his doors and windows, like in our house. What if Johnny does not hear an intruder at night? My mother nagged me to put up the bars.

'My mother was a very frightened woman. She would look behind her in the shopping centre. Others were also frightened of a man who had murdered six older women, so do not take it out of context. But her fear was heightened. She was frightened of bagsnatchers, she carried her key around her neck.' Eva was distressed at her mother's fright.

'My son assures me "I will visit you every day" and that he is not moving far. He is ready to move. He wanted to move when he was seventeen or eighteen. We will do it soon with the proviso that he can always move back. He is very steady, like his father, he does not have panic attacks. You cannot agitate him. He has a steady job. He has his own room, but next door.

'While I lived with my husband and he had to go away the next day, I did not go to sleep, I just looked at him as long as I could. When he was dying I sat by his side so that he was never alone while awake. He also did not want to be left alone.

'After I was widowed I wore my wedding ring like my mother. I was

preparing to be alone permanently like she had been. But unexpectedly I met a man whom I had known as a child in Israel. When I was
nine he was seventeen, in the process of joining the navy. He was
orphaned at the age of nine and he used to visit us as he had no
parents. He had known my husband and we would see him briefly
on our visits to Israel.

'We all thought that he was very nice but I was quite surprised
when he started to pursue me and then suddenly suggested marriage
to me. I said to him, "If you only want to marry me in order to come
to Australia, tell me and we'll help you to migrate without marriage."
I adored him and loved him for what I thought he was. But that
image shattered. I had no option but to file for divorce. I was devastated because my trust was shaken again and it was another loss.

'Separation, separation, separation, it has been a recurring pattern
and trauma. It hurts, it is actually painful. I cannot understand people
who look back on divorces and deaths as things of the past, something that is over. I tend to live in the past because I need the people
of the past. And, spiritually, I still have my husband. I believe in life
after death. In that way I can overcome my lack. He is with me.
I know that he would want to be. And I look forward to being with
him again.

'On the way from the cemetery following his burial a friend of mine
suggested to me that I read a book called *Life After Life*. It completely
absorbed me. I read this book and seventeen similar ones. I did not
want to go to bed. It was too painful to be alone there. That is when
it hurts, when seemingly eternally you do not know what to do with
yourself. So I stayed up reading about life after death. I wanted to
know what was happening to my husband. I have now read and heard
enough to believe that there is life after death and I do not need to
read any more. Yet from time to time I do, for comfort.

'I cannot explain this, but a major thing that happened in my life
is that my husband and I became Baha'is, I thirty-one years ago, my
husband longer. In part it dealt with the problem of prejudice and
not belonging. I am not only accepted by the Baha'is, but because
they like diversity I add value and colour to the community and so I
feel appreciated by them. Because the Baha'i world centre is in Haifa,
Israel, there is a convergence with Judaism in the reverence for Israel

and the prophecy of return. There is a good relationship between the Baha'is and Israel.

'The Baha'i religion answered many of my spiritual needs. My mother could not explain God to me, so I grew up not believing in Him. But I always asked questions about God. As a child I fell in love with a Christian neighbour, a childhood romance which lasted eight years. He was a Catholic Palestinian-Greek kid. But my mother could not explain Christ to me either. In sixth grade I wrote in a free essay that, as Christianity was a world religion, Israeli teachers should teach about Christ in schools.

'The Baha'i religion enabled me to put the whole jigsaw puzzle together.' I asked if it explained the Holocaust. 'No, that is too difficult.' Eva ignored my interruption. 'But it shows that there is the same God, called differently in each religion. God sends a teacher or prophet or messenger in each specific age to different parts of the world and they are the founders of the great religions. I was astonished at the similarities between the eightfold path of Buddha and the ten commandments. I studied all the religions before I became a Baha'i. Now all mankind was put together for me. The Jewish religion had its place along with the others on an equal footing and shared the spiritual needs of honesty, justice and other values. I am a Baha'i but I have not lost any of my Jewishness.

'All my pre-death readings dovetailed into the Baha'i teachings too. They explained why there are similar beliefs about life after death in different religions. I accept this and rejoice in it, and I am waiting to be with my husband again.

'In the meantime I am very keen to help people overcome their prejudices because I know that pain is everywhere, like in all school playgrounds. Baha'i gives me the tools to help, the language. I can say meaningfully, "The world is but one country and mankind all its citizens . . . Ye are all the fruits of one tree and the leaves of one branch." It gives me a very healthy feeling. It feels nice to be part of a big family, to belong with those people.

'I love people. I am very open with them. The Baha'is teach not to be estranged from others, but I trust people too much, open myself too much, talk to anyone about anything. Perhaps I want to be accepted too much, but I cannot curb this.

'I feel comfortable in the Child Survivor group, but I do not make it obvious to them that I am a Baha'i. And yet to mix with them and not say who you are is wrong. That is why we stayed away from the Jewish community. At times I have stayed away from the Child Survivor group and I have even thought of stopping going altogether, in order not to upset anyone. I told some committee members that I should not be there, but they remained warm and inviting. And I need to share with other child survivors. I read the same books that they cannot put down.'

Comment

What does 'Separation, separation, that is the trauma of my life' mean? By the age of four a normal child confidently takes pre-school in his or her stride. For Eva there was a crescendo of forced separations and losses in her early life, culminating in the loss of her father and daily forced separations from her mother. By the time she reached what was called 'pre-school' in Teresienstadt the small child cried interminably for her mother and became physically ill.

That is the story, but what is the experience? Eva herself had not put it all together. It is as if emotions cannot be owned and validated until someone else confirms them. Eva's mother, for all their later closeness, was too involved in her own separations and losses to confirm her daughter's feelings. They became much more real only after their confirmation by Sarah Moskovitz and Eva's fellow inmate, Litzi. Eva found the words and acquired clarity for some emotions only in this interview.

For instance Eva came to identify the sense of clinging as her family was rent asunder at the station as having haunted her throughout life. Similarly, she came to remember father's love in his goodbye kiss and was able to acknowledge the deep sadness at the loss of his protectiveness which had pervaded her life. There was a clearer memory of Eva's total preoccupation with and waiting for mother's appearance in the 'pre-school' in Teresienstadt. The child's desperate longing; the hopelessness and helplessness crushed her chest with the pain of her mother's absence. The terror of abandonment and being left alone merged into the traumatic feelings of separation pain felt in the chest. This is what Eva tried to avoid for the rest of her life. These pains were greater than the fear of seeing the dead or feeling her head ringing from being thrown at the wall. Yet, let us remember that Eva's total preoccupation with her mother was congruent with her survival. Without her she had nothing. Without her she would have died.

In addition to being wrenched apart and left, there was the feeling of being excluded because she was different. This started with the bars at the playground in Slovakia and continued in the bars on the cots and windows in Teresienstadt. The social bars were confirmed in Eva's first school experience. She still has metal bars on her house.

Eva's own feelings were highly influenced by her mother's. Mother's anxieties at night, her relief at liberation, her lasting anticipation of Eva's father's return, her need of a male protector, all communicated themselves to Eva and ruled her life.

Even post-war, dealing with all the deaths and separations was sometimes too painful for mother and daughter. So at times when their post-war situation dashed their wartime hopes, they returned symbolically to the wartime situation and its still alive hopes. For instance mother and daughter kept sleeping together in very modest conditions as if in 'a bunk'. In Australia Eva's mother worked hard for Germans and hoped for her husband's return.

At times hopes seemed to be fulfilled, for instance in the case of Eva's husband who became the family's protective figure. Unfortunately, even there history seemed to repeat itself. Eva was left a widow with only her one child to cling to, while waiting to be reunited with her husband.

Eva noted the repetition of the problematic separation pattern with her child. Her son also seemed to be excluded from the world, this time through his deafness, having only his mother (and father) persevere against great odds to give him life. There had been a compulsion to be very close to him, even in the dorms, and separation from him even now evokes panic.

Eva continued to live her own natural life as well as her traumatic life, and sometimes the two combined in creative ways. Her marriage was satisfying and the couple did help their son in a unique way against great odds. From the time when Eva saw children lined up against a wall in Jerusalem, reminding her of the cots lined up against the wall in Teresienstadt, she knew that she could make life better for pre-school children. Her devotion to the children was clear and many of the children benefited as a result.

Eva was blessed with a visual memory and a capacity for putting events on paper to get things 'out of her system'. Perhaps from the earliest scribbles in Teresienstadt to paintings of houses now she gained mastery over her feelings. From being homeless in the world she created her own houses everywhere.

Similarly, Eva was able to find in the Baha'i religion a philosophy which embraced her experiences in a creative way. Not only did her fragmented experiences gain some meaningful cohesion, but she also came to be a valued member of a group where she could belong for the first time.

So today we have the striking mature woman whose beauty speaks of the knowledge of suffering. It is hard to overcome the wrenches and wounds which a cruel world imposed on a small child. Eva's life has been pervaded to a large extent by these events, but she has also grown tendrils of connection around her wounds. A nice child has grown into a nice woman. But Eva's wounds still cause her, in part, to feel excluded from normal life, wrenched from protection, and to crave desperately for the lifeline which only another person can provide.

George

—•—

'I DON'T LOOK BACK

TOO FAR OR TOO DEEP'

I VISITED GEORGE IN *a bayside suburb one and a half hour's drive from Melbourne. The Spanish style house which George built seventeen years ago, and of which he was very proud, stood some streets back from the beach. George and his wife Margaret welcomed me.*

We went into George's study. The bookshelves contained history books of various periods, The Rise and Fall of the Third Reich *being but one of them. There was a small section on Jewry, which seemed to be the only clue to a casual observer that Jewishness was of some interest to the occupants. A chess table which George had made separated us as we sat down. George himself had a rustic appearance, was fair and blue eyed, and spoke with a German accent. Disconcertingly, George could have been an assimilated German Aryan. As well, over the years George had very little to do with the Jewish community. But looks can be deceptive.*

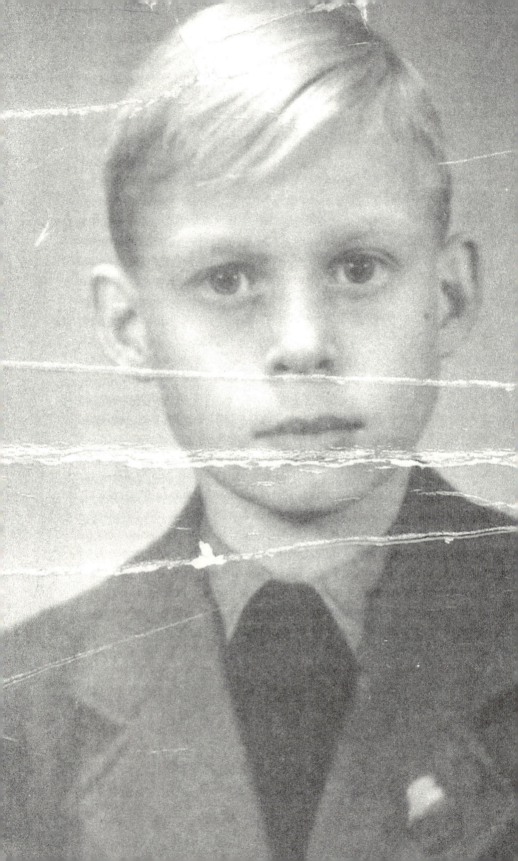

$\mathcal{M}$Y NAME IS George Hammer-
schmidt, and I was born in 1934 in Zwickau, Saxony. My father was
born in Schneidemuhl, East Prussia, and he came to Zwickau before
the war. He worked there in a Jewish store. My mother was Christian
and she converted to Judaism. My parents then returned to Schneide-
mühl where they had a Jewish wedding. There my father sold second-
hand goods, travelling with his horse and cart in the countryside.'

It took me a little while to become accustomed to George's way of
speaking. He tended to report facts, and sometimes in great detail.
Yet he skipped or scrambled information which would enlarge on
important conflicts, emotions, or personal meanings. Or in the space
where such words might be, he would lower his voice, and speak too
fast to understand, or simply make the appropriate sounds without
the words. During this interview I asked many questions, not all listed,
in order to clarify matters and to elicit more specific subjective
information.

'My grandfather was a horse dealer and my very first memory is of
his yard, full of animals. As a child I had toys such as a train. I played
on my own. I remember going to my grandparents on the Sabbath.
But as far back as I remember there was tension. I knew things were
not right. My father's friends visited and they talked about leaving
Germany. My father's cousin left for Israel after his shop was smashed
up. But my grandfather could not be persuaded. He said "I am
German, I served in the German army".

'I always knew that I was Jewish. We may not have been orthodox
Jews, but we went to synagogue and ate *matzoh* [unleavened bread]
on Passover.

'When I was five, my father was taken to Sachsenhausen [a concentration camp in Germany]. His father was already there, I think he was arrested for political reasons. A British Jewish banker whose funds were frozen in Germany was allowed to haul out to England a contingent of Jews, my father among them, in lieu of his money. My grandfather was left in the camp. My mother saw my father for one day in Berlin on his way out of the country. He decoded German messages for the British for some time, and then he came to Australia on the *Dunera* [a ship which carried many refugees who became valuable citizens]. He was interned in a camp for enemy aliens in Hay for some time, following which he joined the Australian army. He was stationed near Melbourne, not far from here.'

Typically, George added as an afterthought, 'It was the time of the Kristallnacht [November 1938] when they burnt the synagogues and smashed everything up that my father was imprisoned. We went back to Zwickau.'

George assured me that he remembered all events well. I asked, 'What do you remember about the impact of these events on yourself?'

George replied, as if puzzled by the question, 'Myself, to be really honest, I have not given it much thought. At the time I just accepted things as they were. I just took each day as it came. But I was devastated the day after my father was taken to the concentration camp. We visited his mother, and on the way I saw the burnt-out shell of the synagogue near her place. And when we returned home the Gestapo had smashed up our furniture, hacked the cupboards with an axe and strewn everything around. The next day we returned to Zwickau to my grandfather.'

'Do you remember how as a little boy you felt when you returned to your destroyed flat?'

'Maybe I felt a bit frightened, I don't know. Maybe I felt a bit unsure of things. But as far as I can tell, I just lived through things. I never look back. It happened, so it happened. We had to go on. I don't look back too far or too deep into things. I don't try to hide things, it doesn't do you any good. But so many things happened which I didn't like. My family got killed. All right, you can hate the Germans. But how much can you hate? Where will it get you? My father finished up as a suspicious recluse. Well, I, we all became suspicious. But I try to not let my whole being be taken over and distorted by hate. I have all my memories, but I cut off my hatred. I try to live my life really without hate. I cannot change what happened. So what can I do? My father was a very bitter man. I don't like that. I like to make the best of what comes.' There followed some confused words.

'So I have gone through life, I would not say happy many times. Sometimes I have lived in my own little world, not thinking about what would happen tomorrow. Today is today, tomorrow is tomorrow. I did not think what would happen tomorrow.'

'Do you think that you developed this way of thinking in childhood, at a time when you had no power to influence your tomorrows, or even know for certain that there would be tomorrows?'

George replied readily, 'Yes, and I have tried to not worry too much throughout my life, because it does not do you any good.

'So my mother and I went back to my grandfather in Zwickau. But she did not get on with her father. He was very German, a Nazi. He blamed the Jews for losing all his money in the depression. Once he had stopped my father in the street and said, "Look you are not going out with my daughter. You are a Jew." So my father gave him a black eye. My grandfather never forgave my father; nor my mother for marrying a Jew.

'So my mother could not stand living with her father, plus it was dangerous to stay in a small town where everyone knew who we were. So we moved to Berlin, to a one-room flat in Judenstrasse. My father's mother and two sisters lived there in a small Jewish community. My mother worked for my uncle in an antique restoration shop, while I stayed with my aunt and two cousins, and grandmother.

'During this time I thought about my father, but things changed so quickly all the time, I just had to go on each day within my own little self. Time came when I had to wear the star of David. I did not like being pointed out as a Jew.

'In the summer of 1942, when I was seven and a half, I developed measles, and meningitis as a complication. I very nearly died. I remember looking down on myself from the ceiling, seeing a doctor punching injections into me. I remember dreaming that I was on an island surrounded by reeds, with my father. In another dream I came through a door and everyone stood on either side. Then they opened the door and I went out again. At other times I dreamed of jumping into a pit, but I floated down and could jump out again. Jumping down heights and coming back again was a recurrent dream in my childhood. I stayed in [the Jewish] hospital for six months.

'I recuperated in Zwickau for some months. When I returned to Berlin, kids called me names and threw stones at me in the streets, so I had to stop going to school. My mother had had enough. I joined her in her flat, and I just stopped wearing the star.

'I spent my time going to picture theatres, art galleries, museums. I also became a member of a street gang, and fought other gangs. I told them that my father was taken prisoner of war in the Africa Corps and was held in Australia. By then there were no Jewish children around, the gang was not preoccupied with Jews at all.

'My grandmother was summoned to report for a transport to Teresienstadt. However, she was given a deferral till my aunt had her baby.'

'Was your own deportation delayed because you were half Christian?'

'No. I lived as a Jew, and I stayed alive because of luck. Once, by chance, I accompanied my mother shopping. As we returned, we saw the SS evacuating all Jews from our house. They were putting my pram on a truck. That was a very close shave.'

'What did Teresienstadt mean to the family?'

'We knew what went on in concentration camps from an SS man who was a lodger with a non-Jewish cousin of my mother. He was Hitler's French and English interpreter. He had been with Hitler while Hitler watched films of concentration camps. He was disillusioned with Hitler, saying he was half mad. He knew our circumstances, and he did not denounce us.

'I did not equate Teresienstadt with death. I never thought of death, those sorts of things. When my grandmother was eventually deported, actually to another camp, it did not really go that far that we thought that much, we just hoped. Really, as a child I just took things as they came. I knew, but I did not go into the depths of things.'

'Do you think that Germans who deny knowledge of concentration camps also did not go into the depths of things?'

'Some did not know. For many it did not register. But other

Germans knew there were concentration camps. The Germans themselves were coerced and humiliated. For instance, the SS lodger's fiancee had to go through humiliating physical examinations to prove that she was of good enough Aryan stock to marry an SS officer. There were Germans in my father's camp, and though there were no mass killings there, the prisoners were badly treated. They were hosed with cold water, they were made to scrub floors with toothbrushes. My father was hit on the head with a rifle butt. We knew what went on in Poland. The Germans have generally been anti-Semites.

'The bombings got heavier. While we were sheltering in the cellar our house caught fire as a result of incendiary bombs. My mother was ordered to help put out the fire. I really went hysterical, I just screamed and screamed. My mother said, "I just can't leave my son" and she stayed. I saved my mother's life, because those who went were hit by bombs.' George could not explain why he behaved in such an uncharacteristic way, that is not just taking things as they came. He said, 'I think it was some kind of survival sixth sense. I still have it today.'

'Those of us left in the shelter tried to escape the fire by opening a passage to the shelter next door, but smoke forced us back. As we ran out of the house, a huge beam blocked the exit. There were burning buildings everywhere. My mother and I crossed the street. A plane swooped low and machine-gunned the side we had just left, killing a man. We just ran to my aunty's place. Then we went to Zwickau.' Characteristically George skipped the feelings and implications of this near-death experience. When questioned, he said, 'Maybe I was frightened a little, but really, there was no time to feel, you just ran. My mother, like older people generally, probably felt more.

'My grandfather in Zwickau was quite militaristic. On our Sunday walk I had to "Step out, stomach in, chest out, walk straight, don't slouch" and everything had to be done exactly, with strict obedience. You certainly did not cry. My experience of my father before the war was the opposite. All my father's family had been kinder than the German side.

'Soon after arriving in Zwickau my mother was summoned to the Gestapo. She was told that I had to go to Teresienstadt, and they gave her the details of where and when I had to report. She could not argue or deny anything, because she saw all the facts about us recorded correctly.

'My mother always believed that my grandfather denounced me. I really don't know. I know that one evening a group of Hitler youths ambushed me and took away my money. People just knew who you were in the small town.'

George's voice fell uncharacteristically to a whisper. 'Anyhow, my mother told me, "They are taking you away from me. You have to go to Teresienstadt. I can't do anything about it."' I asked George how he had felt. After a long pause he said, 'I did not cry.'

'We went to the station. They took my fingerprints, gave me an identity card with J [Jew] on it. We had a cup of tea and I went off on the train.'

Again I tried to peer into the invisible gap. 'Did you say goodbye to her?'

'Oh yes, she was on the platform. I walked on to the train with the others, and the SS men. In Dresden we changed to a cattle truck. We stayed on the sidings during a heavy bombing raid. I was not frightened. I curled up and went to sleep. The next morning I saw the SS guard dirty and pale, a bomb must have exploded near him. We were marched to a school and had something to eat, then back on the train, and in the afternoon we arrived in Teresienstadt.

'"Out! Out!" they shouted. They went through the rigmarole of going through papers, they searched our possessions. They left one man with his pocket watch, another with tobacco, thinking it was tea. I went with the men to a barrack, and slept on a bunk in a small room on the third floor. But the next day I was moved to the children's quarters, which used to be the post office. There were twenty to thirty boys in my dormitory, mainly from Germany and Czechoslovakia. We palled up quickly.

'Soon after I arrived there was a children's show in the attic. The camp commander watched too. There were rules against drawing and singing, but they relaxed those rules with time. Later we were moved to other quarters because of massive infestation with bed bugs. Now I shared my room with nine other German boys. A nice German woman looked after us. We had chores, such as fetching food —

soup, bread, a little margarine, horse goulash, barley pudding. I can't have barley in the house to this day.

'The rest of the time I just walked around. I met up with a fourteen year old boy who lived with his mother, and we talked about what we would do after the war, how we would return home on a horse and cart. But most of the time I walked alone, I was a bit of a loner. I walked to the wall and looked out to the mountains. I walked to see the transports come in. I saw people come off the trains, and the dead people stayed on. One train did not have a single survivor. It had just been left on a siding for many days in the cold.

'On my tenth birthday I walked to see the transports come in. On this day an old lady came off the train and I offered to carry her suitcase for her. I told her who I was and that it was my birthday. She assured me that I would rejoin my mother soon.

'Then we parted and I was in my own little world again. I bumped into an SS man as I turned a corner. I expected a clout, but he patted me. Then I saw Himmler [the chief engineer of the genocide] in his black uniform, the camp commander and guards.'

'What impression did Himmler make on you?'

'He was two hundred feet away. I just went home, I was not going to stay around.' George laughed.

'What was your response to seeing all these dead people?'

'I don't know. I felt sorry for them. I remember one man sitting in a corner covered with a blanket. He reminded me of my grandfather. Umm . . . I did not have nightmares. Then we saw a dogfight. One of the fighters swooped down and machine-gunned the SS barracks.'

George spent about half a year in Teresienstadt. I asked, 'Overall, what was it like?'

'What can I say? People walked around. It was like a self-governing community, with a mayor, its own money, little shops selling stale vegetables, ersatz coffee. You could have a shower for money. There was a fire brigade, theatre. All the policing was done by Jews inside the camp.

'We children kept to ourselves. We played. Sometimes we played war games, but not Germans and others, just ordinary kids' games. One day I fell on a stone, and the wound festered. There was nothing

I could do about it. No one had taught me what to do with wounds. I still have the scar from it today.

'One of the Czech women who worked for the Gestapo gave me one hundred crowns, and bits of food. Then my hair was shorn because of lice, and I stopped seeing her because I was too ashamed to let her see me like that.'

'What was your worst experience in Teresienstadt?'

'I used to peer over the walls. I just wanted to go home. I was homesick, but I occupied my mind. I never cried. My experiences were nothing special, nothing worse than the bombings. I only saw dead people on the trains, not in the camp. Torture and killing took place only in the small fortress. It never occurred to me that I might die.

'When the SS left, they threw hand grenades and machine-gunned us. One or two people got killed and one boy lost a leg. I was sheltered in a cellar at this time. Then the Russians came through with their tanks, masses of them. For two weeks they came, with prisoners of war, cattle, carts, everything. The Russians threw cigars to us, that is where I had my first cigar.' George guffawed.

'How did you feel about the Russians coming in?'

'Oh, it was great,' George said a little offhandedly. On further probing, he continued in the same vein. 'Yes, it was one of those emotions. We were free. But because of looting we were not allowed out again. The Russians took over the SS quarters. One day some Russians came into the camp with a bucket of beer and a big tin of bully beef, and we joined in with them. Another day, a Russian was so drunk that he shot randomly with a revolver.' George laughed, 'They socked him to the ground and took the gun away.' It was like a soldier's story with the high points, the comic, little of the cruelty or sadness of war.

'Yes, when the Russians came there was singing and dancing in the streets. They brought in the mayors of surrounding villages, sheared their hair in the middle of their heads and painted swastikas on their pants. They sheared Nazi women's heads too. They made them all do menial work for about a week, while people heckled them. I just looked, I didn't heckle. I saw one SS guard hit over the head with a piece of wood, and he bled. If anything I felt a bit sorry for him. I just looked, just saw that this was what was happening.

'Cholera broke out after prisoners from other camps arrived. They were in a worse state than us. They were just skin and bones. Some went mad.

'People from my home district organised a bus. I collected a card stating that I had been in Teresienstadt, some provisions, and we went. The Czech border guards robbed us. The man with the pocket watch was robbed of it there.

'We arrived in a town near Zwickau, and I was put in the charge of two women in a hotel. But they found a lift to their town. "I am coming with you," I insisted. I was not going to stay there on my own. Maybe I did not feel very safe. I just was not going to stay there. I jumped up and down, and forced them to take me with them. They arranged for me to stay with a family, who knew that I was Jewish. They gave me a bath, tended my sores and blisters. I was a mess.

'The next day an American captain took me to Zwickau. I directed him to my grandfather's house, thinking my mother would be there. I rushed upstairs. People came to the landings to look. They asked me where I had been. They knew me, and I told them. But there were strangers in my grandfather's flat. I was directed to my mother's new address. So I went there.

'My mother had a very small room. She was extremely thin and sick, lying in bed. Of course she was very happy to see me.'

'How did you feel when you saw her?'

More readily than usual, George responded, 'We were happy as anything. My mother was very happy. She was very sick. She had suffered a lot. Things improved from then on. We had more food, I had a suit made, and I went to school. But I could not settle there, so I had a private tutor.

'Then the Russians took over from the Americans. They were quite different. They weeded out the Nazis. An ex-red brigade fighter in the Spanish Civil War became mayor. He advised us to join the Communist Party. We did, and got extra food. Joining the party was to help us leave the country too. In fact we went to Berlin to start emigration proceedings to Australia. They had a May Day procession there.' George was tickled, 'I had the Communist flag in one window, and a Jewish naval flag which I happened to have in the other. I had to remove the latter. My mother got the papers and we crossed to the American sector.'

'My father met us at Spencer Street station in Melbourne. That was a bit horrific.' George struggled and made a few false starts. 'We had not seen each other for six years. He did not like the way I looked at him. He always held that against me, I don't know why. I didn't throw my arms around him, he was a stranger to me. But he felt that I did not like him. In fact I think that he was jealous of my closeness to my mother.

'He had totally changed. He was a distant, suspicious man, full of hate. He always picked, found fault, and could never be pleased. He was very dogmatic, everything had to be done his way. I think being hit by the rifle butt in the concentration camp, plus his parents, two sisters, their children and most of the Hammerschmidts having been killed, engulfed his life and ate him up.

'Hatred and suspicion ate him up. He even accused my mother of wanting to poison him when a few drops of fly spray accidentally fell on some potatoes. He had normal times, but we were very seldom if ever close. I felt that my life was hard, and my mother was unhappy.

'My father bought five acres of land near where his army unit had been stationed, and went into a poultry business which failed. Then he worked in town in a Jewish store. His last job was as a security guard.

'My father took me out of school after three years, because we needed the money. I worked on farms, and became a flower gardener. I had my own business at the age of sixteen. I worked seven days a week, ten hours a day. My only break till I married at the age of twenty-two was three months in the army. I worked to pay my business off, and I even helped my father with his car. I had no money for our honeymoon.

'I met Margaret at a friend's place and fell in love with her. I had no Jewish friends, and she was Roman Catholic. Her religion did not matter to me. We agreed to marry in a registry office, and to give our children choice of religion. Of the six children, one chose to be Jewish.'

'You and your environment were non-Jewish.'

'I was too busy to think about these things. Friends and I took each other as we were. It just happened that way. But I still feel Jewish. My father was Jewish, my grandfather was Jewish, he died in a concentration camp, and I wore a star. I could never convert. One day a kid at school called me a Jew. I poked him hard with a ruler, and said, "Next time I'll ram it down your throat." We became best of friends. It was one of those kids' things. Generally I did not experience anti-Semitism. So over the years I worked hard, supporting six children.

'To be honest, I only wanted one, but I finished up with six, they just came along. Well, I wanted my line to go on, and I don't dislike them, I love my children. I always tried to do the best for them. We are like friends, open with each other. But until the twins, the last children, I was not maternal, I did not kiss and cuddle them. On the other hand, I did not discipline them too much, I am a bit of a softie really.

'I wanted them to have a better life than I had. I told them my story, about concentration camps, the things I did not want to happen to them. I brought them up to be independent, to survive in the world. I wanted them to be educated, not to have to do manual work like myself.

'The eldest is thirty-four, she has four children and is a special aid teacher working mainly with autistic children. The next daughter has three children and works for an insurance broker. Next is a son, a bricklayer. Jane has a child and is going to marry an Israeli. The twins are doing well in their studies and are going to university.

'Only one child has a Jewish partner. I probably would have liked them all to be Jewish, but that's the way it is. I have a Jewish grandchild and that makes me happy.'

'What did the others choose?'

'They don't go to church. Jane leans to Judaism. She is the only one who goes to synagogue. My eldest son is more Jewish than anything else.

'My children were called Nazis when they went to school because they had a German name. Another time a priest told them at school that the Jews brought leprosy to the world. The kids were devastated when they came home. This was one of the few times when I was very angry. I didn't do anything. I told the children he was a liar.'

'Have you thought that not being Jewish is best for survival?'

'In that sense I could give it away too. But we have to make a stand, be candid like everyone else, say what you believe in. Survival — you can get killed on the roads.'

'In summary, how did the past affect you over the years?'

'It made me hard. I believe what's black is black, what's white is white; what's right is right, what's wrong is wrong. I don't like this in-between business. But I am soft underneath too. I can't do enough for my children. We have differences in our family like everybody else. They have a life to live, I have a life to live. Once they are married, I can't dictate. They have to live with their own conscience.

'It made me hard in my marriage too. My wife thinks so. Though I can be passionate sexually. Maybe I can be too dogmatic, impatient, irate when things don't go my way, though I am not as bad as my father. I can be hard to live with.

'Two years ago I took redundancy and returned to the market garden which I had sold. I could not stand the owner's inefficiency and I became stressed. He forgot everything I initially taught him. I had to leave the job.'

'Are you a bit Germanic?'

'Probably a bit. Previously I just worked, to support my children. There was a job to do, that's all, for years. Often I only slept four hours a night, I had to go to the markets early mornings. I never stopped still. But I have softened in recent years.'

'How was your outlook on life affected by your experiences?'

'It's always at the back of your mind. Maybe I became serious, more concerned with protecting my children. It has made me hard, suspicious, always looking for the ulterior motive.

'It took me years to shed a tear. The first time was when they separated the twins at school and they were really broken up. They became nervous, one chewed at his jumper. Finally one day they just came home devastated. It made me angry to the point that I cried, I had tears in my eyes. I talked to the teachers and insisted, "You can't separate my children". They were brought together and were weaned slowly the following year.

'Another time I had tears in my eyes was when I first stepped off the plane in Israel. It felt good to see Israeli soldiers standing there with guns, for the first time in two thousand years. And I felt that I belonged somewhere for the first time.

'I hate the Germans for what happened. I hate anti-Semitism, and that humanity is unjust. But I try to not let my hatred get to me. I don't hate God, I see him as almighty nature. It has not bothered me to work with Germans, and I see German tourists like anyone else, some good, others bad. I buy German goods, and I don't mind talking German. I try to do the right thing. I try to not hurt anyone.

'It is difficult to explain what I do with my hatred. I feel that I am better than they are. And maybe the Germans want me to hate them. I say that anyone who hates gets eaten up in their own hatred. And they won't get me to do that. That would mean defeat, and no one has ever defeated me. I will win by not hating, being better than they are. Have better educated children than they, so we can think better than they do, because these people don't think. If they thought they would not do what they did.'

'What do you feel about neo-Nazis, revisionists?'

'I think they should be shot. I don't know if I would shoot them, that's cold blooded, but these people should not live. I mean, we have had enough suffering.'

'Do you hate them?'

'Oh, yes, I hate them. Maybe they don't know what they are doing, they are not smart people.'

'Have you contact with your German family?'

'I have no contact with them and know very little about them. I met an uncle after the war, he was a sergeant-major in Russia, his son was on a U-boat. I am not interested in them. I have not visited Germany.'

'What other consequences have there been from your experiences?'

'Whenever I see films with any tension in them, such as murder films, or when things don't go my way, I sweat a lot. I try not to worry, but subconsciously these things are still there. You can't hide from it. The tension is in you when you lie in bed. No thoughts or feelings, just the tension. Can't get rid of it. You can look at things from a rosy perspective, but subconsciously you can't get away from it. You smile all day, but a bit of stress, and you break out in a sweat at night. I think it is there subconsciously from the bombings and such things. I have never slept much, three to four hours a night. I do not have nightmares.

'I have not had physical illnesses though I was run down in this last job. Couldn't shake the flu, had tonsillitis three times this year. I was angry with the boss, but only in fantasies. I had more cold sweats than usual at night, like I do when stressed and worried.

'I have also had depressions all my life, feeling very low and vulnerable. But I get out of them after a few hours by shutting them off, and giving myself a talking to.'

'How come you have mellowed in the last few years?'

'I have become more maternal with my twins. They were the apple of my eye. The others were too, but these were special. We did not expect twins. The doctor offered me a cigar, then another. I was flabbergasted. He said I could go into the labour ward. That was the nearest I ever approached the birth process. It gave me a different view of life. And I held my grandson when he was circumcised, that made me feel close to him, even closer than my children. My rigidity softened, work became less important.

'Four years ago, by chance, I came to learn that there was a meeting of children who survived the war in Sydney. I met Litzi who had also been in Teresienstadt. It was good to talk for the first time with others who had had similar experiences. I did not feel alone any more. Litzi was younger, so I could explain to her about the camp, explain a part of her life to her. That felt good.

'Two years ago I went to a Child Survivor conference in Los Angeles. Some of the stories there were too tense, it was too chilling to hear stories similar and even worse than your own. It made me frustrated, "Why did this have to happen?"

'I did not attend the Melbourne Child Survivor group, because I was too busy, and did not know many Jewish people in Melbourne, I felt an outsider. But they are lovely people and I am glad that I started to attend. It makes me feel a part of things. It has somehow allowed me to be closer to Margaret. Subconsciously I am more relaxed with myself.'

'What was the very worst experience?'

'When I had to go to Teresienstadt on my own. When I look back on it, you are torn away from your mother. It was heartless. She suffered more than I.'

'If there was anything good, what was it?'

'I suppose when the Russians came to Teresienstadt, but at the time it did not sink in, because we still could not go through the fence.'

I pointed to an article which George had shown me. It said that of fifteen thousand children who entered Teresienstadt only one hundred survived. 'What do you make of being one of the hundred?'

'When I was there, I did not think about it. For me, I was just with the children who were there. I did not think that there should have been a lot more of us. After the war I never thought about it, till I read this article. Then it shocked me.'

'And you are the only German child survivor you know in Australia?'

'Yes, and I only met two overseas.'

'They did a good job,' I commented.

George said sadly, 'Well, what can you say about it? It's horrific. It's a lot of lives. It should not have happened. There are no words to describe it.'

Comment

There are no words to describe genocide and the human tragedy which the word signifies. On a more personal scale, George did not have the words to describe for himself the threat of death and the shattering of his own world during the years of persecution. In fact, we see how the little boy survived by making sure that day by day he did not think far enough or deep enough about his predicament. Had he done so, feelings of terror, hatred, grief and despair would have threatened his survival.

George could not physically defend himself against the murderous world about him, but he could defend himself mentally against aspects of himself which might expose him or make him more vulnerable to his predators. Acknowledgement of what was happening, and emotions, were internal dangers which he could control. George built up a psychological fortress with an elaborate system of defences against knowledge and emotions. He was cut off in his own little world.

Behind the protective walls within his mind George lived each day as it came and refused to think about the meaning of the many days, or where tomorrows were heading. He had to not know and not feel the coalescence of available information — that his turn would come to be one of the disappearing children, that deportation meant death, whether for his grandmother, or for himself. Each fragment of information, each traumatic situation, was parcelled off into a world of its own, a separate logic to be adapted to at the time, but not connected with meanings.

The small George used another kind of internal wall to survive. This wall divided the world clearly into good and bad. George then ignored the bad with its threatening doom and clung to the good and the secure. This was often a very small area of life, such as George's mother, a fleeting substitute for her in Teresienstadt, or his own internal world in which George sought security.

Much energy was needed for not thinking or connecting. George kept his mind obsessively busy with thoughts and details whose content and order he could control, such as the adventures which did not threaten him.

When meanings threatened to break through, George dissociated, split and disconnected himself from them, and so it appeared to him that others, not himself, were threatened. This was clearest in the hospital where he looked down at himself being resuscitated as if he were another person. But it also happened when he considered that it was his mother, older people, the SS man at the railway siding, the dead in the carriages, who were threatened by death, not George himself.

Manoeuvres like these enabled George to cut off his dangerous feelings. The ability to cut off these feelings was felt as a strength, a precious weapon, and indeed it was at the time.

It is important to note that this system of defences was not immutable. When circumstances demanded George was capable of unequivocal expression of feeling. His uncharacteristic and unremitting screaming enabled George's mother to stay with him rather than help put out the fire during the bombing raid, and this saved her life. Similarly, George expressed his fear of being left alone in the hotel near Zwickau and this was instrumental in the two women taking him with them.

George's usual measures of protection had limits, however. George's early severe illness may have been partly the result of the intense stresses which were consuming George at the time. When George was near death, and his defences were overstretched, or possibly were not needed any more, he dreamed of death (though always bouncing back), and being reunited with his father. The craving for his absent father emerged in this extreme situation.

To a large extent George maintained his defensive system over the years, with work being the obsessive diversion. In the interview defences were reflected in the content and form of his speech, for instance describing two fragments of experience contiguously but not allowing himself to extract their combined meaning. Again, there were limits to this adaptation. The past continued to erupt in sweats and tension without words. It was difficult to sleep and dream. Perhaps seeing his father's corrosive bitterness and hatred reinforced in George's mind the value of not thinking and feeling too much. But the cost of this fortress mentality was that it made it difficult for those who loved George to connect with him and he was hampered in enjoying positive emotions, which were cut off along with the negative ones.

Perhaps one of the greatest problems for George was one of identity. When George said that he did not like half and half, that he knew what was what, without ambiguities, he denied that he was himself a mixture of half and half, and that the halves themselves were ambiguous. Certainly George's persecution as a Jew made him feel unambiguously Jewish. The Nazi machine ignored George's Christian half. And yet George's Christian relatives cared for him at times, while his Jewish father was unavailable to him during the war and later turned into a persecutor. It was ironic that both George and his father developed some Germanic qualities which they hated in the Germans. It was also ironic that George could not hate the Germans because the corrosive nature of hatred reminded him too much of his father. And outsiders were not always clear about the

Hammerschmidt (a German surname) identities. George's father was interned as a foreign alien in Australia, and George's children were called Nazis at school. Lastly, though George felt at home in Israel, it is possible that that country would not recognise him or his children as Jewish. So though the Nazi persecution was clear, original ambiguities could still cast their shadows. George did not think about this in depth. He lived in his own little world, part of it Jewish, part seemingly assimilated.

To drive the irony home even further, perhaps some of the ambiguities were identifications with George's father. After all, he had married a non-Jewish person and assimilated outwardly. When George said that he only wanted one child, perhaps he meant one child like his father had one child — one Jewish child. In this sense George does have only one identified Jewish child, who also has one Jewish child. And like his father, George has a devoted Christian wife who not only cares for his children, but cares about George's Holocaust experiences and his Jewishness.

In later years, George has mellowed. He allowed himself to be overcome by the bounteousness of life when his twin boys were born. They represented something over and above survival. George has been able to find his own identity as a survivor in Israel, and with other child survivors. He has started to bridge gaps, to find words, feelings, people. Perhaps he has started to reconnect with his original loving pre-war parents and those devoted people, especially his mother, who kept him alive during the persecution. Although still tentative, George has started to go far back and deep.

Eva M.

—•—

'I PUT HOLES

IN THE DOLL'S

HEAD AND BACK'

I ENTERED EVA'S HOUSE, *a cultured Edwardian home in the 'Jewish' suburb of Caufield. I could see Eva's pottery on display. She had many stuffed toys behind the cupboard door in the hall. Her adopted grand-daughter's bedroom was crowded with soft toys. Half her bed was covered with them, dolls and teddies, every assortment of comfort a child could desire. Eva had been a talented craft teacher and magazine commentator on arts and crafts. She had made most of the soft toys in her home. Currently she was devoutly repairing a prayer shawl salvaged from Auschwitz for the Holocaust museum. Eva had red hair, a youthful face and a moderate Viennese accent. She was slightly plump.*

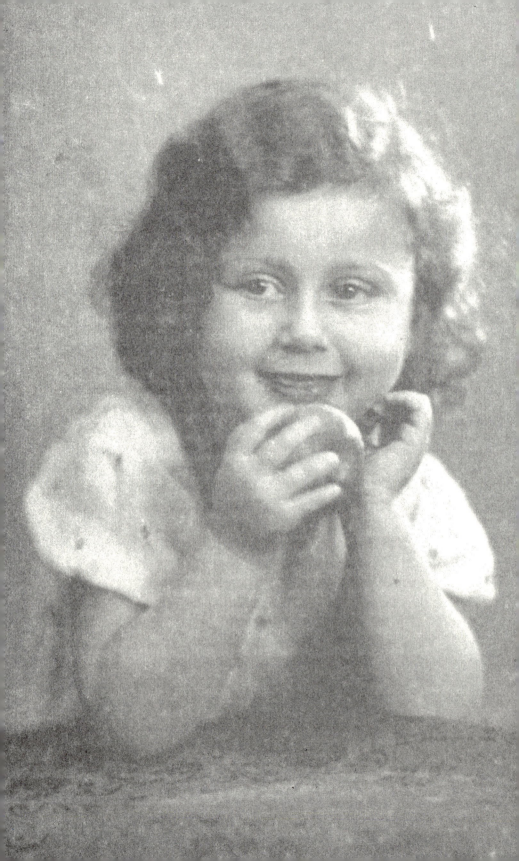

I AM EVA MARKS, and I was born in Vienna in 1932. I lived with my mother and father in Vienna, but my parents separated when I was three. We left Vienna in 1938. We left one after another. It was a very bad way my mother left.

'My parents separated before the war. I have a sense that there was discord at home before my father left. They were arguing a lot and I was caught in the middle. My father said I could not suck on a dummy and my mother said I could. My father put the dummy in salt, but while they were arguing I wheeled the pram to another room, took the dummy out and sucked on it.' Eva gave her naughty chuckle. It had a tenacious gutsiness to it — "They will not get the better of me."

'I hardly remember my father from that time. I know he left Vienna when I was six and I do not remember if he came to say good-bye to me. I have no memories of my father until I saw him in Australia when I came here at the age of eighteen.

'My mother remarried soon after she separated from my father. My step-father worked as an accountant in my mother's export-import fashion business. We became fond of each other. Actually I led a charmed life because my mother and her two sisters, as well as my two grandmothers, had only me as a child to dote on. I could have anything I liked, I was very spoilt. For instance I refused to wear the same dress twice to birthday parties. I was taken to cafes where I could have all the cakes I wanted. The women borrowed me for weekends.' Perhaps they treated Eva like a doll.

'With the Nazi Anschluss in 1938, things changed drastically for me. For one thing my step-father disappeared, being the first to go to Latvia which at that time was used as a point of departure to America. But in Vienna things became ever worse. I was not allowed to play in parks and other places which had signs "No Jews or Dogs allowed". I had to go to a special school for Jewish children. Outside Hitler Youth teenagers threw big rocks at us. I asked, "Why are they doing this to us?" and my grandmother said, "Because we are Jewish." I asked "What is that?" Jewish did not mean anything to me. I was taken out of school.

'One day I was outside my grandmother's shop. Some people dabbed "Jew" on it and I saw my grandmother physically thrown out of the shop. I was standing in the street, and that's when I had my first migraine attack. I also threw up, I was sick, and I felt tremendous anger. I was so angry I thought my head was going to blow off . . . My grandmother was a war widow, and the shop was one given to help support such widows. As a child I felt very helpless, but I saw that even adults were powerless. They made Jewish men scrub the pavements with toothbrushes and clean public toilets. So I had to control myself when they attacked her . . . I thought one day I would be one of those girls giving Hitler flowers. But I would stab him with a knife. My grandmother came to live with us then.

'And then my mother left and I have really bad feelings about that. I was very, very upset and I still feel it was the wrong thing to do. I used to sleep with her in the bed after my step-father left for Latvia and one morning her night clothes were still there but she was not. I asked, "Where is Mummy?" and my grandmother said "She has left". "What do you mean she left?"' Eva had tears in her eyes.

'It took me some time to understand that she was not coming back and that I would join her one day soon. "Why did she not take me with her?" "Why did she not say goodbye?" I received no suitable answers. Much later in life I asked her, "Why did you do that? It was so painful! You should have explained." She said she just could not say goodbye to me. It would have seemed final. "You just could not understand," she said. But it was wrong.

'I slept with her night clothes each night because I could still smell her body smell. I only lived for the day when I would see my mother again. That anticipation made my life in Vienna tolerable. We had to move a number of times into ever smaller apartments. There was ever less money, there was no more pampering. Restrictions increased. There were fewer people around. My father, step-father, mother, and now one of my aunts had left. It was a blur, a loss, a not belonging. At night I had mother's night clothes. During the day I had the satchel she gave me for my sixth birthday. And always I yearned for my mother. That allowed me to cope with the other fears, because they would stop once I went to my mother. Sometimes I felt great fear that I might not see her again.

'Then one day Aunt said, "It is time, we are going to see your mother". I did not want to leave my grandmother whom I had always loved and to whom I became more attached while my mother was away. But we took a train to Berlin. Aunt went to a hotel where it said "No Jews or Dogs allowed". I whispered, "We can't go in here" but she dragged me in and told me to pretend that I was not Jewish, we were simply on holiday, and I was Aunty's daughter. At dinner a German officer bought us a drink. I was very frightened.

'The next day we went by train to the airport at Königsberg. Aunty was going to leave me and I was to go on the plane by myself. We got to the gate where we were to part and I started to be sick again, I vomited. I told her I was not going on that plane. It had a swastika painted on it, it was German. She screamed at me and eventually she gave me a gold watch. She reassured me. I screamed, "I want my grandmother. I love her one per cent more than my mother". I knew something terrible would happen to me in the swastika plane. Everything bad had been done by people wearing swastikas. Even today I would hesitate about sending a six year old child from Melbourne to Sydney with a stewardess. How frightening it must have been then!

'So I arrived in Riga with vomit on my dress. My mother and stepfather were there to greet me. It was a wonderful feeling. I was still a bit angry, but my mother was so happy and relieved to see me that the anger dissolved. I did not ask her then why she had left me.

'It was waiting time for the US visas in Riga. In the meantime my grandmother joined us. In fact three visas arrived but no visa for grandmother. We were not going to leave her behind. Her visa would arrive too, and we would all be safe. And so I went to school in Riga for three years.

'I was picked on in the choir. Maybe I did not sing well. "You, you, with the red hair! Get out!" yelled the teacher. I felt that I would have liked the ground to open under my feet. I slowly left the room in front of the whole choir. You know I cannot remember a single Latvian word to this very day. I have no memory of the Latvian voice.' Perhaps it was thus that Eva retaliated for her humiliation.

'In 1940, when I was eight, the Russians occupied Riga. I remember soldiers looting, and a sense of oppression. The biggest change to my life however, was having to learn Russian at school. But in fact there was a much bigger change. I slowly realised that the family would not go to America. A light had gone out. I was bewildered and asked, "So if not to America, where are we going to go?" And my mother and then my step-father just answered, "I don't know".

'Because our family had German passports (even though designated with J for Jewish) we had to register as aliens. Then in 1941 the war broke out.

'A day or so before the Germans invaded Latvia we were ready to be evacuated. My parents said that I might as well have my birthday present now, and they gave me a doll. There I was sitting on the suitcase with my satchel in one hand and this beautiful doll in the other, wearing the gold watch. I was frightened but also excited thinking this could be an adventure. There was a siren and we went to the cellar. When we returned the Russian soldiers told us in the last minute that we could only take two suitcases between the four of us. This caused chaos. But I kept my three precious objects — the satchel, the gold watch and the doll. They took us by truck to a high school for the night. There they took our valuables and they ripped my watch off. The next day they drove us to a railway station, they separated the men and women, placed most luggage in the end carriage, and loaded us on to cattle wagons. I still understood that we were being taken to safety away from the Germans. But I asked myself, "What has safety to do with separating us and shoving us into locked cattle trucks?"

'And so we travelled packed like sardines for six weeks from gulag to gulag. None wanted to take us because they were all full. You lose your sense of being, the sense of your body. Not being able to walk you don't sense your legs. You're hungry, you're thirsty, it is hot, there is a terrible smell, people have diarrhoea and are dirty and soiled and cannot wash themselves . . . There was no toilet paper, no modesty. Some played mental games. Others just sat and sobbed all the time. I did not cry. I just sat between my mother and grandmother all the time. I put a pillow over my head, shut my eyes and fantasised about nice things in Vienna and America. I could do this for very long periods.

'Yet the time seemed eternal. There was an ever greater sense of disorientation. I had my ninth birthday on the train. I felt that I would spend the rest of my life on it.

'One day the train stopped and the doors opened. The light was absolutely blinding. The first thing I saw was a chain gang. But I was relieved to see my step-father (even though shockingly bedraggled) come out of one of the other wagons. We were taken to a camp which turned out to be sixty miles out of Novosibirsk, in Siberia. Dogs, barbed wire and Russian guards with machine-guns greeted us. We had to live in brick buildings which housed a hundred people per room; on long bunks, forty centimetres per person. If one person turned over, everyone else had to turn too.

'Actually, you know, Siberia is beautiful. There were these silver birch trees, and I told myself that if I survive this, I'll plant one. I did just that here, thirty years ago. It was some kind of symbol — of life, perhaps.'

'You had become aware of death?'

'Oh yes. Well over a third of the camp inmates died. A friend of mine died of diphtheria.' Eva's voice became apathetic.

'It is extremely hard to describe the next six years. Somehow, those years became an infinity, yet also a condensed blur somewhat akin to the six weeks on the train. It is as if the six weeks were an introduction to the six years. You could not believe that it was happening. You were somewhere in the middle of nowhere and your desperation turned into conviction that this would be eternal. Being imprisoned for murder would have been better because there would be a predetermined end, however distant, and you would know why you were imprisoned. Unlike days worked in normal life, which are an investment in the future, the days survived in camp seemed to lead nowhere. I had to struggle against the senselessness and limitlessness of the situation. I tried not to give in even though I had so little control over my life. I also felt bitter that the Russians were supposed to save us but instead mistreated us for so long.

'Some events were highlighted in these otherwise dreary terrible years, when threat to life peaked for some reason. However, this was against the background of constant threat. Each day was a saga of challenges, unremarkable only because these days were like other days in a long continuity. If you read *One Day in the Life of Ivan Denisovitch* and multiply it by six years, that is how it was.

'We put our energy into surviving day by day. If one did not freeze, did not get burnt, did not have one's ration stolen, did not have a major disease, that was a good day. One tried to make each day a good day. But there seemed to be no end of days to surmount.

'The daily background included tasteless food on which one could hardly survive. Also there was systematic degradation. For instance, the weekly showers were controlled by outside taps which were turned hot and cold at will by guards who also peeped at us naked females. Towels were not provided. And again, quite senselessly, we were given absolutely no information about the world, such as how the war was progressing.

'Inevitably I felt a sense of resignation, but I also felt an underlying terrible fury because I did not understand why I was there — I had not done anything wrong. I had a lot of migraine and vomiting. That is how I react to stress.' Here stress meant suppressed fury.

Eva became wistful as she recounted her precocious resourcefulness. 'I knew that I was starving and that I would die if I did not do something about it. Around this time a prisoner returned from the Novosibirsk hospital looking quite strange — because he was well fed. He described the plentiful hospital food he was given there when admitted with scarlet fever. I noticed that he still had scarlet fever spots on his hand and I touched them in the hope of being infected with scarlet fever myself. When I did contract it a few days later I was elated. And further, I was taken to Novosibirsk hospital according to plan. And after I recovered from the illness I did eat plenty, whatever I could scavenge around the hospital. However, just as I was putting on weight I contracted chicken pox and mumps, and I nearly died. I vividly remember feeling that I was in a tunnel being whirled at great speed toward a light at the other end. I said, "I don't want to go. I don't want to go". I started to improve soon after that. And after recovering again I did return to camp well fed. People laughed at my funny fat appearance now. Then I developed severe scabies and what with the migraine and vomiting I could not eat. I am sure that having improved my condition in hospital saved my life.

'One day without any warning whatever they told us that we were going to be shifted to another camp. The train journey was cruel. Grandmother had bad dysentery so we three females were put in the wagon carrying the sick. A friend of ours from Latvia called Mr Stern was bleeding and dehydrated. At each stop we pleaded for water for him but each time we were refused. After three days Mr Stern died. We requested to bury him and were refused even that. Because of the heat we had to dispose of the body. We were forced to push him out of the train. I still remember the thud his body made on the rough stones. It was total degradation and indignity. I liked Mr Stern.' Eva's eyes filled with tears.

'We prisoners were taken to the flat steppes of Kazakhstan. The physical conditions were much worse than in Siberia. Temperatures now ranged from +40 degrees centigrade in the summer to −40 degrees in the winter. Winds were so strong that we had to go to the latrines in small groups linked arm in arm in order not to be blown into barbed wire and then be shot as escapees. Food was poor. Clothes were rough next to the skin. I was forced to work in the fields. But otherwise the endless drudgery and misery continued.

'At one time both my mother and grandmother took ill, my mother with jaundice, grandmother with dysentery again. They were taken to the camp hospital. An older girl swaggered up to me and said, "My family are taking these lower bunks. You won't need them any more". My sick mother and grandmother needed the prized lower bunks so I said, "No, you're not having them". She said, "Yes, I am. Your mother and grandmother are going to die, so I am having them." And with that, I don't know from where I got the strength, I hit her so hard in the mouth that I knocked one of her teeth out. I was so angry. I thought, "Enough has been taken away, she is not going to take this." I kept the bunks and my mother and grandmother returned.

'I became aware that my mother's and step-father's marriage was disintegrating. This upset me very much. I also saw that my step-father was physically deteriorating, and I knew that he would die soon. Again I knew I had to do something. I was twelve and I took stock of my resources. I had been robbed of my gold watch long before. I had my satchel but in the camp it had no value because there was nothing to put in it. But I did have one big treasure in camp — my doll.

'It was very precious to me because it connected me to my normal childhood. But the doll was precious to all the prisoners because it represented normal childhood to them too. It was the only doll in camp. People would ask me if they could touch it. So I devised a barter situation. The tailor wanted the doll for his daughter and the cook wanted pants other than the horrible uniform ones from the tailor. I arranged for the cook to give extra rations to the tailor who then passed part of them to me in exchange for the doll. I gave these rations to my step-father and saved his life.

'But,' Eva added with her look of defiance, 'before I gave up the doll, and I really did not want to part with it, I made little holes in its head and back. Perhaps I was nasty,' Eva chuckled, 'but that way they did not get the same doll which was my precious birthday present.'

'To what extent did anger sustain you?'

'Anger did keep me going; for instance that the cook had food to eat while other people died of starvation. They were not going to get at me. The will to live kept me going. I also realised that people could be both strong as steel and fragile as eggshells at the same time.

'Another one of those unwanted highlights occurred later in that year of 1944. One day we were collecting food in the fields and it was getting dark. The guards were impatient and hurried us on. As I was running I fell into a cesspool — a collection of excreta in a seven-foot deep pit, lightly covered by earth. I screamed as I felt myself being sucked in. A friend grabbed my hand but she too was pulled toward the pit. A second friend came to the rescue. The muck was up to my neck by then. Eventually the two other girls pulled me out. The guards laughed as they checked me into camp. To this day I have nightmares about this. I am still scared that I might be buried alive and I still feel that I smell. I am fussy about mess and smells around the house.

'The next year I was thirteen. I had abdominal pains which were written off as periods coming on. The pains became severe and I was diagnosed as having peritonitis from a burst appendix. The commandant had me moved to a nearby prisoner of war camp where there was a German surgeon. His face was terrifying. He said that there were no anaesthetics. I was strapped down. I still saw the sadistic eyes of the German surgeon. I screamed for my mother but also out of deep animal pain. I remember vividly the excruciating pain of cut skin, the horror of seeing my blood, my green and blackish intestines piled up on my abdomen, the pain of being stitched up and clipped.

'"Now stand up," said the surgeon,"to settle things down inside." I was shoved into a vertical position. Back in our camp I was in a coma for nine days and nearly died for the second time. I had the same near-death experience as before.

'And then one day in 1945 we were suddenly told that the war had finished. We thought that we would be released soon but we were not. They kept us imprisoned for another two years. By then we realised that we might stay enslaved forever and we went on a hunger strike. People started to die like flies. Eventually some officials came from outside and apologised for having wrongly detained us in the first place. And so in 1947, we re-entered the cattle wagons, though this time they were not locked. We had another six weeks trip, on three weeks' rations.

'I was still wearing German prisoner garb as I got out at one of the railway stops. Suddenly I saw a Russian soldier a few metres away raising his rifle at me. It was an incredible irony that I should be slaughtered so senselessly after all I went through. "I am not a German!" I yelled throwing away the dead German's hat. "Nazi!" he called. "No, I am not a Nazi!" I screamed in Russian. People around went about their business oblivious of what was happening to me. Then I exposed my breasts trying to prove that I was a girl, but I had no breasts. Eventually another soldier from the slave labour camp convinced his comrade that I was not an escaped Nazi.

'At the Austro-Hungarian border some Austrian officials came to look at us and said, "My, my, you look terrible. I don't think we could possibly take you to a train station where they unload people, the Austrians would be too upset. We will take you where they unload goods and cattle." That was a nice homecoming!

'We were put up in a derelicts' house. Liberation did of course have its joys. Being able to have a shower, privacy, toilet paper, were luxuries to be savoured. And yet at first beds were uncomfortable, and the rich food made me sick.

'And then there was a great anticlimax. Really there was no welcome home. In fact, sixty-three of my family members had died. The only distant cousin still alive was embarrassed by our presence. There was no one to welcome me back as a child. My relationship with my mother had changed irretrievably in the camps. I realised that she really could not protect me. At times I had to protect her. The concept of mother had become lost. I had lost my childhood, a whole way of life.

'I had no father and I missed my step-father. To my child's mind my mother had "got rid of" two of my fathers. I vowed that I was not going to get attached to any of her husbands again. So when my mother quickly remarried I was not impressed. She married the man who came back well fed from Novosibirsk hospital after he contracted scarlet fever. My mother married him because, among other reasons, she had a passionate hope that someone at last would look after her and her daughter. The hope backfired and from my point of view the only good thing that came out of that marriage for me was that on his insistence I became educated. Within two years I caught up and got my matriculation.

'But Vienna haunted me. I was terrified of the Russian soldiers and hid in doorways. I had to escape.'

'I came to my biological father in Melbourne in 1949 when I was seventeen. It was very sad because my father and I were strangers to each other and he was not interested in me. His wife saw me as an intruder. But I met Stan, my husband, in my father's restaurant on that first day. I was still seventeen when I left my father and lived and worked on my own.

'I was nineteen in 1951 when I married Stan in London. A strange thing happened there which I could never understand. My mother had come specially from Vienna for the wedding and was leaving again that day. But I left the wedding without staying to talk to her, or to say goodbye to her properly. I now realise that it was a payback — for leaving me in Vienna without saying goodbye. This time *I* did not say goodbye.'

'What kind of person had you become as a result of your wartime experiences?'

'I think I am cynical. I am a strong person, I don't suffer fools gladly. I am quite independent, for instance I have never relied on drugs, I want to be in control of my life. However, sometimes I eat too much but I tell myself that after all the starvation I deserve a bit of indulgence. I hoard things, I think that one day they will be useful to me. I try to be kind to people because many people have been kind to me. I try to be a good friend.'

'I have not lost my capacity to love — my husband, children, my work. I am able to have sexual satisfaction. I don't know. I just tell myself if I am depressed, that there is only one way to go — up.'

'What did the years of nastiness do to your sense of morality?'

'I never did anything wrong. I did not steal, did not hurt anyone on my own account. When I knocked that girl's tooth out, it was because she wanted to steal my mother's and grandmother's bunks. There is nothing I feel guilty about. I don't feel shame either. I was not the only one who was covered with shit. Perhaps if I had walked like that in the streets of Vienna, I would have been ashamed.

'Of course my experiences have left their mark. I have recurrences of similar abdominal pains as I had in camp, though not as severe. But I have had two emergency abdominal operations. Matters reached emergency states because I could not stand doctors and avoided them as long as possible.

'TV shows on the Holocaust bring back nightmares of my experiences. But apart from these obvious relivings of the war, I have an overall sense that the war has made me indelibly different. You cannot live through six years of total lack of freedom and not be affected.

'Some effects are subtle. For instance I had little early schooling and no school friends. Altogether I have no peers with whom I shared my childhood. And even the local Jews have no idea. What could I tell my mother-in-law who said that Australians had it tough in the war — they had to ration butter, and nylons were hard to buy?'

In 1952, at the age of twenty, Eva gave birth to her daughter Lee. 'It was a difficult breech birth. Lee was difficult from birth. She was a self-assertive, demanding child.'

In 1954, when Eva was twenty-two, she saw her mother for the last time.

'Mother was forty-seven and was already ill with lung cancer. I think this was caused by the raw tobacco and tree leaves my mother smoked in the camp, though she also had a problematic life at the time. She died five years later.'

In 1955, Eva's daughter Lee was aged three, the age Eva was when her parents separated. Peter was born and had to stay in hospital for six weeks. Lee developed chicken pox and had to be sent away to her paternal grandparents.

By the age of nine, Lee was a stubborn, wilful child. To the grudging admiration of her mother, she went without pocket money for a year rather than relent on a matter of principle. At the same age Eva forgot every word of Latvian. At the age of seventeen, like Eva, Lee left home. Again, like Eva, she married at the age of nineteen. However, unlike Eva, who had established a stable marriage, Lee was on a self-destructive course. She was simultaneously openly angry and suffered abuse. Eva had a hysterectomy that year (her second emergency operation).

The turmoil continued for the three years of Lee's marriage. In these years Eva developed stomach pains and diverticulitis which have persisted to the present day. After the three years a daughter was born. Lee's husband left her while she was pregnant.

Whatever the subsequent distress, Lee was always loving to her daughter. When the daughter was aged three, Lee remarried, in the belief that the new husband would help to look after her daughter. Lee quickly realised that her husband was not going to fulfil her hopes, and that the marriage was disastrous. In the process of leaving her husband, Lee suddenly died. The coroner's verdict was open. Eva was totally shocked. She cried a lot over the years over this worst tragedy of her life. She again had to contain her anger about it.

Eva and Stan adopted the three year old granddaughter Cait — 'the consolation which came out of that tragedy'.

As against this, Peter grew up to be successful in both career and marriage. He obtained law and economic degrees and important jobs. He expressed his deep love of music as a horn player in the Melbourne Symphony Orchestra.

Over the years Eva developed a stomach ulcer, osteoporosis, arthritis and, in 1985, around the age her mother died, a myocardial infarct. Malnutrition and scarlet fever from camp and her other stresses may have contributed to Eva's illnesses. Eva also nearly died for the third time after she had an allergic reaction to an injection for migraine.

Eva was both wistful and defiant in looking over the latter part of her life.

'It is not time for me to give in. It is very important for me to do something nice each day and I appreciate and am grateful for each day of life and health which I still have. I do not believe in my family's tradition of ending marriages when they were not going well. I work out things with Stan and compromise when necessary.'

Eva has been very creative with her craft work. There were the many many soft toys which I mentioned. Referring to the many dolls in her grand-daughter's bedroom she said:

'Maybe it is for the doll I lost in the camp. Maybe it is for my lost childhood. The children had to use sticks for dolls in the camps. It is a challenge to make something nice from scraps. I love making donkeys. Sometimes they are a misunderstood animal. They are not stupid, like people say. They are tenacious, they dig their heels in a bit, they are a bit stubborn.'

We laughed as we recognised why Eva felt warmth for the donkeys.

'They are a bit mournful,' Eva added.

Eva joined the Child Survivors group.

'I am the treasurer but there is not enough money to abscond with.' She laughed. 'I was not sure whether I would belong. But though I find the meetings very traumatic, they also provide relief and I get a lot out of them. I can talk without feeling self-conscious.

'I also enjoy working in the Holocaust Museum. I like the company and preserving the truth for posterity. The truth should not be wasted or destroyed by revisionist propaganda. My story is part of this truth.

'And the truth is that there are some things you just cannot get over. I lost nine years between when I left and came back to Vienna. Six years in camp is just too much time, too great a chunk of my life. I had enough excitement in my life to last me two or three lifetimes. Whoever dealt me my cards put a few jokers in and a few very hard hands but I tried to play them as best as I could.'

Comment

Indeed too much happened to the richly loved spoilt little Viennese girl as her life's fabric tore around her. In passing we may note that to the extent the term Holocaust is used only for Nazi-occupied Europe, Eva experienced 'only' the 1938 harassments. But Eva's experiences show clearly that the Holocaust extended its tentacles beyond Nazi occupied areas too.

Eva's experiences demonstrate the cascade of increasing stresses typical for the Holocaust. First the stigmatisation, exclusion, then uprooting into ever more congested places, leaving one's town and country, deportation, imprisonment and slavery with deprivation, humiliation and death. The only mitigating circumstances for Eva were that she was not in an extermination camp, and the fact that she was surrounded by her mother and grandmother, with her stepfather nearby.

In Eva's case the stresses did not decrease at the end of the war or even with liberation. There was the disillusionment, the dashed hopes, new father and changed and unavailable mother. As against the major near-death experiences which kept intruding as clear memories or dreams, subtle effects left indelible marks on Eva's daily approach and moods, relationships, and physical symptoms. These were like concentric ripples taking a long-term toll, including across the generations.

It was notable how many physical illnesses Eva had suffered. Starting with her migraines, we may speculate that some of Eva's other illnesses were also related to physical and emotional stresses directly or indirectly related to the Holocaust.

On the other hand, what gave Eva her remarkable resilience? It is possible that the presence of her mother and grandmother, their loyalty to each other, and their devotion to Eva were very protective. And even if her mother's initial disappearance was traumatic for the little Eva, at least she reappeared and survived. So did her other closest relatives. And Eva was given opportunity, even if delayed and covert, to feel anger. So she preserved some sense of security and some measure of defiant anger of the normal child. This defiance gave Eva spirit in her grey eternity, hope even as she was giving up her doll to save her step-father.

However, perhaps it is impossible to unmake such a long brake on normal development and expression. For instance, until recently Eva has been unable to express overt outrage and rebellion, and to fight openly for principles and values. We may wonder whether her daughter expressed some of these feelings for Eva previously. On the other hand, Eva has been able to express her feelings of love and care in her new family and in the use of her artistic talents to provide pleasure and comfort for others. Her toys and dolls make sure that other children will not be robbed of them. They also help Eva to retrieve some of her own robbed childhood. Eva is making the best of her difficult hand.

Danial

—•—

'I DEVELOPED A

VERY SEVERE

EXPLOSIVE STAMMER'

*D*ANIAL'S BIRTH OCCURRED AT the same time as his family's Holocaust. How does major trauma around birth manifest in later life? And how do these manifestations differ, if they do, from other, not infrequent traumas around the births of children? Is the lack of memory for the events protective, or an excessive burden? These were some of the questions which went through my mind before I interviewed the youngest child survivor.

Danial arrived punctually. He was mild-mannered and very softly spoken. When I asked him to raise his voice, he could do so only for a short time. At times Danial had a mild stammer. At such times he repeated, or had difficulty expressing a word. At times he withheld his p's and b's and then they exploded with some excess of breath.

I AM DANIAL KOGAN. I am married and I have a five year old son. I am an artist. I was born on the 30th of October 1943 in Vichy, France.

'I think it is best to start with my parents. My father was born in Czarist Russia into a very wealthy family who lost all their possessions in the Russian Revolution. The family emigrated to Rumania. My father studied accountancy in Vienna, and then settled in Paris in 1928, where he established a wholesale leather business. This went bankrupt at the beginning of the war. His brother, a doctor, was employed by OSE, which cared for Jewish children whose parents had been arrested, or who wanted the organisation to give their children shelter. His brother obtained employment for my father in OSE.

'His main job was to obtain food for the thirteen staff, and over one hundred children in one of their homes in Brout Vernet near Vichy.

'My mother's background was very different. She was one of seven children. Her father died in the First World War, and the family was very destitute. She only had one or two years of schooling. From about the age of seven she looked after the house and the youngest child who had a deformity. Eventually she followed an older sister to Paris, and my parents met at a Jewish Rumanian ball there. After marriage they lived a prosperous middle-class life. Mother was not able to have children at first, but my uncle organised an operation, and she was able to have two children — Fanny and Albert. From my mother's account this was an ideal time for her.

'Fanny was almost seven and Albert was two and a half when I was born. My mother was nearly forty when I was conceived. My cousin Betty, who was living in the home at the time, told me that she overheard my parents having a very bitter argument about my mother conceiving. I gather I was . . . I was . . . I was . . . unwanted.' This was the first evidence of Danial's stammer. 'Because of my mother's age, and the wartime situation, abortion was not available or not thought of. When the time came, my mother went to the Vichy hospital. She was obviously anxious, and she arrived too soon. The doctors, knowing about the circumstances, gave her the opportunity to have the birth induced, which she accepted. Three days after my birth my father, brother and sister were arrested. Again my cousin Betty is the source of my information. She kept a diary of the events and she read it to me one day. She described being in her room, hearing the sound of jackboots echoing around the house. Eventually she was summoned downstairs. She had false papers indicating that she was a non-Jewish local. Because she had played a lot with Fanny and Albert, she was worried that they would give her away as part of the family. She described how my father was sitting down, very calm, very tranquil, and the children followed his lead. They showed no recognition of Betty. The three were taken to Drancy, a transit camp near Paris. Fanny had her seventh birthday there. In December they went on convoy 64 to Auschwitz. The documents of my father's death list that he died of pneumonia. There is no documentation of the children's deaths.

'There is another account dealing with the arrest.' Danial went on without a break. 'It is from Betty's mother but she sometimes distorts facts. She was also there at the time of the arrest, working as a domestic, also on false papers. She described how the Germans searched all over the institution for my family and could not find them. As they were leaving, a French woman told them that they were still in the house, so they kept searching and eventually found them in a wardrobe. My cousin, and one of the boys, Shimon, who was fourteen then, also mentioned that they had hidden in a wardrobe.' I had the impression that Danial would rather not have had this fact confirmed, perhaps because hiding in a wardrobe contrasted with the description of his father's quiet, exemplary dignity at the time of the arrest. Danial described the following with affection and pride.

'Not having met my father, I tried to obtain information about him from many sources. It seems that he was easygoing, and liked to play practical jokes. At the same time he was not so much imposing, but someone you could trust. Shimon related how father had tactfully sidelined a difficult teacher. He inspired people to keep going. So my father's arrest was a great shock to people like him [Shimon].

'When my father gathered food for over a hundred people at the home, he travelled around the countryside with my mother, and with some of the older children, such as Shimon.' Danial conveyed how close and yet how infinitely far was this father who gave shelter and nurturance to a multitude of children.

'The people in the home decided not to tell my mother about the arrest of her family. When she eventually had to be told, she went temporarily blind, and tried to commit suicide.

'I received this information from my mother only some years ago. I still do not know exactly when mother attempted suicide, or how she attempted it. I was not so interested in information then as I am now . . . The hospital kept us as long as they could, but after some months they had to discharge us. Then for some further months we roamed the countryside, going from contact to contact where food had been obtained for the home previously.

'But then the money ran out, and there was no food at all. I only know this because a palmist asked me when I was thirty why I had starved as an infant. At that time I had not taken interest in my early life, but my mother confirmed that there was a period of starvation during which she fed me walnuts which she had first chewed up herself. Her milk had dried up when she heard the news of her family's arrest.

'During this time . . . my mother came out with this story out of the blue while we were having a cup of tea. In the home there had been a Dr Bass. She was decorated in the First World War, and she knew some Vichy generals. Through this contact my mother obtained a pass to visit the Gestapo headquarters. Her mission was to try and find out where her children were. She arranged for a couple to look after me and keep me if she did not come back. She was kept waiting all day at the headquarters. Then she was seen by a minor official. She was given no information.' Danial skipped to another period.

'After the war we returned to Paris. My mother married someone she had known before my father. He was divorced, and had an eight year old daughter. Mother had a husband, an older daughter and a younger son once more.

'Monique, my new sister, related this story much later to me. It was my sixth birthday. My mother transformed the candles on the birthday cake into a *Jahrzeit* [memorial candles] for her two children and started to cry for them. Monique screamed at Mother in anger. This episode was also my first ever memory.' Danial said even more softly than usual, 'My memory was that something happened that I was responsible for. I hid under the table. It was too dramatic.

'We were still very poor. I had no toys. It was good to have a family around, but my mother was still very distraught. I remember once rushing into my step-father's workshop telling him that she had died, because I found her on the floor. My mother told me much later that she suffered blackouts at the time. My mother's emotional state did not allow her to be ready for a relationship. Her relationship with Monique was also disastrous. The marriage ended. I met them eighteen years later.

'About six months into the marriage I was thought to have TB, and I was sent to an institution outside Paris, run by nuns. I was there for six months. During my therapy I recalled the excitement of the preparations for going to this place. I was happy in the train. It was an adventure. I was interested without being anxious.' And now came one of those offhand stories akin to mother dropping something momentous out of the blue over a cup of tea.

'I already had a history of being separated from my mother, because she had had a traffic accident and she was in hospital for nearly a year. I was about a year and a half old then. It was after the war already. I was placed with some farm people. My cousin Betty had visited me there, and she told me later that I seemed dirty, but nevertheless very happy.'

Danial changed smoothly back. 'But on the train my mother took me aside and whispered to me that I was going somewhere where it was important that I did not reveal that I was Jewish. She was extremely well meaning because she believed that the nuns would treat me better if they did not know that I was Jewish. However, my only understanding of being Jewish was that my father and brother and sister were killed in a most horrible way because they were Jewish.' Now Danial paused between words. 'This set up a conflict within me, because the people looking after me were my potential enemies who could kill me. I had to be careful but I did not know what Jewish was, though somehow I was Jewish. I had not previously connected me being Jewish with my father and brother and sister having been Jewish.' Danial had no idea about the significance of circumcision. His mother had not explained it.

'My memories lead me to believe that I was highly anxious during that time. One memory involved Betty who was twenty by now. She and her fiance arrived with a large parcel. I unfolded many layers of newspaper and there was a book at the end. My memory is that I was so enraged, really angry, that I kicked them.' Danial's voice was very low. 'My memory was that I was bitterly disappointed with the present. But in my therapy I learned that I had wished that they would take me away. When I was thirty-five, I mentioned this incident to Betty. She remembered the incident quite differently. She remembered me undoing the paper layers very, very quietly. At the end I just looked at the book and then I stayed in a passive state until they left and then she turned to face me and I was still holding the book looking very . . . empty. She cried.

'Another memory was me walking along a corridor, and there was a lady, and children who were having a really good time. On the way there was a room, and in it were Jewish children who were very misshapen and ugly, and they were Christ killers. There were other shadowy figures and in the dream [till now Danial had not mentioned that this was dream] I did not know where to go. So I presume that I picked up information about Jews and Christ in this place.

'In another incident I was sick, in a dormitory. The bed adjacent to me had a statue of Christ and I remember making a deal with Christ that if he made everything okay, if he brought back my father, and I got well, I would become Christian. And I remember getting out of bed and praying.

'The last incident there was in a chapel, on a Sunday I think, and it was a beautiful day, with sunlight, and I was sitting next to a really young nun, who was very effervescent, very full of life. She showed me these little cards which were reproductions of paintings of the life of Christ. As I remember the incident I thought that these images were just the most beautiful things. Something happened in the exchange between her and myself. My fear . . . perhaps I came to realise that I was not in a position to be harmed. That was a very major exchange . . . My cousin Betty used to take me to the Louvre with Michel, her later husband — I think this was when I was four, so I think I had a grounding earlier with art, and this was a connection with a good time in the past. And I still feel a glow. It was a very important moment with the nun. It gave me an understanding that there was a connection through what I saw as art . . . that I was connected to . . . that I wasn't as separate. I think it had a very important influence on me choosing to be an artist.'

'My now separated mother and I went to New York for six months and then we arrived in Sydney in May 1950. My mother's sister Rachel and my cousin Betty followed us to Australia.

'During this time in Sydney Betty taught me how to play, and I played with children in the neighbourhood. I was invited to birthday parties, and Betty threw me a birthday party too.

'I was eight, and I cried on that day. It was not until my therapy that I did not cry on my birthdays.

'When we left Sydney to come to Melbourne, that was probably my most traumatic move. I was back in isolation. I was in my room all day, my mother being at work. The children in the street were different. They were Jewish, but I did not identify with them. One day I left my room and bought six ice blocks. I presume I bought them to give one to each of the children in the street. But I just rushed past them, back to my room.

'We rented a room at the back of a house. In the front was the first intact family I ever knew — a mother, father and child.

'I was amazed by normal home life. For instance, instead of tiptoeing around an ever tired mother, Merv woke his mother one morning, and lo and behold she got up to make his breakfast, and apologised for sleeping in.

'That had a very strong impact on me because I realised how much

I had missed out on. I came to realise that my father was absent and I cried every night for my father ... We played a game where I stood in front of the house and looked out for Merv's father. When I glimpsed him on his bike I would rush in and tell Merv. He would then come out and greet his father. The game was that he pretended to pay me by the minute for my watching. Years later he told me he must owe me thousands of pounds. I used the situation to fantasise that it was my father coming home.

'Also, the only time I invited a boy home, I just cried the whole time. I didn't know why. Perhaps having a friend pointed out to me my emptiness. It was just emptiness.

'My mother worked long hours in a factory. She was fifty by now, and wanted to marry. One time she went to meet a prospective husband. In the house there were visitors, laughter in the kitchen ... good times happening. I got a whole lot of paper, piled it up on the floor and I lit it. I rushed in and told the people. It shows me how disturbed I was.'

'Why did you do it?'

'Well, I was extremely angry that I was not in the kitchen. It was a cry for attention.

'I coped by fantasising a lot. There were no books, my mother did not read. There were no pictures, magazines, or toys even at that time. I developed the ability to fantasise in the institution, where we were forced to rest a lot.

'My mother did remarry. This time the marriage lasted twenty-five years. My new step-father was a concentration camp survivor. He was also fifty, and he had also lost two children in the war. A daughter older than myself had survived but had no contact with her father.

'My mother and step-father battled and argued all the time. My mother told me not to antagonise him, because he would take it out on her. They argued in Yiddish. Eventually I secretly learned Yiddish.

'And my mother used to get back at him by, for instance, putting garlic into everything she could — he did not like garlic. She never fought him openly, it was like in *The Color Purple* where she spits into her husband's lemonade. My mother also gave me the best cuts of meat.

'Soon after my mother remarried, when I was nine and a half,

I started to develop a chronic stammer. I had a slight stammer before, but now it developed into a very severe explosive stammer. I used to jerk and dribble with it. I had it worst between ten and fifteen.

'My step-father was extremely angry, raging, though not physically violent. Looking back, they were both purging themselves of what had built up. My mother was very guilt-ridden, and this was a sort of punishment. But I was trapped in the middle. Also, by now, I was an extremely well-trained child. I was very quiet and introverted. I never rebelled, and yet through things I could never understand, I did things to upset my step-father, just by my presence. So there was no other means of release for me . . .'

'Release for what?'

After a long silence, Danial said tentatively, 'It was a form of anger . . . and rage.'

'Why was your mother guilt-ridden?'

'Basically for surviving, abandoning her two children. I mean I have sifted through the things that have happened, and I have built up a picture of the relationship my mother and my father must have had.

'Some years ago I met a teacher called Dybnis from the "colony", as the home at Brout Vernet was called. A few minutes after we met he took me aside and he said he wanted to tell me a story about my father. The story was that my father had built up a strong relationship with the local policeman. The policeman came to my father and he told him that he had received notification that my father's family, and the Dybnises, were to be arrested. The Dybnises of course made arrangements to escape, taking with them several children, and they managed to escape to Switzerland. Miriam Dybnis told me that she pleaded with my father to [at least] allow her to take Fanny. Fanny had been their bridesmaid, they had a strong relationship. And he wouldn't. She said that my father sat down and played a game of patience. He would leave it to the cards to determine whether he would leave or stay. Obviously the cards told him to stay.

'I talked about this to my father's brother, the one who got him the job in the colony. He told me that OSE had understood the situation to be critical and arranged for both my father's and my uncle's family (his wife was also pregnant at the time) to escape to Switzerland. This was in August. They chose November the 6th. It was already arranged that they would be accepted in an internment camp in Switzerland. My uncle was shocked by my father telling him he had decided not to go — that he felt reasonably safe, and that my mother didn't want her children to be in a camp. My uncle told my father this was absolute madness. But he did not change his mind. My uncle told me that where it concerned my mother, my father was not actually dominated, but she had the final say.

'After the policeman warned my father, he rang my uncle and told him. My uncle pleaded with him to escape. My father said that my mother would never forgive him if he took the children away. I don't think my mother connected these things, but she had strong guilt. She did attempt quite successfully to project some of the guilt on me, because I grew up thinking I was responsible; because she used to tell me that they did not escape because she was pregnant with me.

'And the pattern was established fairly early on, because my cousin Betty used to visit me in the hospital when I was only a few days old, and I was covered with a rash, and I cried the whole time, and Betty was very upset and she came to comfort me, and my mother said not to bother because she said I was crying for my brother and sister (that is, for what I had done to them). She would never acknowledge that she contributed in any way. She could never do that. But I think unconsciously it was there for her.'

This was a roundabout way of answering, yet not acknowledging why Danial developed his explosive stammer.

'How do you think she saw you at the time — denying you comfort, attempting suicide?'

'I really don't think she had the capacity at the time to focus on anything other than the loss of her two children. I mean she looked after me very well materially. She denied herself many things. But emotionally she was not able to give very much.'

We took up the thread of the story. 'I went to a speech therapist between the ages of eleven and eighteen. He was someone that I really focused on. I went to see him once a week, and it was like a haven. I also liked school very much because compared to my home life it was a very safe environment. It was predictable.'

'How did you get on with your mother during this time?'

'I had been her main focus till this classic step-father came on the scene. I tried to induce her to concentrate on me. One way to do it was the stammer. Another way was having pains in my legs, for which doctors and hospitals could find no cause, so they were probably psychosomatic. As a younger child I was sick a lot, but apart from the TB I don't know with what.

'At the age of twenty-five I met my father's elderly aunt in Paris. She and her husband managed to escape to the mountains in France during the occupation. My father rang her too from the home when he found out about the impending arrest. She told him to come up to the mountains with the children. It was relatively safe there, and they had enough money to live on. She said that he refused. At that time I did not question things more deeply. I did not ask why he refused. I did not even know why she came out with this story all of a sudden during lunch. I did not understand what she was saying. I subsequently understood. I also discovered that my father had a live sister in Rumania, and an uncle in Israel.

'I also met an early friend of my father's. She said they went to Charlie Chaplin movies, and my father laughed himself silly. I got all these little glimpses. Up to that time the only information about my father came from my mother, and she never really talked about him. If I did something she was displeased with she said, "Well, really, you are not like him," especially if she thought I was aggressive, which I wasn't.

'I may have given the impression that I was extremely compliant, and to a degree I was. But there were some instances where I did not do what my mother wished. Then she came out with these statements. When I came back from overseas [at the age of twenty-five] with slightly long hair she got unbelievably upset, to the point that she ripped out her own hair, and her false teeth came out. Admittedly at the time I had decided to move to Sydney, and I did, for six months.

'I also went overseas in 1991. This time I was much more prepared, I asked questions, and I found out more. Basically the things I mentioned. My father's father came from a family where he did no work except study. When the family lost their money it was my father's mother who opened and ran the business, while my grandfather continued to study and pray. These background things possibly explain more my father's decision to stay.'

'How do you understand that decision now?'

'Well, I don't really. After I gathered the information I let it go. It is not for me to work it out. It was like, it was his decision . . .'

'It is not for you to blame?'

'No, no way! When I told my story to the Child Survivor group, some asked me if I blamed my mother. I don't. The blame lies totally on the people who worked out the programme of annihilation. My focus is very clear as to who is to blame. My father was a very ordinary person, and he didn't have all the information. He had a kind of armour around him which protected him from seeing the real menace. He just focused on domestic things. I mean I can't blame him for that. He did not know what would happen in the Holocaust then.' Danial was unusually emphatic defending both parents.

'And yet you grew up steeped in an atmosphere of personal guilt and blame.'

'Yes, everything was permeated by the Holocaust. I mean food . . . if I didn't finish my food . . . I mean your brother and sister needed that food, how can you not eat it?! It was like a criminal act. And there were no books, magazines, in the house. Only photographs of dead people.'

'How did you feel toward those dead people?'

'I did not have strong feelings toward them. When I attended the *Yom Kippur* (Day of Atonement) *Yizkor* (memorial) service [at the age of eleven], I read through the passages for my father, brother and sister. I felt absolutely nothing. I tried to, I felt abnormal. But in my prayers I could have been referring to the Queen of England. Actually I had more feeling for her at the time. In my therapy I came to feel wronged at having been robbed of a brother and a family, but it was not specific, and it was idealised, according to what I have come to learn about families.'

'What made you go into therapy, and when did you first go?'

'I started when I was twenty-five. I attempted suicide, and it was suggested that I go to a psychiatrist.' This was another piece of information which dropped out of the blue. 'I went for a few years without gaining much. But then my psychiatrist started primal therapy and I found that fantastically useful. That's where a lot of my anger and rage surfaced. The therapy was in a safe room, all padded, and there is a person called the sitter there all the time, basically to protect you, and help you to extend yourself.'

'What anger and rage?'

'It focused primarily on my mother at first. I hadn't allowed myself to be angry with her as a child. Now I had a chance, I was very angry with her. I spent a very long time, I mean a couple of months, eight hours a day, five days a week on that.'

'Anger and rage for what?'

'It was her not seeing me; looking at me but not seeing me. I'd try to reach in . . . it was very early in life. I could never retrieve actual memories, it was more a feeling . . . It was entering a tunnel type thing, it was kind of never ending, never reached a point of contact.'

I felt that Danial was describing the tunnel between a baby's and a mother's gaze, but for him the tunnel was empty, never reaching the end station of mother's eyes.

'Then I spent a lot of time on trust, quite a few months . . . My experience was that nothing was as it seemed. All my childhood my mother taught me not to trust anyone. My mother doesn't trust anyone. When I came out of the primal, I had a lot of respect for my mother, I'd got through the anger and rage to a certain extent, and then I saw that, given the limited resources she had, she had definitely done the best of her abilities. This is the way I came out of therapy. I was a lot closer to her, and a lot more open in my relationships. I was more trusting, and it enabled me to fall in love, get married and have a child.

'But interestingly, although I had done so much therapy, and put so much focus on trust, it's only very recently that I've felt comfortable with the outside world. Going to the Child Survivor group has made a very big difference. For the first time I was in a group where, no matter what I said, there would be certain people in that group who would understand what I was talking about. It was also very important to be in a group where people had been through similar experiences to me in some ways, and had survived. Because I had heard of others who had suicided.

'Also the group has helped me to feel grounded, to belong and even to be uplifted at the *Rosh Hashanah* (New Year) service for the first time. I had been disillusioned early with orthodox Judaism when a rabbi answered my question about the Holocaust in a pat way, "We cannot judge God." I persevered with reform Judaism, but even there at first it was like in the kitchen. Everyone was happy, and I was alone. Even more recently, when I went regularly, in the process of my wife converting, she came out radiant, I came out tortured. But this time I felt comfortable, so that's what I mean — trust.

'It is interesting too that since going to the group, I have been able to remember my dreams for the first time. In one dream I was in a concentration camp. As a boy I had very bad nightmares.

'I see my story as one fragment of the stories which make up the Holocaust. It's almost beyond being a witness now. I am an artist now. Some of my art deals with Holocaust issues and that's very much where I try to project my own intensity. What I experienced at the *Rosh Hashanah* service indicated that I wasn't caught up in the Holocaust thing. It's like I'm . . . I'm nearing fifty, and it's like I've found a tribe, I can go beyond the Holocaust. My work, I have several projects to do with the Holocaust. It is very firmly part of my life, but now it is not . . . well, for the first time at *Rosh Hashanah* I was not personally lumbered with it. Though I still accept that it is my right and my obligation to do work on the Holocaust. It is part of what I've earned, to do this, but it is not as if it was going to purge me of anything, or anything like that.'

After a pause I asked, 'Danial, why did you attempt suicide?'

'When I started to gain some control, when I started earning money, I wanted to control my whole life. I had been very influenced by my speech therapist. I tried to emulate him. I dressed like him. I looked exactly like him. So I ended up at the age of twenty-one as fairly WASP [White Anglo-Saxon Protestant]. It wasn't that I denied being Jewish, or that I denied my Holocaust background, but it did not seem to have any relevance to the direction I was taking in my life. I also started to be a homosexual [I was amazed again] and I chose to be part of that group. I had several relationships, one very successful. I owned a house and I was offered a lectureship in an art college, and I was only twenty-four. I was successful. I no longer stammered. But I wasn't basically satisfied. I was deeply unhappy. I assumed the identity of what a successful person was without actually integrating myself. Then, too, my mother did not treat me as successful. She wanted me to be a doctor. She never accepted my direction.

'Then one day the weather changed. It was January, it was very hot, then it was stormy. I just went to a doctor for tablets in order to commit suicide. I took enough to knock me out for three days. It was a touch and go situation. I never really planned it, never thought about suicide, I just did it.

'Then I went overseas, and the first thing I did when I came back was to change my name from Cogan to Kogan. My father had changed it from Kogan, because it indicated that he was foreign and Jewish in France. After my contact with my family, it was my first step to acknowledge that my background was very important to me.

'This was also the time I went to Sydney and I took six months off to paint. I started to paint Holocaust themes.'

'Can you tell me about your sexual development?'

'At first I chose a lot of older men, obviously father replacements. I feel very positive toward my homosexual experiences.' Then less certainly, 'Looking back at my childhood and what happened to me, there was very little possibility that I could develop the kind of relationship I have now with my wife. Basically trust was the problem. I felt I could trust men more than I could trust women. My mother was so all-consuming to me, I just could not have another relationship with someone like that.

'I changed my orientation gradually after primal therapy. I married at the age of forty-two, and I have a five year old son.' Danial spoke with much affection of his new family. 'On my recent trip Liz [his wife], joined me and my uncle on our visit to Drancy. That was a real bonding experience for the three of us.

'One of the reasons I wanted to join the Child Survivor group was because I knew I was putting some feelings of the Holocaust on to my son. I have looked after him quite a lot from the time he was four months old . . . The main thing is that I never had a father, and he has one twenty-four hours a day, and I spent a lot of time and energy with him . . . It is not a big deal for him [we laughed], and he does not treat me with the respect . . . He is growing up to be very stable, and he is generally very wonderful. He has a lot of toys, like, a huge amount of toys. He got to the stage where he wanted more and more and nothing would satisfy him . . . A couple of days after my talk,

I felt a furious rage with him for not being content, and I realised that I definitely overreacted, I thought it had to do with the talk. So I did a primal session. In it I got very quickly beyond anger with my son. I got into an absolute rage with the German people in the Holocaust period, the Nazis, something which I had not allowed myself to do before. It had not seemed relevant to get angry with them. They'd be eighty years old now. But in the session it was relevant. I was extremely angry and disgusted. In the past I had been angry with myself, my mother, my therapist, but never with the perpetrators. I feel much stronger since that session.'

'What damage did the Germans do to you?'

'Well, they made my family into . . . they caricatured my family, they transformed my family from a very ordinary normal mundane family into something to exterminate. They robbed a two and a half year old boy of his life and they made the last few months of his life most horrendous, as well as my sister's life. And I can really identify with my father now that I am older, of having to watch the disintegration of his family and the inhuman treatment given his children. Nobody has the right to do that.' Danial's voice rose. No stammer here.

I asked Danial what the lack of memories had meant to him?

'Even though I don't have the memories, I have the scars. It's like waking up and wondering "How did that get there?" I've had to spend a phenomenal amount of energy working out how it did get there.

'And much of what got there was through my mother. She never surmounted, never got beyond those events, they were always there. The crime was always there, in every aspect of my experience. She was just an ordinary person. She did not have the resources to deal with such events. They really had no right to do that.'

We reviewed the traumatic circumstances around Danial's birth. We agreed that from his mother's point of view Danial was the wrong child, at the wrong time in the wrong place. He prevented her being with her two children, in death or in Switzerland.

'You may have had to carry the blame for your mother's messed-up life all your life. What about the counter blame, that she messed up your life?'

'I don't really feel that. I don't feel that my mother has messed up my life.'

'Why that rage with your mother?'

'It was an infant's rage. For not being nurtured. I don't have a rage with her now. I am angry with her. Basically she pisses me off a lot of the time.' Danial's speech was uncharacteristically fast and well modulated. 'But I'm not enraged with her. I do feel an obligation toward ending our relationship in the best way possible.'

We returned to Danial's art.

'My first Holocaust painting was a portrait of my grandfather. He was very religious. I knew little of the Holocaust, but one thing I knew at the time was that there had been deeply religious Jews who went to their deaths praying. My grandfather was holding up his hands, which could have been as in an arrest, but could have also been praying. This represented for me the ambiguity of the whole Holocaust question. It did not relate to my actual grandfather, who did not die in the Holocaust, but it related to my personal experience.

'Then I did other Holocaust prints and paintings, but the most successful one is "Mother Icon" which is really my experience of my mother. Most of my paintings are psychological ones. "Mother Icon" refers to my mother and her loss. It is fragmented. I am trying to make the fragmented process of the work reflect the actual content of the topic. I have not attempted to resolve what my mother's experience was, or to make a whole which would explain it, but a larger fragment which I think is all I can do with the Holocaust.

'I wanted to do a series of paintings on adult survivors, but it was not right. Now that I have met child Holocaust survivors, I am really keen to do the series. I can use my own experience, because I can really identify, and because I feel a part of this group. But I want to use my experiences to try to get beyond the personal, that is looking beyond issues just relevant for me, making it a part of the whole human experience, not just Holocaust ones.'

Comment

Yes, children can be affected by traumas which they were too young to remember, and be influenced by them throughout their lives.

Danial's story is a clear indication of this. Danial also demonstrates that the lack of memories is indeed a lack, a deprivation, because without memories the scars one carries in the form of emotions and behaviour are believed to be senseless and irrational. This is because the scars cannot be connected with the original wounds. Further, because there are no words or concepts for the original traumas, they cannot be integrated into higher level views such as of parents, blame and identity. Thus Danial did not have the tools to know about his unhappiness, nor even why he had the impulse to kill himself. Danial needed to apply himself to much detective work about the past and himself to reach the original traumas, and the unspoken haunting dilemmas which were spawned by the hideous wrenching apart of Danial's family.

Danial first attempted to take control of his life in his late adolescence. He rebelled against his mother and tried to merge into a new group identity. Danial became a WASPish Australian, and he modelled himself on older homosexual men. Yet the falseness of this identity overwhelmed him. It was better to be dead than false, to be forever not seen for himself. Possibly, too, death was where paradoxically he could be most recognised. This was because mother only recognised dead children. Or perhaps he could expiate his guilt at last. Then again, maybe he could be together with his father and siblings. These are of course my speculations, not Danial's, and they may or may not have elements of truth in them. The point is that, at the time, Danial could not know who he was. He could not speculate about his unhappiness in a constructive way. Without memories Danial was vulnerable to unidentified forces within himself.

We see then that the extra vulnerability of the younger child is not only physical. Danial was not only physically at death's door as a young child. He was also totally helpless psychologically and socially. He was at the mercy of carers, mainly his mother, whose life and ability to care were severely distorted. From the start, Danial's mother saw his birth as wrong, and she blamed Danial for the family's Holocaust. She idealised the dead and blamed Danial, her living child.

It is a tribute to the human spirit and the ingenuity of the human mind, that Danial not only survived, but started to flourish.

After his suicide attempt, it was as if Danial had paid death its due. He now started to struggle with life. He affirmed his identity as a Holocaust survivor, and later as a Holocaust painter. He entered therapy and he achieved space from his mother.

Into that space came anger. Primal therapy deals with the earliest conflicts in life. Danial was able to express the infant's rage for his mother not recognising him. This allowed him to recognise that, considering her condition at the time, she also devoted as much as she could (a tremendous amount) to his survival.

But one anger was not allowed. It was blame of the parents, especially of mother, for the three deaths. Of course Danial is right in saying that his parents were ordinary human beings whose foibles could not be blamed for the Holocaust; that the blame rests with those who engineered and perpetrated the hideous crimes. But in the psychology of human beings, much of which evolved to deal with crises at the family level, family blame and guilt arise. Someone had to be blamed, and it was Danial. He had to carry both father's and mother's guilt. Even though mother purged and punished herself, she still blamed him.

Danial suppressed his own anger at his misfortunes, except for his loud explosive stammer. In therapy he expressed his infantile anger for not having been recognized. After the Child Survivor group, Danial became enraged with the Germans. His stammer disappeared.

Danial returned a number of times in the interview to the matter of possible escape before the arrest. But he always stopped short of blame and anger. It is hard to be angry with a dead father and a long suffering deeply bereaved mother. In fact, Danial protected them both and had not wanted this part of the story to be published unless it was seen as important. It is a mark of Danial's courage and integrity that he raised no objections to the current comments.

How did Danial extract himself from his inauspicious beginnings? In his deeply deprived background, with not even a toy to hang on to, Danial nevertheless found objects of hope, beauty and love. His cousin Betty supplemented the meagre rations of maternal recognition and care. Later there were male objects whom Danial found, such as the gentle speech therapist, and perhaps his primal therapist to whom Danial could scream out his anguish. Finding a group of people similar to himself further enhanced Danial's sense of personal validity.

Art has been very important in Danial's life. It connected him to the early caring Betty and a future life of hope and security symbolised by the vivacious nun. His paintings perhaps serve Danial as a vehicle to create something meaningful from his own fragmented past, which could in turn be meaningful for other children whose lives have been fragmented. This is what his father did with the children in the home.

Against all odds, Danial did carve out a space for himself in the world, a niche of love and belonging, giving and creativity.

'Anne'

—•—

'I WANT TO STAY

ANONYMOUS'

I HAD BEEN SEEING *Anne in weekly psychotherapy for over two years. I have not asked any child survivors in therapy with me for interviews for this book. However, Anne approached me for an interview. She considered that having one could be beneficial to her and her family. After some discussion, I agreed.*

Anne stipulated that she wanted to remain anonymous. She still feared retribution from her persecutors who had threatened to kill her if she ever exposed them, and she was still ashamed of her story.

What follows coherently, Anne had told me over two years in fragments, each fragment costing her great hardship and suffering. This interview was the first time that Anne integrated the fragments in a thread which unequivocally made up her story.

We met in my rooms. Anne felt more comfortable surrounded by the walls 'which know it all'. She sat in her usual seat. Her voice throughout the interview, as in her sessions, was slow, soft, and anguished. She sighed.

$\mathcal{T}$HIS IS GOING TO be difficult. I have only talked about these things once before in fifty years.' Tears crept into Anne's eyes.

'I have to start my story from when I was three and a half. Many may say, "What does a child of three and a half remember?" I have no doubts about what I remember. I have talked to myself about it, I have seen it in front of my eyes, in my pictures, slides if you like, and I can see myself in them.

'So, I am three and a half or thereabouts. I have no memories from before this. We are in France, and my mother, father, two little children younger than myself, and myself are moving into an apartment in Paris. I remember the apartment very well. It was a one-room apartment in what I now know was the eleventh district. Many people like us [refugees] moved into that area. There was no furniture nor suitcases being moved in, just the family moving into a furnished apartment. I was very happy.

'I do not know how long we were in the apartment. It was long enough for me to remember to this day the worn carpet, curtains, all the furniture, pictures and outside surroundings. I remember my father sitting in the corner sewing. I found out that he was a tailor. He seemed to be a tall man, very red haired, and very white skinned. I do not remember his voice very much.

'My mother seemed to be short and fat, but thinking about that later in life, I realised that she had two children after me, and so her pregnancies would have made her appear fat to me as a child. I do not remember her voice. I do remember my voice, and the children crying, but there was peace around. There was cooking at one end.

'I so wanted to go out and play. It seemed to me that I had not had much opportunity to play before, and I was not allowed out. But one day,' Anne blew her nose, 'my mother said I could go and play. I ran down the two flights of stairs to the courtyard, surrounded by tall buildings. I was happy to be out. It must have been close to winter, when the afternoons were short. I remember that my ball had rolled down a lane. I ran after it but there was a person standing at the entrance to the lane. At first I only noticed his strange, black, shiny boots. As I looked up, I saw the pants tucked in the boots. I remember the khaki heavy winter material. I looked up further and saw some red on what I suppose was his uniform, because he did not wear normal clothes. I stopped bursting with energy. I did not get the ball. I decided to run back home.

'I ran up two flights of stairs and into the apartment, full of excitement. But it was empty. I looked around. The children were not there. My mother was not there. My father was not there.' Anne wept. 'However, this did not deter me, I was not upset. "They just went out, and will be back," I thought.

'After a while I went to see the *concierge*. I can see her now, coming up the stairs to meet me. She said, "Your parents have gone away for a while, but they'll come back." And I believed her fully. I went happily with her.

'I am not sure what happened after that. She must have got in touch with an organisation which looked after Jewish children during the war.

'It did not bother me to leave the apartment, as long as my parents would be wherever I was going. So I walked with this lady from the organisation, somewhere in the country, I have no idea where, on our way to a French family. We must have walked some days, because I remember sleeping nights on the grass. I remember my clothes, because I wore them for the next almost seven years. A blue skirt, red shirt, singlet and pants, cardigan, a blue-grey coat, long socks and black shoes.

'The lady left me with the family, saying that she would return after three months. She gave them coupons for food and clothes for me, and money, to care for me and I suppose as payment for the danger in looking after me. The family consisted of a man, a woman, and an elderly lady. We all lived in one room in an isolated house.

'I had to stay in the house while they worked in the fields. I suppose they were in a difficult situation, me being so young and them not knowing what I would be up to. So they decided it would be best to tie me up on a chair while they were out working. They bound my legs and arms, and then tied me in a kneeling position to the back of the chair which was placed as far away from doors and windows as possible.

They left a piece of bread for me for the day, which I could just reach with my mouth. They warned that they would beat me if I made a mess. So I was left, aching and in agony. When they came home late at night, they untied me. They put me out, like you do a dog, to perform my toilet needs. But I was a fussy little girl, and when you are told not to mess, and you are not left out long enough to relax, you can control it. So I never wetted or soiled. And even now, as then, I can control and not go to the toilet for weeks, or even months, in spite of the stomach cramps and headaches. Because the way I was left that first day, I was left the second, and the third day, for three months.

'They screamed and yelled at me, called me names and hit me. I felt I was a nuisance, a worry to them, and I felt sorry to be causing them so much trouble. So I said very little, and took my punishment. I slept on the cold winter floor, but I learned not to sleep. Maybe I was too tired or cold. My clothes were taken off me after I arrived, and I next saw them only when I was leaving. I was left in just my singlet and pants, socks and shoes.

'I do not know whether I was cold or hungry, nor what I thought or did during this time. I just stayed, and it seemed a long time. But I do remember that I did not cry. You see, there was no need, because my parents would find me, and all would be well. So the agony did not matter. I waited. I just knew my parents would come. They were clear in my mind, as they are to this day, the way they were when I left them in the apartment. I was totally convinced that they would materialise, if not today, tomorrow. And if not tomorrow, definitely the next day. And we would continue in the apartment, or possibly somewhere else. This was more important than hunger, or anything.

I just adapted to the new conditions, did exactly what I was told, and waited. Whatever they did to me did not matter. I lived in a dream world in which I waited. Compared to the next seven years, that experience was not so bad. I could take it.

'After three months I was dressed in my good clothes. I was told that I looked spotless and lovely. So the organisation lady (they were always different women) took me to the next family. Each lady was nice. None asked me how the previous family had been, and I did not tell them. I became very, very quiet in a very short time. It was because I was thinking of my family, and anyone talking to me was an intrusion into my thoughts. I had no one in the world who was mine, except the family I thought about. I also did not talk because I was threatened a lot. If someone said that they would kill me, I believed them. And there was no time limit to the threats. Nor were there other children whose experiences could soften the threats for me.

'So again we slept out. My next memories may relate to the next family, or the one after that.

'The lady left again, and as always, I felt strange in the new family. Some things were always the same. For instance, like the others, they took all my clothes off, just leaving me in my singlet and pants for three months. That used to worry me greatly. I was fussy about my clothes, they were mine. Again, there was a place on the earth for me to sleep, never a bed or a pillow. No toilets, no mirrors. I remember clearly that I could never see what I looked like. The food was again bread and potatoes. I did not know what a vegetable was. I do not even remember drinking the water.

'So I behaved as I had learned to do in the previous family. I was four and a half or five and keen to please, so I knelt on the wooden chair. But this family did not want me to kneel on a chair. Instead, when they went to work they rolled a sort of sheet around me, and tied me up against a long plank at the end of the room. I was left standing against this plank, unable to see anything but the wall in front of me. So I looked at the wall, and waited again. They did not have to tell me to control my bowels, because by then I was fully trained. They also threw me out for a while at nights.

'Their threats were slightly different. They still yelled and screamed at me and blamed me. But this time they told me that they hated me because I was a problem, a nuisance, I was the cause of the war, whatever that was, and they did not want me. They hit me with their hands, and a leather whip. They liked using it, I think it got rid of their aggravations. I had no idea at the time that they benefited from my coupons.

'There was nothing else around, so I could not run away. And anyway, how could my parents find me, if I ran away? But it was taking a while now. I was beginning to be lonely, I started not to feel so well. Apart from my constipation pains, I had pains from the hard sleeping conditions and the beatings.

'In addition to the usual couple and old woman, there was a younger man in this family. He was big, and was always friendly and laughing.

'I liked the fact that he took notice of me, while the others hated me. Then as well as laughing at me, he started to tickle me. I did not laugh back, it did not feel amusing, but I looked towards this man. Then at nights he took my singlet off and brushed himself against me. And he took my pants off. I did not think there was harm in that. He was taking notice of me and I felt good when he looked and smiled at me. I suppose it was nice when he paid me attention.

'But, I don't know, he had no clothes on, and I had never been near anyone naked. I did not like the feel. He told me not to make any noise because it was night time, but I was on the floor, which was cold and hard, and it hurt my back when he lay on me. Then one day he threw himself on me. I was only little, so this hurt and crushed me, and I could not breathe. I could not cope. I became constantly sick with coughs, headaches, stomach aches, leg aches, the gashes where they hit me. I ached from top to toe.

'I do not know how he did not squash me to death. I came to hate the whole thing, him. I hated him playing with me, rubbing himself against me.' Anne's voice shook with suppressed sobs. 'And he . . . wanted me to play with him, his penis, and every part of him. Well, I did that. It still did not worry me as much as him squashing me. It became a regular ritual.

'I remember saying something to the lady about him squashing me. She yelled and screamed at me. She called me a liar, and said she would punish me by putting me in the oven. She took me to the oven, opened it, lifted me, and I thought I was going into the roaring fire. I did not fight, I was too afraid, and shocked. I felt the heat. Sometimes I wished that she had put me in there . . . because now it meant that this man would continue as before. And he did.

'Well, I became dumbfounded, terrified and speechless. I did not cry or scream. I did not say a word to anybody any more. I put up with his body . . .' Anne blew her nose.

'Came the day, I was dressed up nicely again, and the lady took me away. I worried about many little things, for instance lice crawling in my hair. But now I had this new fear, of a man smiling or talking to me. I was very glad to leave. And I thought my mother or father must come now. I needed them, so they had to come. But we walked toward another home.

'The lady talked happily, and told me stories. I trusted her enough to go to the toilet. But she did not ask about my experiences, and I stayed in my own world. Sometimes I asked the ladies about my family. Some said that they would come shortly. Others overlooked my question. I was trained to not burden others with my questions.

'The war must have been in full swing by now. But I knew very little about it, or indeed about anything. Religion meant nothing to me, and not having seen other children I did not know about them. I was quite afraid of the new home. The people in it seemed to be the same. Again there were two men, as well as a younger and an older woman.

'Like the other families, they all screamed at each other, and at me. My own family never screamed at me. They were quiet, I cannot even remember their voices. But these people's screaming I can hear even now. I did not talk now. I did not cry, I just did what I was told . . .' Anne's voice trailed off. She blew her nose and became silent.

'They had beds in that house, though not for me. The man lay in after the others went to the fields. And I lay on the floor. He invited me into his bed, and I went. The bed was very high, so he pulled me up. I saw nothing wrong with that. I just needed someone to take notice of me. And I thought this was going to be good. But he was rough. He picked me up and threw me around. I became frightened and remembered the last man. This was not what I was looking for.

'Then he pushed me between his legs, and he wanted me to put his penis in my mouth. I did not know the purpose of this, but if I was told to do it, I did it. But it was too much for my mouth, and I started to dry retch and feel sick. He held my head down and kept me there with his legs. He was moving up and down, and my throat was aching, my mouth was not big enough. There was this odour, this liquid. I could not stand the smell, the sight, I could not get away. I just wanted to be sick and I could not be, because I could not get away. He became rougher.

'He threatened to tell the others. I was afraid of that, I did not think anyone else should know. Not because I knew it was wrong, only because I did not like it, and I felt sick. To me, I suppose, that was life. I believed that what happened to me happened to everyone.

'Then he began to use me from the other end. He pushed my legs away and tried to . . . I did not know what he wanted, nor what to do. Whichever way I put my legs, he threw them some other way. He hurt me, and he tore me. I was full of blood, and I was very afraid. I could not have screamed or cried if I tried. I was just numb. I would have done anything at this stage, just to finish whatever he wanted to do and be left in peace. But it seemed to go on and on. Everything was sore and stung. I could not even breathe properly.

'Then he threw me on the floor and left me there while he stripped the bed. Then he hit me and screamed saying what a terrible girl I was. I could not understand why I was terrible. I found a cloth and with my spit I cleaned myself up as best I could. I could not stand or lie, or move, so I just curled up and stayed there for the rest of the day. The others did not notice anything different about me. When they threw me out that night to go to the toilet, there was no way I could go.

'This ritual took place many times, perhaps once every two weeks. He was a big person. I can see him, me, the room, the surroundings. He was determined to penetrate me, and he did. I certainly wanted to die then.' Anne cried. 'I was quite a small girl, and I ate little by this stage.' Anne developed violent head and neck aches as she was talking, just the same as she had during the period which she was describing. 'I still suffer a lot of these headaches,' she said.

'I still did not think there was anything wrong in what was done. No one told me it was wrong. As a child, you have to be told something is wrong, otherwise it is not wrong. I was often told that I was the cause of whatever anxiety was going on in the world, and I accepted that. I thought that I was wrong.

'The man kept asking me to hop into his bed. He spoke with a soft lovely voice at first, and each time I thought that he liked me. I liked that, even though I knew what I would have to do. But there was no way out, so I did it. Obviously I did not respond well, because he always became very angry, angrier and more violent each time. I had bruises everywhere, I was blue.

'I do not know if there was ever any satisfaction for him. But he just did it again and again, me bleeding from the time before and the time before that. I can feel the sting and the pain now . . . I just feel sick.' Anne cried for a long time. 'I came to not be keen on him at all. Nobody noticed my aching and bleeding.

'I started to wonder what was going on — why were my parents not there? Seeing as I suffered so. They obviously could not know, otherwise they would be there.

'I could not stand up any more. I could not even make it into the bed. So he slapped me, threw me to the floor and yelled at me.' Anne cowered. 'I can hear him yelling. I became very, very ill then. I could not move. I was so sick that they had to take me to a hospital. Not the family, but the lady from the organisation who picked me up. She carried me to one of their hospitals. I could not walk.

'I was suffering from malnutrition, I was told. That is why my stomach protruded and I could not see my legs. I had pneumonia and tuberculosis. They shaved my hair off because I had lice. When they undressed me they found out. I did not tell them anything. They had to work it all out. I was told not to tell, so I assumed you do not tell — ever. I could not forget, so I only told myself and just suffered within myself. I did not tell anybody, until a few months ago, after fifty years.

'I was in hospital a long time, perhaps a year, and I was happy for the first time since my parents disappeared. I had doctors looking after me. They gave me mustard wraps, and they drew fluid off my lungs with a flame and curved glass. Somehow I trusted them, perhaps I was too weak not to. But I still waited for my parents. I was sure that I would see them, because here in hospital people visited the sick.

'I was very, very happy to be in hospital. So happy that I missed the fact that my parents had not come. I had all these people to look after me, and I liked that.

'However, I had to leave. I was seven and a half now. I was feeling so good, I was healthy, almost as happy as when I was three and a half. And this lady picked me up to take me to another home. On the way there I found out,' Anne's voice quivered, 'that I was not going to see my parents . . . I asked why . . . And she said that they had died. I asked about the children. She said she did not know about them. I could not understand all that. Maybe I did not want to. Here I was so happy, and everything that had happened flashed in front of my eyes. My parents had been the only people I was going to tell, and now they were not going to be there to listen to me.' Anne was anguished and incredulous.

'All of a sudden I did not know which was worse — the sickness before or now. I was sick again, but this time differently, mentally. That was the first time I cried since . . . since ever. I cried, and I was so sick, and yet I had just come out of hospital feeling so well. It was not a bodily ache from beatings and abuse, it was an ache in my head. I had such headaches suddenly, and I developed such mental blocks!

'My parents were not there, and they had not been there previously for long enough for me to remember enough of the good times. So now I imagined them. I saw them in fantasy, I lived with them, talked to them. I was off the air for periods of time when I did not know what I was doing.

'In one short time I came to see things so differently. My whole life changed. I came to think that everything that had happened was because my parents had not been there. You could say that I blamed them. I was angry with my family in fantasy for not being there to help me.' Anne cried with intensity. 'I needed them, so I blamed them . . . But I forgave them. I said to myself, "Oh, well, I feel better now, so it doesn't matter." I had grown up quite a bit in that little time. But I was concerned about how I would lead the rest of my life without them, as well as having now lost faith. I had lived in such hopes till now, and they had virtually carried me through. And so I worried. I had nothing tangible from my parents, such as a toy, doll or book. I did not know what they were. I only had what was in my head, and this had changed now.

'So I went on to the next family. This external lifestyle obviously had to continue. But this time it was different. I was going there knowing there would be no parents to rescue me. So I was very depressed. I had been quiet before, but now I became really quiet, and moody. I was in a different world. I tried to live in the past, the little bit of the past which I could remember. And then I tried to imagine what life would have been like had my family been around. How different it would have been.

'I still had no idea about Germans, that there was a war on, or about the world generally. So I could only imagine what life might be like if normality had persisted. I still had not confided in other children, nor shared fantasies with them. I missed my little sisters more, I wanted to hear them crying, to tell them off. I missed my parents, and the apartment, the only home I could remember. I thought more, but had no one to share thoughts with. I had no relations, I have never had relations, not before, and not to this day.

'I felt very miserable to be alone. I did not forget what they looked like . . . but their comforting . . . them being around . . . Many things had happened since I had been that happy three and a half year old. To know that I would never see them again changed me completely. White to black. I became frequently quite depressed. I had trained myself not to talk before, but now I really did not talk. I was in a world of agony of my own.

'So again this family had four members, two men and two women. I was old enough to work in the fields now, so they made sure I did. I had to go barefoot on the stubbles of harvested wheat, in an old dress and no pants. My job was to collect the heads of the wheat. My feet bled from the cuts, and I could hardly walk by the end of the day. Within a few days my legs were full of sores and blood.

'In a way I was happy to do the job, because it allowed me to forget the bad news. But it was tiring, what with the work and my having trained myself not to sleep at nights. This was in order to be awake in case my parents came, and to be on guard against the men. I definitely just could not sleep. And it is amazing how this became a lifetime habit. I sleep two hours these nights with a tablet. Without it, I do not sleep.

'So one day I fell asleep in the sun for a while. I was woken up by this man standing over me wetting my mouth and face with urine from his penis. I was really frightened. There was no one around. Then he put his penis in my mouth. But after being forced to swallow two mouthfuls of urine I could not face that. I screamed for the first time in my life. I had a different outlook by now.

'So he hit me about, lifted my dress. I had no pants on. He went about it in the same manner as the previous men. I can still feel the wheat stubs piercing my back. I was fighting it a bit then, trying to twist about, but he was stronger than I was. So he penetrated me with such strength, such force . . .' Anne trailed off and wept silently. 'And he squeezed me, he wanted me to hold on to him . . . I thought that he was going to go through my body, and he was hitting me as well. I still did not know what to do. Then he left me, and I stayed there for a while, until I could pick myself up and take myself back. The others saw my cuts, but said nothing. It was a lesson for me not to sit down on the stubble.

'From then on he would grab me suddenly from behind as I was bent over working. Sometimes he used his hand, sometimes he tried to push his fist up, ram it up. I think I had changed. I knew I did not like this way of life. All these smelly people who did not have baths, I was sensitive to smells, and I was starting to smell like them. I could not say anything, and no one would have believed me. And then they were doing me a favour having me, though they were cashing in on it.

'I had to have my tonsils out, because I always had bad throats. I was eight and a half now. The lady who picked me up took me to a small hospital. This was one of the very few times that I saw other children, though from a distance. I thought they were small adults.

'They wrapped me up in a sheet. I had to be placed on a man's lap while the other operated, without anaesthetic. I do not know which hurt most, the operation or sitting on the man's lap while he held me. I hated that. In the end I managed to not sit on his lap, but to stand between his legs. Then I had my first icecream, and went on to another family.

'This family had three children. The youngest was twelve. I was approaching nine, but I still did not know how to behave with children. We all slept in a bedroom. There were beds, but not for me. The two oldest girls and the mother went off to work early (the woman did most of the work on the farm). The youngest daughter was in her bed, and I was on the floor.' Anne squealed in pain, and sighed.

'The father asked me to come to bed and lie next to him. I never said no. I still had hopes, I think. I lay there for a few minutes. The daughter pretended to be asleep. Then he was nice to me. And he squeezed, hugged and kissed, all the things I thought I would want. But of course it was the same thing again. It started with the mouth, he got desperate quickly, I was in agony. Then he started with my backside. I already had enough trouble with my backside, but he forced himself in there. It absolutely took my breath away. I thought that I would choke. The daughter did not move, though this was hardly silent work. I was in so much agony, I did not care any more, it was better to die. If I had to lead a life like this, without parents to help out, I might as well be dead with them. I did want to die,' Anne said in a grim whisper.

'I went to school for the first time in my life. But the youngest daughter told them at school what I was doing with her father. I still did not realise that it was so wrong, except that it caused such agony. But the children told everyone, pointed at me, teased me, and they all kept well away from me. After only two weeks I had to leave and stay at home because I was causing such an uproar. I so wanted to die.

'I thought that maybe I could find my mother and father. So I cut my wrist with a pair of secateurs. But I could not stand the blood and I fainted. So I just lived . . . existed, with that family.

'He threatened that if I told he would put my head into a large bucket of snails which he collected in the garden. Eventually he did. He turned me upside down and put my head in a bucket of water full of snails, with foam at the top. I screamed and screamed, until my head was submerged, and I swallowed the water. I am petrified of water to this day. I also learned that there was no way I could fight anything. I had to put up with anything he wanted me to do till the three months were up. And I did.

'Whether daily or weekly, I cannot remember, but I had to put up too frequently. He tried anything, but I could never satisfy him, and then he bashed me. One day he poked a broom up. Another day he pushed the broom up my backside. I would have to do the sucking, and oh . . . And the rest of the time he would speak and behave nicely to me. The three months came and I went in the same clothes. This must have been near the end of the war, because I was taken back to Paris and I was placed with a Jewish couple.

'They were very nice, but I was difficult. I would not talk, I was always sick, and I could not eat or sleep. They did not know what to do with me. Another couple came and said that they wanted to take me to Australia and that I would be happy there. I did not like the people who wanted to adopt me, and I did not want to go with them. The husband was meek and mild, and I was not scared of him. I probably kept away from him. But I was afraid of the woman's loudness and accent. It took two years for them to be able to adopt me, an eternity to wait for the promise to make me happy. Another reason I did not like these new parents was because they had asked me what I would like the most. I had heard about dolls, so I said a doll. But it had to have shoes on. They promised they would get it for me, but I am still waiting for that doll. I was very unsettled.

'I wanted to stay with the couple who looked after me for those two years. They worked in an OSE hostel, caring for children who came back from concentration camps. It was only now that I learned about the war and religion, and being Jewish.

'I played up a lot on my new adoptive parents. For instance, I pretended I could not see and needed glasses. I thought people would like me with glasses. The trouble was I could not see with them, but it did not matter, because I got what I wanted for once.

'I was also becoming very aggressive, stubborn and obnoxious. I decided I'd had enough, people were not going to tell me what to do. However, I had no say about my adoption.'

'So I came to Australia in 1948 without dolls or toys. I still did not know what fruit or chocolate were. I was eleven, but I still could not read. Prior to coming here I changed my name. I wanted to forget the name which my parents had given me, to make the past gone. I wanted to feel a different person, who had started a new life.

'It took my new parents ages to teach me how to read the time. They became exasperated with me, and they started to hit me. It was a bad start to the new country, but now I see it could not have been easy for them either. I felt that nothing had changed. Promises were still being broken.

'And the desire for the past to be gone was only imagination, because there was no way I could forget the past. I kept thinking about it all the time. I have spent the last fifty years thinking about it. Hardly a day goes by without me thinking about it, and that is why I remember quite vividly. I have remembered only important events, others I have pushed aside. So what I have talked about is not every moment of my young life, but some occasions of the seven worst years.

'We lived in a country town, and I went to my first real school. I liked it. Children were interested in me, I was different. A rich local family paid for my private education, and I visited them on weekends. My step-parents punished me for this. I wish I could have done better with my step-parents. They were not the family I needed. The years with them are not joyous to remember. But I cannot put all the blame on them. I have never put the blame on all the men either. Maybe there is something about me that people do not like, something about my character that people cannot cope with. I may be difficult for strangers to like. And yet I was prepared to like them all.

'It was a relief to marry a nice man, ten years older. It is strange, I have a husband and children who could not be better to me, I have been really very, very lucky . . . and yet, I am very lonely, never happy. How dare I be happy? Whenever I am happy, something pulls me up and says, "How dare you!" I know it makes no sense. Sometimes I forget and am happy, and then I suffer, and become depressed. Because my whole life comes before me and reminds me.

'I was very determined to have my children. Being literally an only child in the world, I missed children, especially my own two sisters. So I was determined to have at least three children, to make up. Also, perhaps through their lives I could see what I could have had. I had three lovely children, but I have not been able to get my memories out of my system.

'My children, and their children, are the most important things in my life. And yet, I am upset when I am with the grandchildren, because I see . . .' Anne cried with grief, 'I see what good lives they have, and how different mine was. So when I should be happy with them, I am really sad. I know it is wrong.

'Yet I can love my husband and children. I can even have sex, up to a point.' Anne sighed and was silent a long time. 'I do not know whether there is not still a fear there sexually. I do not know if I ever enjoyed sex.

'I have been able to develop a few intimate friendships. But . . .' Anne added emphatically, 'they know nothing of my past. To outsiders I appear as a very happy person, good fun, always sick, but without a hang-up. I keep the tears and the sadness to myself.

'I have not been sick enough to be in hospital, but I have never been well. I have shocking headaches, bad backs, terrible necks, and I am very often depressed. Since the children have left home, I cry a lot which I did not do before. Slightest thing, I cry. One wrong word, look, I feel sorry for myself. I hate myself for this, I really do. My family has now seen me cry like this many, too many times. I do not talk to them, and they just overlook my behaviour. They do not know what to do with me.

'When I look at my family, I think that I have every happiness, yet not a day goes past when I do not have a bout of tears. My whole life comes before me, too vividly. It is very hard to forget, or even put aside all that passed.

'I would like to think that what is in my head is not true, I would love it if someone could say that some of it is wrong, that I imagined or read it, it is someone else's story. I would almost be happy if someone said that. But no one could do that. I have seen no one from three and a half onwards, family or friend, who could say that to me. I have been in touch with people in France, in Israel, the OSE. No one knows anything about me. OSE said that during the war they destroyed all papers relating to me for my safety. So I only have post-war documents about my parents and me, and what is in my head.

'I went back to Paris to the address of the apartment. I did not go in. I did not want to recognise too much, I still do not want to. I discovered that it was not the Germans who took my family, but French *gendarmes* who collaborated with the Germans. The Germans were not even in France at that time. I have read about these events only very recently. I could not and did not want to till now. I was afraid.

'I worked out that my family must have been denounced by a neighbour, a friend, or the *concierge*. Many families were collected like this in trucks which went up and down the streets of the eleventh and twelfth districts. Why I escaped, I am not sure. Whether my mother knew, and she sent me out to play to possibly escape; or whether the *concierge* let me escape, I do not know.

'Really, I still do not want to talk about these things. When I do, it is not like reading a book, it is having to live through it again, and I have never wanted to keep feeling the misery of it. And I particularly did not want my children to know, especially about the sexual parts. I did not want to explain what I had to do. It is not nice, nor something that they have to know. They can read about these things.

'I think I was afraid . . . well, I was embarrassed, I still am. I was not ashamed then, but I am now. Having read about these things I have learned that you are a disgrace for having done things like that. I do not think of the age I was then, or the force upon me, I think of the act of it. I feel as if I have just done it, because I can feel it, still feel the agony and the ugliness. I know that I am forced, but I am the one doing it. It is me who is there. I don't know, I have always taken the blame myself. I am ashamed of myself.

'I have had moments of regret about starting therapy. I do not know if it has helped yet. Well, it has taken a long time to get this far, now I will see if it will do me any good.

'I belong to the Child Survivor group. I have ups and downs about it. I will never tell my story to the group. I do not really think the group has made me feel better, but I do not like missing it, in case something may be said that may just suit me to a tee, and make me feel better. Perhaps a name will be mentioned, a link to my family. I know that my parents and sisters are dead from reading the French book of convoys and their names are in there as having gone from Drancy to Auschwitz. I have the dates of their deaths. Actually I was about seven and a half when my mother died. I found that out only recently.

'I am not sure that anything can make me feel better. I am a very pessimistic person. Israel does not mean much to me, so involvement in it does not make me feel better. I am happy to be Jewish and I would not wish to be different.' Anne cried, 'But I just wish I had not been born Jewish. Then I might be a slightly different person. I am still not sure who is better off — those who have gone, or those who are left. Maybe it is my fault that I have not done the best to help myself.'

'Why are you doing this interview?'

Anne cried. 'Well, first out of selfishness, hoping it will help me. Then, I think, for my family, yet I do not want them to see it. Lastly, because it may help others. But it does not change anything for me. It does not make it any easier . . . Not yet, anyway. Maybe in the future. I hope so.

'I still do not want to say my name.'

Comment

Children suffered cruelly in the war in many ways. Anne shows that it is not only tangible injuries and destruction which affect children. Nor are concentration camps, the ultimate solid monuments of inhumanity and torture, the only places where the very fabric of children can be torn apart. Children in hiding could suffer as much as anyone. Anne suffered being torn away from her parents, isolation, intimidation, physical cruelty, mental cruelty, sexual abuse and moral depradation. These attacks on childhood life could be worse than hunger and illness, and even death.

Anne shows clearly the courage, perseverance, and ingenuity which even small children can manifest in their struggle to survive, even in the worst of circumstances. Numbing her feelings and fragmenting the knowledge of what was happening allowed Anne to survive. And then, she lived with the inextinguishable hope that tomorrow, or the next day, or the next, she would be found by her parents. She imagined the relief of telling them everything, and how their comforting would make her suffering go away forever. And so Anne lived day by day, maintaining her connection with her past. Her fantasy was so strong that she could make what was happening to her in the present unimportant.

Anne demonstrates the power of memory and hope. The small child had very few memories to guide her to a normal world where she might grow into a normal person. Perhaps that is why she clung to those memories, literally for dear life, cherishing every little detail.

Involuntarily, Anne sought in each of her abusers, time after time, a personification of her good parents. Perhaps the instinct to satisfy caregivers and to thereby evoke nurturing in them was always present. But with each disillusionment, she sustained herself through her memories and her hope. There was a major crisis when she learned that her parents were dead. However, she used her more mature mental powers to both accept that, and simultaneously to create a more intense and complex fantasy life built on the few memories she had. This allowed her to survive, but at the cost of depressions and other symptoms. She continued this pattern throughout her life.

Anne again gives us cause to reflect on the perversion of morality where innocent victims take on blame. As a child she experienced a deep conflict between the natural desire to seek security from an adult caretaker, and the reality of that person threatening her life at the very moment of promising protection. Two moralities arose side by side out of this situation: a 'biological' life-preserving morality, which said that what was so painful and threatening was bad; and another 'parent-child' morality, which accepted parents and caretakes as gods whose actions and judgements determined good and bad. Anne's abusers told her that their actions were good and that she was bad. Compounding the two moralities Anne deduced that her sufferings were punishment. She could not be angry, except with herself. However, Anne still remembered in another part of her mind her original non-abusive caring parents. Anne tried to hold on to their morality and to pass it on to her children.

Throughout her life, Anne relived almost constantly all aspects of her trauma, including the moral conflicts.

It has not been a coherent internal life. Anne's images have manifested themselves in fragments of memories, unconnected feelings of depression and anxiety, surges of shame and guilt and physical symptoms. But coherence would have re-evoked the suicidal despair associated with truly knowing.

It is a tribute to her strength, to the probable early affection which she had received and to her tenacious hold on it, that Anne developed her healthy side. She was able to work, raise a family and to lead a normal, even 'fun', external life. However, she has always felt that her hidden internal life was the significant part of her.

Anne is still struggling to establish her identity, which she senses may include grief beyond endurance. So she still has her family vividly in her mind. Sometimes I represent that family, at other times others do. Committing herself to the present means abandoning her old life-sustaining fantasies.

Yet through genuine care she is learning to trust and grieve. She is also learning to discern present and past. For instance, to play and enjoy herself is not always leaving her family to die. To expose herself is not necessarily to show her shame and guilt. Growing within her is a sense of herself as a nice innocent child to whom very evil things happened. Both that child and the adult she became deserve compassion and admiration. Perhaps Anne will soon dare to put the love of her parents in perspective, and come to enjoy with fewer complications the love of those who surround her.

Conclusions

— • —

Our ten child survivors were part of the ten per cent of children who survived the extermination machine of the Holocaust. They have bared their souls to us in order to show us what happens to children whose physical, psychological and social lives are murderously attacked. They want us to think about the damage done to children in wars and other traumatic situations, and to consider that children, hurt and are not are not expendable. Attacking children is attacking the most vulnerable and the most precious in humanity.

Further, our child survivors have shown us that an assault on a child is particularly cruel, because it lasts for life. The Holocaust became such an immense part of the survivors' childhoods that it wove itself into every intimate aspect of life. It was the backdrop, the overshadowing principle which accompanied every childhood development.

Children can also be assaulted by assaults on their parents. They are not unaffected appendages in adult dramas. Rather, they are vulnerable victims of adult powerlessness, inability to care, absence, pain, anger and scapegoating.

So when we examine how the genocide impacted on the surviving children's individual worlds, we must realise that we are dealing with issues of life and death for both children and their parents, and their ramifications over a lifetime. It is obviously difficult to summarise and do justice to such complexity. However, we must attempt somehow to digest what our witnesses have told us.

As we do so, let us bear in mind that our children came from normal pre-war Jewish families. Except for Eva M, the children's families had been intact. All indications were that the children were loved, except where the tensions of the Holocaust were already present. With the same caveat, the children had normal early developments and were physically and psychologically well. So we are dealing with the effects of the Holocaust on normal children.

For the sake of some coherence, let us now see how the Holocaust affected our children over the different chronological stages of their lives.

Wartime

Our children suffered the whole range of Holocaust experiences— the anti-Jewish laws; ghettoes; hiding in cupboards, forests and villages; arrests and imprisonment; separation and death of parents and family; slavery; physical abuse; sexual abuse and rape; mental cruelty, perversity and betrayal; shootings and bombings; heat and cold, starvation and disease.

These took place not only in concentration camps; but also in gulags, at home and in hiding. Anne's story is just as horrifying in its own way as Eva Slonim's. It is unwise to grade suffering according to where it took place.

Most children died in the Holocaust. Did the child survivors in this book differ from them? In fact, all these children had been near death and could have died. George, Eva M, Eva S, Anne and Danial had all been literally at death's door. Without belittling their individual triumphs over death, each child could have joined the majority who were dead, but for luck.

How clearly did children understand that their suffering was part of a plan to annihilate them? This varied enormously. Eva S came to know exactly. Anne hardly knew that there was a war on during her trials. Others only knew the terrors of their own parcel of the war. As George said, he was only aware of the children who were in Teresienstadt, not of the many more who had passed through it to their deaths. For most, as for Frankie, the true magnitude of the Holocaust only came home after the war. But (like for adults) there was probably a world of half-knowing. Like George, all the children in their different ways stopped themselves from thinking 'too long or too deep'.

How did these children adjust subjectively to their threatening worlds? They accepted it. 'That is how it was,' said George. And, 'At the time it was normal,' said Richard of his cupboard experience. Only when Richard became fully aware of his and his family's inevitable deportation to Treblinka and death, did he acknowledge, 'This is not normal any more'.

Powerful parental examples moulded the new realities too. Richard's parents did not question the cupboard. Parental admonitions and threats were absorbed by the children along with their life and death connotations. 'You must not let on that you are Jewish!' So new realities were acted out with great conviction, while old realities were enclosed in another part of the mind. Children as young as four, such as Juliette and Bernadette, could order the new and old realities as required.

Children also adapted by being busy. Eva S ran messages. George went to museums and galleries and joined a gang. Richard did his physical and mental routines in the cupboard. Danial fantasised. Such activities gave the children a sense of some purpose and control, and took their minds away from acknowledging their realities.

It was important not to think, know or feel. Richard explained, 'If you feel, you die.' Partisans could not afford to grieve while fighting for their lives. These children were constantly fighting for their lives and especially at times when they might have felt most deeply. So children did not cry as they were separated from their parents, nor did they show fear when threatened with death. They came to hide their feelings in their everyday lives. George described this as not looking too deeply, Juliette described it as being level, Eva S equated it with animal cunning.

And yet, just as there was knowing and not knowing, there was feeling and not feeling. For instance, as Eva S said, there was constant fear underneath. In an untapped core part of the children, there were unexpressed emotions. They were always there, and yet they could be stifled into the background.

In summary, children concentrated on daily survival, busied themselves as best they could, and did not acknowledge in their minds or hearts what they knew and feared.

But reality always prevailed in another part of them. They could adapt and obey, even to the extent of forgetting to see, but they could not totally eradicate their unexpressed knowledge and feelings. At times the expression of knowledge and emotions served survival. When George's mother was about to leave him after the bombing raid his screams enabled her to stay with him. Similarly, Eva G's loud crying prevented her parents from being shot. Thus, at such times children's expression of emotions could save their own, and even their parents' lives. Emotions could burst through in more benign circumstances too, as when Juliette cried with joy when she saw her teddy.

So children adapted according to parental models. They depended on their parents to protect them from the threatening world. While parents did that, children stayed close and obeyed. But when parents were helpless, children could reverse roles with them and rescue them.

All our child survivors experienced their parents being suddenly wrenched away at some time. As noted, children's responses at such times were surprisingly appropriate to the situations. Examples were Bernadette's flight and Juliette's obedience. At the same time, the children could not process the meaning of what was happening and felt stunned, bewildered and confused. Yet they were able to behave as required, and in their sudden new situations, assume new identities. Older children grew up very quickly and assumed semi-adult or even fully adult roles, such as Eva S, Eva M and Richard. At times they actively protected their parents, and Eva S even saved her community.

The traumatic separations created not only unexpressed emotions in the children, but also unacknowledged meanings such as: 'My parents are vulnerable.' 'My parents cannot protect me.' 'My family is gone forever.' 'My parents have abandoned me.' They in turn encompassed unspoken yearning and grief, anger and guilt, outrage and shame. It is in this unspoken area that physical symptoms developed, such as Eva M's migraine, Juliette's asthma and Anne's headaches, nausea and constipation.

Occasionally emotions associated with separations were not repressed. Then they were very intense. Eva G felt the physical pain of separation, which was worse than illness, starvation and having her head smashed against the wall. Similarly, Anne acknowledged her despair for short periods. But generally such emotions, especially if felt for prolonged periods, would have threatened survival.

Children clung to their parents mentally, when they could no longer do so physically. This hope was an important means of survival. By remembering the happy past and projecting it into a future hope of physical reunion, children could make mental detours around their current distress. Anne described poignantly how she countered her tortures by imagining reuniting with her parents and telling them of her pain. Others also clung tenaciously to their parental images. George looked over the wall and fantasised returning to his mother. Eva S maintained contact with her father in Auschwitz by talking to the stars. Bernadette clung to symbols of her parents in the form of bags and glasses, Juliette through games and music. For the older children, Eva M and Richard, hope was mixed with hatred of the enemy, and thus hate was sustaining. Here annihilation of the enemy would return the good times before.

Beyond immediate survival, how did these children make sense of a world gone mad, a world where harmony and morality ceased to exist? Children felt confusion and horror as the old order crumbled. Eva S was confused when her nurse greeted the Germans with joy, when she was taught German culture even as the Germans persecuted her family, and when her father overruled previously sacred religious behaviour. Frankie was horrified at adults causing disorder, destroying furniture, and relieving themselves in public. Lying, for instance about one's Jewish identity, became the norm. However, thus far the values and norms within families and among Jews were maintained. It was permissible to lie to murderers. There was no question for Eva S that it was right for her to lie about her Jewish identity while a gun was pointed at her head.

However, intense guilt and anger accompanied acts which compromised one's own. Eva S felt very guilty for momentarily choosing life for herself while allowing her sister to die. The children in Auschwitz felt guilty when their games selected other children to die.

On the other hand, children felt anger when others betrayed them. Eva S felt rage when a Jewish woman stole milk from the children and when past friends exploited her. Anger could be directed towards parents too. Eva M was angry that her mother had left her suddenly. Frankie was angry with her mother for having fits. Richard was angry with his father for misjudging situations and dying. But these feelings were felt when they did not threaten survival.

It was extremely hard to acknowledge that Jews could act badly to Jews. But the perception that family members could betray each other was untenable. So among the frozen emotions at times of separation and danger were spontaneous moral judgements of shame and accusation, guilt and anger. 'I betrayed my sister.' 'My mother and father abandoned me.' Thus did children lose their innocence, their childhoods, sense of order and goodness.

Anne shows the different levels of morality available to children. At a core biological level she knew that the tearing of her flesh was bad. She hated the sexual abuse. But on another level her abusers were her parent figures on whom she depended for life and interpretation of reality. To survive, Anne accepted the rightness of her adult abusers' actions, and took on the shame and guilt that was rightfully theirs.

Mengele consciously manipulated children into feeling guilt for his own torturing and murders. This cynical perversion of morality has the stamp of ultimate evil.

Suppressing anger against the true perpetrators while blaming parents and themselves continued to be very burdensome for our child survivors. But it says a lot for them that on a deep level they could appreciate the difference between their parents' love and their enemies' hate. This did not resolve all moral dilemmas, but it preserved the desire for loving moral relationships.

The dark greyness of suffering which permeated the children's lives was most tangibly seen in their physical illnesses. In the inexorable push toward death, children were deprived of basic needs such as food and shelter. Anne nearly died of starvation. Starvation made children vulnerable to infections of various kinds. Danial, Frankie, Eva S and Richard had tuberculosis; Eva S had diphtheria at the time of invasion, rheumatic fever and tonsillitis later, and typhoid in camp. Eva M had appendicitis, and Eva G had impetigo in camps. George had meningitis and Juliette had boils at particularly stressful times. Most children had recurrent tonsillitis and minor infections during the war. Eva M developed migraines associated with suppressed rage when her grandmother's shop was vandalised and Juliette developed asthma when she was transferred to her new family.

Some children developed further psychophysiological stress symptoms. Anne developed headaches, nausea and constipation, Bernadette and Juliette bedwetting, and Juliette head banging.

One last comment must be made as we try to understand children's wartime lives. Despite the Holocaust, the children were still children. They played games, scared each other, had adventures and developed creatively. They could usually tell the difference between childhood games and reality, as Frankie could discern fears of monsters and soldiers in the forest. But sometimes the two could merge, as when living with partisans became for Richard, in part, a boyhood adventure.

The children made the most of their meagre supplies to enhance their creativity. Richard's creative memory possibly received a spurt from his time in the cupboard. Danial's experience with the angelic nun and her beautiful pictures connected with earlier good times with Betty in galleries, and together they seemed an inspiration to Danial's artistry. Similarly, Juliette's music seemed connected with her good musical experiences. Eva M's creation of many dolls no doubt made up for the loss of her original one as well as connecting with her mother's talents, and Eva S determined to create children when she saw them being destroyed. She was also following her parents' example. So we may speculate that each of these creative impulses was also connected with the children's most precious loves.

In summary, child survivors lived through the Holocaust immersed in the daily realities of survival. Like their parents, children tried not to think about or acknowledge the meaning of events, and they suppressed their feelings. This was even more true in traumatic situations such as partings from parents. But in a core part of themselves children *did* know what was happening.

While in their care, children obeyed parents and other adults implicitly. When required, children could grow up quickly. But, children always maintained hope, and looked forward to continuing their previous lives with their families. Yet we saw that part of children's traumas were moral conflicts which could be as intense as the traumas themselves, especially if they involved parents or siblings.

Children's suffering could be overlooked even when severe. Sometimes only physical states drew attention to their sufferings. As already noted, a large proportion of our children nearly died from illnesses.

$\mathcal{P}$ost-war

As with other wartime experiences, children often absorbed the happiness and joy of liberation through the feelings of adults. On the other hand, there was no doubt about the moments of joy when children reunited with parents, as described by Bernadette, George and Eva S. But for others, such as Juliette, reunion with her father meant loss of her new family, so it was not a joyous occasion.

Indeed, many of our children's post-liberation experiences did not match their wartime hopes. There were no 'happy endings'. For instance, most children learnt that at least one of their parents and many other family members had died. Even the surviving parents, for instance George's and Juliette's fathers, had changed drastically from their pre-war selves. Step-parents and adoptive parents came on the scene, some of whom did not attach well to the children. Also, some children had to give up familiar religions to become Jewish, which was frightening as Jews were killed.

There were no welcoming societies for the children either. Eva M was too unseemly to enter Vienna at a normal station. Richard was declared non-existent as he was about to reunite with his childhood friend. Children in eastern Europe experienced anti-Semitism in schools. In Poland there were even anti-Jewish pogroms.

On top of that there were more separations from parents after the war. They were sometimes even more painful than wartime ones, because they made less sense, they dashed wartime hopes, and thus they were felt as deliberate rejections. Bernadette, Frankie and Richard were very resentful for having been sent away. Even if not sent away, at times children had to look after their parents. Frankie looked after her sick mother. Danial was made to bear the burden of his mother's guilt. These separations and role reversals were necessary because of the children's own illnesses, such as tuberculosis, and because of the collapse of some parents after years of tension. But the children added post-war traumas and related anger and guilt to their frozen emotions.

To sum up, for some children the post-war stresses were as bad as the wartime ones. How did the children respond? In some ways, they responded as they had done in wartime. Children again adapted to inevitable realities and obeyed their parents. They still arranged their minds as was demanded of them. They accepted that their survivor parents had gone through a lot and needed special consideration. They did not see themselves as victims in their own right. They continued to live day by day, accepted further uprooting and migration, kept suppressing their thoughts and feelings and hoped that some time in the future things would come good at last.

Children still had physical illnesses and some symptoms of distress such as head banging and poor sleep. Some like Richard suffered delayed resocialisation into normal civilian life.

Period of Rebuilding

After migration, the child survivors entered a long period of rebuilding their lives. The war apparently receded into the background. However, this appearance was deceptive.

As adolescents the children put in much effort to assimilate with other Jewish children and the wider community. Though they pretended to be like anyone else, they often gravitated to each other as friends. However they never talked of their Holocaust experiences.

All in our group achieved reasonable education, occupations and financial security. All but one of the children married and had children. Danial and George married non-Jewish spouses. Eva G and Richard in his first marriage married fellow child survivors. The rest married local Jews. George, Danial and Juliette took external assimilation the furthest. The others were overtly Jewish. Statistically our group does not stand out as extraordinary. At Child Survivor meetings participants are struck with how normal the groups appear.

But this is a measure of how much can be concealed. As Anne said, she is the life of the party while inside she is tormented. Child survivors have been adept since the war at concealing their emotions and in leading double lives. Without such skills they would not have survived.

On the other side of the coin, almost all the children had some typical childhood distress symptoms in the early post-war years.

These included severe thumb sucking, night terrors, head banging, bedwetting, stuttering, constipation and eating disturbances. Some symptoms persevered into or developed in adolescence. Frankie developed fits like her mother, and Danial stuttered. He attempted homosexuality trying to find an identity, but it failed, and he attempted suicide. Juliette remained troubled and level, and Eva G could not bear to separate from her mother. All suffered periods of anxiety and depression.

That other side of the coin continued in some form throughout the survivors' adult lives. Holocaust terrors are even now particularly prone to emerge at nights, when survivors are alone, or when current events remind them of the past. Bernadette and Eva G cannot tolerate being at home alone in the dark. Richard to this day dreams of Germans chasing him. Eva S feels she is in the concentration camp when in a dentist's or even hairdresser's chair. Various other symptomatic outbreaks occur at different times. Eva M continued to have migraines and she developed abdominal crises and arthritis thought to relate to the war. Others have also suffered arthritic problems. A number have been overweight. Eva S could not conceive at first and had a psychotic breakdown after her newborn baby died. Anne has suffered depressions akin to when she found out that her parents died. Other psychosomatic symptoms represent other traumas of her past.

A number of our group would have qualified for psychiatric diagnoses at some time. About half of our child survivors have received psychiatric help, with benefit. We know that others not in our group have had long-term psychiatric illnesses and a number, as Richard noted, did suicide.

But perhaps even more important than overt symptoms are the subtle pervasive influences of the Holocaust on later life, even in their creative aspects. Looking at occupations, for instance, Eva G and Frankie made clear links between their passion for caring for children and their own childhood cravings for such care. Eva M taught children how to make dolls and toys, the loss of which had been very significant to her. Richard learnt that money meant survival and he devoted himself to accumulating it. He also beat the Poles and the French in bridge.

Yet the Holocaust casts its shadow even on child survivors' greatest passion — their own children. For each child survivor, his or her own survival is confirmed by having children. They are the victory over the Nazi juggernaut, the genocide. Eva S described most clearly the deep desire to produce children as an answer to the murdered children. Life defeats death. But the shadow over work and family stems from imbuing them with excessive survival needs. This can interfere with normal peacetime fulfilments.

While the Holocaust could merge with some creative aspects of survivors' lives, most influences were unambiguously negative. For instance, in spite of their efforts, child survivors stayed with a sense of being different, not belonging, of not being truly accepted. Putting so much of themselves into abeyance made it difficult for the survivors to be in true contact with themselves and others, and to feel whole and genuine. This restricted their ability to love intimately, as Richard noted about himself. They loved passionately where survival was concerned, but the important little empathies and sympathies, the trivial everyday joys and pleasures of life, often passed them by. They found it difficult to be optimistic and to trust in a moral, caring, orderly world.

Contemporary Period

Identity

Till recently child survivors were simply not recognised, and therefore they did not have a label, an identity. Even parents ignored their children's Holocaust experiences, giving the children a sense that those experiences were not valid aspects of themselves. Eva G expressed this graphically.

There were three identifications available to child survivors — religion, Israel, and being Jewish. Yet none of them recognised child survivors. As far as religion, most child survivors were not religious and some, like Bernadette, felt more at home in a church than a synagogue. But most importantly, as Eva S found, religion had nothing to say about the Holocaust. It failed to explain how God could have allowed it to happen.

Child survivors have identified with Israel as the place where they could be Jewish, and defeat the Holocaust. This was the place where the Holocaust would never happen again. Israel's victories seemed to be proof of this, and of the fulfilment of the promise given to Eva S by the Israeli soldiers: 'They will never again do this to you. You will never be helpless again. You will be at home in Israel.' Eva S, Frankie, Bernadette, George and Eva G did have a sense of feeling at home in Israel. Israeli child survivors have expressed to me the satisfaction in holding a gun knowing that for the first time in two thousand years Jews would not be slaughtered without consequences. Eva S expressed this even as she was putting gas masks on her grandchildren during Iraqi Scud missile attacks. So in Israel one could be Jewish and reverse the Holocaust identity.

However, Israel did not identify with child survivors, like the soldiers who denigrated Holocaust Jews to Eva S. Similarly, Eva G, who felt at home in Israel as a modern Jew, nevertheless felt her war experiences remained unrecognised. Thus Israel's denial of the past in its attempt to create a safe future avoided the reality of the Holocaust nightmare.

Lastly, each child survivor was Jewish. But what made one Jewish? It was not religion, Israel, nor physical features, social class, place of birth or language. For child survivors it was the persecution experiences which made them indelibly Jewish and which forged a common bond. This was as true for George, who was biologically half-Jewish, as for Anne, who had not known what Jewish meant. But other Jews did not recognise this definition of Jewish child survivors.

It was only recently that the term child survivor was coined, recognising both the suffering and the feat of children surviving the Holocaust. With increasing recognition child survivors have come to give more credit to their experiences and to value themselves more. In child survivor groups members recognise each other even more intensely. Here at last they feel really accepted, here they really belong, and such groups develop a sense of siblinghood. For the child survivors in this book, survival has become a source of pride, not shame. It is on this new basis that they talk to the world and other child survivors.

Memories

Child survivors have achieved middle age, security and children. That is, they have achieved the future toward which they had been striving. There is no need any more to live day by day, be busy, to not think, acknowledge or feel. It is also not enough just to know that one is a child survivor. It is time to know what it has been all about. And it is in this context, sometimes to their surprise, that memories of the past return to child survivors and they demand further memories and explanations. Bernadette demonstrated the intense need to retrieve and understand memories. Why are memories so important?

The Holocaust is now only memories. Child survivors are living representatives of the Holocaust, and only their memories give it flesh and blood. One is one's memories. One cannot exist without memories. Memories connect the past, present and future, they connect oneself with the world. Without memories there is a nothingness, an irrational deadness, symbolised by Danial's suicide attempt. Bernadette needed memories to fill the holes within herself.

It is certainly not true that an absence of memories means an absence of suffering. The lack of memories may be, in fact, an added burden. As Danial said, the scars are there but you do not know how they got there. He could not make sense of what was affecting him. Thus one may be more at the mercy of memories one cannot remember than those one can.

Why did our child survivors not remember their childhoods? There seem to be three reasons: the innate biological limitations of immaturity; parental desires; and the pain of remembering. First, there are innate age limitations on the capacity to remember. Children between four and six, such as Juliette and Bernadette, remembered only some images, like slides, of childhood. The youngest children, Eva G and Danial, had almost no visual memories at all of their early traumatic childhoods. What memories they had were little fragments. Often the only memories were in the nature of seemingly irrational emotions, sensations and behavioural impulses. On the other hand, after seven, children's capacity to remember seems to be similar to that of adults. We saw maturation of Richard's capacity to remember as he reached seven. We also saw how Frankie remembered much more than Bernadette, though there was only eighteen months difference between the two sisters. Similarly, George's memories of Teresienstadt were more total than Eva G's.

However, there were exceptions. Anne had a clear memory of her parents at the age of three, and Bernadette had clear memories of the arrest at the age of four but no memories from before. It seems that major shocks can leave a precocious imprint on memory. Anne also clung to her memory of her family as it was the only connection she had with them.

Some went to great trouble to fill out their memories. Bernadette and Danial returned to wartime places, others read and talked to older people and to each other. There could be great relief and even joy at refinding memories or validation of memory fragments.

To a large extent parents continued to filter, buffer and arrange their children's minds. As before, parents wished to protect children from threats, but they also wanted to hide their own vulnerability, guilt and shame. Examples were Juliette's father, Richard's mother, Frankie's and Bernadette's mother and Danial's mother. So child survivors were given messages by their parents, 'Do not know, do not remember, you cannot remember, you should not remember, what you remember is wrong.' If child survivors asserted their unwanted memories parents could become anxious, offended, hurt and angry. The children then felt guilty and sacrilegious. Yet as Eva G noted, memories needed to be validated by others for them to feel real. For those whose parents did not validate their memories, memories remained elusive. It sometimes required parent figures, such as Sarah Moskovitz was for Eva G, to validate child survivors' memories.

Sometimes adults kept deliberate secrets from children making it impossible for children to integrate major influences on their lives. Juliette could not know that Mama Mijn did not love her and was not going to keep her. Nor could she understand the silent hatred of her relative who envied her existence, nor her father's angry distance due to his secret guilt.

Lastly, remembering was painful. It released previously frozen feelings and meanings. Some were intensely personal, such as Anne's shame of having been sexually abused and Bernadette's shame of having been a 'pisseuse'. Others involved parents. With increasing memory Bernadette had to acknowledge her father's terror and helplessness, and she re-experienced her own terror. Danial came to experience rage with his mother for not seeing him as an infant. Eva M became aware of having left her mother at her wedding as revenge for her mother having left her during the war.

As well as an absence of memories, too many memories could also be burdensome. Anne was plagued by constantly remembering her abuses. Eva S and Richard felt burdened by their dreams and flashbacks. Symbolic memories in physical symptoms such as Eva M's migraine and palpitations, and behavioural impulses such as Eva G's clinging, were also burdensome.

So child survivors were caught in the dilemma that to be alive they had to remember, but to remember meant pain for themselves and others. The struggle continues and therefore not all emotions and meanings have been unblocked. But Juliette's story shows that it is never too late to remember or to repair loves. She refound her beloved father when he confessed his guilt to her on his death bed.

Love has been perhaps most painful to remember, because with it came the grief for its loss, the tragedies and the lost years. And yet with memory of love came a discovered capacity for it in today's world. As our child survivors started to identify themselves and share their memories, they came to see that at their core they were just nice, ordinary children from nice, ordinary families to whom the most extraordinary awful things had happened. Child survivors came to like themselves more.

Searching for meaning

How *did* child survivors come to judge themselves and the world around them? We saw that it was very important for children to achieve a moral order. How did the survivors integrate their dilemmas over the years?

The return to acceptable peacetime behaviour occurred reasonably quickly. Richard's special circumstances delayed this when he had to join a gang in order to survive in the orphanage. Child survivors in

Israel had to join the army. Nevertheless, all the child survivors in this book became law abiding civilian non-aggressive citizens. But again, appearances could be deceptive, for their subjective trust in a good just world was impaired.

Where was the justice in the persecution of innocent children and their parents? And why did the world do so little about it? It was impossible to extract a sense of justice from the Holocaust, or to reconcile it with a moral Jewish God. Child survivors became both politically aware and sceptical about world affairs. Events such as those in Cambodia and Bosnia constantly rekindled and reinforced their outrage and scepticism. They have remained particularly sensitive to anti-Semitism. And yet because of their keen sense of political and social injustice, child survivors are particularly aware of injustices to vulnerable groups, especially children, and they try to protect them in the social sphere.

However, child survivors are subject to the vagaries of human moral responses like anyone else. Even while Eva S was still plagued with possibly having to choose the wrong people to die, to her horror she realised that she had identified with medical experiments which she found immoral. And even if child survivors are more aware of suffering children, often they may not sacrifice much more than the rest of the community for them.

How have child survivors been able to integrate the Holocaust into their values and world outlook? It is a tribute to the human capacity for creativity and the need for order that our child survivors attempted to place the Holocaust into a wider world vision. Eva S tried to find a meaning in the context of the Jewish religion, drawing parallels between the Holocaust and the Inquisition. Eva G found in the Baha'i religion, and Juliette in the Gurdjieff movement groups both personal acceptance, and an all-embracing vision of a bigger whole. Others found more personal reconciliations, as when Frankie was pleased that her father had exacted justice on the Gestapo. Others, like Eva M and Richard, simply acknowledged that Fate had dealt them a raw deal. But none of these attempts integrated the Holocaust as really meaningful.

We must return to child survivors' children to see what gave the survivors most meaning over the years. Children were a compound of the broader answer to genocide and of personal rectifications. Thus Bernadette's child was not separated from her mother in the two and a half months of her illness. Eva S's child was safe in the bosom of Israel. Danial's child had his father constantly present. And Eva G's child did not have to cry for his constantly disappearing mother.

Personal creativity was also meaningful in that it symbolically overcame the Holocaust. We noted Frankie's and Eva G's fulfilment in child care. George had his gardening. Danial had his art, Juliette her music, Richard his chess and bridge. Each contained what the Holocaust denied — expression, achievement, triumph, love and connection.

As child survivors have come to identify themselves, remembered, and gained self-esteem, they have started to find specific child survivor meanings and purpose for themselves. They came to see themselves in a unique position to be able to testify to the great evil which adults can inflict on children. They can describe how such events cause suffering over many years. They can also testify to the courage and strength of children, and their goodness. But above all, through their testimonies child survivors can hope to prevent such events happening to children in the future. All the child survivors in this book have made their pain public with this purpose in mind.

Adult, Child and Second-generation Survivors

It is obviously important to know how much we can generalise from our selected group to other child survivors. I believe that these stories are unique but nonetheless representative. The differences are to do with the process of assimilating these traumas.

Who joins child survivor groups and who takes on therapy? My impression is that those who do are not very different to those who do not. Most people vacillate between acceptance and denial. Much depends on the availability of a trusted group or therapist and those who availed themselves of either generally benefitted.

Child survivors overlap with adult and second-generation survivors. We saw that the older children were in many ways similar to adult survivors. And on the other hand, we may say that, after all, adults are only big children. For instance, for them too separations from their parents made lifetime marks on them.

However, there are differences. Adult survivors were more aware of events at the time and could remember them afterward. They had relatively more control to make day to day decisions. On the other hand, they had the added anguish of being unable to protect their children and often losing them. Later, adult survivors were more able to connect their symptoms with their memories, and to form groups of peers. On the other hand they had less flexibility to adjust to peacetime conditions.

Second-generation children were in some ways more vulnerable than child survivors because they carried scars and emotions with no possibility of remembering their origin. While they had the advantage of being born in an objectively better world, they were subject to the memories, anguish and struggles of their parents, who often kept them in the dark about them. We must remember that child survivors were also second generation children.

Thus there is an overlap and sharing of the Holocaust anguish across the generations. Adults and children are both similar and different — they feel about and defend themselves against traumas similarly; but they differ in their capacities and roles. The younger the person, the greater is their vulnerability, the less their ability to know and to speak, or even to know what they would like to say.

Child Survivors and Other Traumatised Children

Very importantly, we would like to know how much our child survivors have in common with other traumatised children. The answer is that all children's fabrics can be rent asunder, not only those of the child survivors of the Holocaust. All children can experience, and far too many have experienced, being wrenched away from their parents, temporarily or permanently. Too many have witnessed their parents damaged, humiliated and abused. Too many have themselves suffered physical abuse and illness, sexual abuse, humiliation and degradation.

Too many have suffered aloneness and isolation, neglect and rejection, shame and exploitation. Too many have grown up feeling unlovable, fearful and lacking confidence. Too many are confused and fragmented, physically and emotionally undernourished. Too many have not had the chance to blossom in stability, security and love. We do not need to detail here the reasons for such suffering: wars, political tyrannies, the tyrannies of home, the tyrannies of fate. But always the children are the most vulnerable, and thought of the least.

Child survivors of the Holocaust can be used as a prototype for other groups of traumatised children. The variety and magnitude of their and their parents' traumas are well documented and have been followed up for fifty years or more. Due to this clarity and magnitude, child survivors of the Holocaust can be used for comparison, or to draw attention to the nature of responses in other traumatised children. What kinds of general lessons do they teach us?

Firstly, that even if silent and obedient, and even if they do not understand coherently what is happening, children are highly vulnerable to events and absorb them deeply into their beings. They are not inanimate appendages of adults even if they seem to adapt silently to the adult world. Sooner or later children need to know the meaning of what happened, why, and who was to blame. Children tend not to question their parents and adults, and often assume guilt. Thus they become morally traumatised as well. Without retrieving meaning and a sense of goodness, they become alienated from themselves and the world.

Next, child survivors alert us to the variety of circumstances which may be stressful to children. Not only the immediate external threats to life, but the threats as transmitted from their parents and others. Some of these stresses are brutal, while others are more subtle. Children respond to them with frozen feelings and meanings such as feeling rejected, excluded, different, worthless, unloved, exploited, humiliated and bad. Such responses can be evoked even when parents are victims. That is why by traumatising parents, we traumatise children too.

Like child survivors, children in other traumas push away painful knowledge, get busy with day to day activities, do not think or feel about what befell them, and look forward hopefully one day to reconnect with good parents and a good world. As with child survivors, they may appear normal during a long latent period. Our group gives warning that even those most saturated with distress can show a normal face, especially in environments which do not wish to know. We may not wish to know about child survivors from Cambodia, Vietnam and South America. It is only recently that we have become aware of the high frequency of physical and sexual abuse of children in our communities. We often reassure too glibly about the variety of physical and mental manifestations which reflect major inner distress.

Younger children are more vulnerable than older ones. For infants, visual and tactile rejection or neglect may be as traumatic as a separation for an older child. Early abuse carries with it greater fragmentation and confusion and greater long-term distress. Child survivors draw our attention to the next generation also being affected.

Lastly, child survivors draw attention to the indomitable courage of children, and their drive to grow, create and heal. Issues of identity, memory and making sense are part of this healing for all traumatised children. It is a relief to know and put words to one's trauma, be recognised for it and share oneself in a group who have undergone similar experiences.

Memories, even with their painful meanings, can fill holes in the personality. Reopened wounds can reopen love and new connections. Along with pain, there is still life and hope.

And so ten child survivors of the Holocaust have exposed their hearts and souls to us. They were particular that not a word be printed which was not genuine. They wanted to tell the truth about what it was like to be among the small minority who survived the greatest attack on children in history.

Above all, these child survivors of the Holocaust wanted to document their stories. They do not see themselves as special people, but they do feel that their persecution has given them voice for a special message. They want to give hope to other traumatised children. But more than this, their message to the world is that we must recognise children's vulnerabilities. They want to bear testimony so that such suffering will not be imposed on children in the future. If they can achieve a measure of success in this goal, their sufferings will not have been in vain.